# DUNDEE UNITED
## Champions of Scotland
## 1982-83

DESERT ISLAND FOOTBALL HISTORIES

CLUB HISTORIES ISBN
Aberdeen: A Centenary History 1903-2003 1-874287-49-X
Aberdeen: Champions of Scotland 1954-55 1-874287-65-1
Aberdeen: The European Era – A Complete Record 1-874287-11-2
Bristol City: The Modern Era – A Complete Record 1-874287-28-7
Bristol City: The Early Years 1894-1915 1-874287-74-0
Cambridge United: The League Era – A Complete Record 1-874287-32-5
Cambridge United: 101 Golden Greats 1-874287-58-9
The Story of the Celtic 1888-1938 1-874287-15-5
Colchester United: Graham to Whitton – A Complete Record 1-874287-27-9
Coventry City: The Elite Era – A Complete Record 1-874287-51-1
Coventry City: An Illustrated History 1-874287-59-7
Dundee: Champions of Scotland 1961-62 1-874287-72-4
Dundee United: Champions of Scotland 1982-83 1-874287-71-6
History of the Everton Football Club 1878-1928 1-874287-14-7
Halifax Town: From Ball to Lillis – A Complete Record 1-874287-26-0
Hereford United: The League Era – A Complete Record 1-874287-18-X
Huddersfield Town: Champions of England 1923-1926 1-874287-66-X
Ipswich Town: The Modern Era – A Complete Record 1-874287-43-0
Ipswich Town: Champions of England 1961-62 1-874287-56-2
Luton Town: The Modern Era – A Complete Record 1-874287-05-8
Luton Town: An Illustrated History 1-874287-37-6
Matt Busby: A Complete Man U record 1945-1971 1-874287-53-8
Motherwell: Champions of Scotland 1931-32 1-874287-73-2
Norwich City: The Modern Era – A Complete Record 1-874287-67-8
Peterborough United: The Modern Era – A Complete Record 1-874287-33-3
Peterborough United: Who's Who? 1-874287-48-1
Plymouth Argyle: The Modern Era – A Complete Record 1-874287-54-6
Plymouth Argyle: 101 Golden Greats 1-874287-64-3
Portsmouth: From Tindall to Ball – A Complete Record 1-874287-25-2
Portsmouth: Champions of England – 1948-49 & 1949-50 1-874287-38-4
The Story of the Rangers 1873-1923 1-874287-16-3
The Romance of the Wednesday 1867-1926 1-874287-17-1
Stoke City: The Modern Era – A Complete Record 1-874287-76-7
Stoke City: 101 Golden Greats 1-874287-55-4
West Ham: From Greenwood to Redknapp 1-874287-19-8
West Ham: The Elite Era – A Complete Record 1-874287-31-7
Wimbledon: From Southern League to Premiership 1-874287-09-0
Wimbledon: From Wembley to Selhurst 1-874287-20-1
Wimbledon: The Premiership Years 1-874287-40-6
Wrexham: The European Era – A Complete Record 1-874287-52-X

WORLD CUP HISTORIES
England's Quest for the World Cup – A Complete Record 1-874287-61-9
Scotland: The Quest for the World Cup – A Complete Record 1-897850-50-6
Ireland: The Quest for the World Cup – A Complete Record 1-897850-80-8

MISCELLANEOUS
Red Dragons in Europe – A Complete Record 1-874287-01-5
The Book of Football: A History to 1905-06 1-874287-13-9
Football's War & Peace: The Tumultuous Season of 1946-47 1-874287-70-8

# DUNDEE UNITED
## Champions of Scotland
## 1982-83

Series Editor: Clive Leatherdale

Peter Rundo

DESERT ISLAND BOOKS

First published in 2003
by
DESERT ISLAND BOOKS LIMITED
89 Park Street, Westcliff-on-Sea, Essex SS0 7PD
United Kingdom
www.desertislandbooks.com

The right of Peter Rundo to be identified as author of this work has been
asserted under The Copyright Designs and Patents Act 1988


British Library Cataloguing-in-Publication Data
A catalogue record for this book is available from the British Library


ISBN 1-874287-71-6

Printed in Great Britain
by
Biddles Ltd


Photographs in this book are reproduced by kind permission of:
Fotopress, DC Thomson (page 83, bottom), Frank Tocher, and the author

# ~ CONTENTS ~

# ~ PREFACE ~

For any footballer, winning a League Championship medal has got to be the height of sporting achievement. When you play for a club like Dundee United, as I did for the whole of my playing career, it has got to be even more special.

Throughout the whole of history of Scottish football, very few players outside of the Old Firm can boast a League Championship medal, so the one I possess from the 1982-83 campaign certainly ranks as my biggest achievement in football.

During 2002-03 there have been several functions to celebrate our title win. These have been very enjoyable and reinforced the tremendous camaraderie between what was a tightly-knit bunch of players, who were as friendly off the field, as they were on it.

And it was that sense of togetherness which was undoubtedly a big factor in our success.

The tension that wet afternoon in May twenty years ago when we won the league at Dens Park will live with me forever.

The tension of the occasion was unbelievable and I can sympathise what it was like for the fans because John Holt replaced me with almost half an hour to go and the pressure of having to sit and watch the rest of the game from the dug-out was unbearable.

Fortunately, we hung on to win 2-1 and provided me with the sweetest moment of my career.

Although I now manage Plymouth Argyle, I am still, and always will be a big fan of Dundee United. To the extent that my office at Home Park is painted tangerine and I have changed Argyle's away strip to one which is predominately tangerine!

Consequently, I am sure that I will enjoy reliving Dundee United's season of triumph through the medium of this book as much as all my fellow Arabs.

PAUL STURROCK

# ~ Author's Note ~

I returned to Scotland from exile in England in January 1982. Given that Dundee United would shortly embark on their most momentous season, my timing couldn't have been better. By chance, it coincided with my first year back editing the programme, a task I had done for a season back in 1967-68. I had previously served my apprenticeship by selling programmes at Tannadice.

When Desert Island Books asked if I would be interested in writing a book chronicling United's Championship season, I thought it would be a relatively easy task. Having kept comprehensive scrapbooks during the 1960s, I had done so again on my return to Scotland, which meant I had acres of material at my fingertips. However, I soon discovered that this was insufficient to provide the detail which such a huge event in the history of the club deserved. Consequently, I am indebted to those who provided additional material, in particular fellow supporters Tom Cairns, Kevin Sheehan, and Fraser Maclean, who, as he does in the United programme, kept me on the straight and narrow statistically.

Other fellow Arabs to assist were Eamonn Malone, Andy Crichton, and Gerry Brady, whilst my programme counterpart at Aberdeen, Kevin Stirling, provided a Devil's Advocate view of United's achievements.

As programme editor, getting in touch with ex-players was not difficult. I still see many of them regularly, and all whom I asked readily assisted. They deserve every United supporter's thanks because without them, you wouldn't be reading this. Gordon Wallace, who arrived as coach just after the landing of the title, was another fount of information, always helpful during my persistent telephone calls.

The pictorial section of the book would not have been possible without Fotopress of Dundee, and in particular Dave Martin, who allowed me the use of pictures from his library which stretches back over 30 years. The few photographs which he did not supply came from either DC Thomson or Frank Tocher, to whom I am equally appreciative.

Finally, I thank my publisher, Clive Leatherdale, for the opportunity to write a book about the club so close to my heart

PETER RUNDO

DEDICATION: To my wife Kathleen, who is married to a football fanatic. I apologise for turning to her at 4.45pm on 14 May 1983 and saying that was the greatest moment of my life. It was, of course, 3pm on Saturday, 16 September 1972 – the timing of our marriage.

Introduction

# ~ DENS DELIGHT ~
### (MAY 1983)

Dundee's Cammy Fraser kicked the ball away in disgust as Edinburgh referee George Smith sounded the final whistle at Dens Park at 4.42pm on Saturday, 14 May 1983. For the Dundee skipper, it was the frustration of another derby defeat by the club that had shown him the door as a schoolboy, but for Jim McLean's men it was the final chapter of a modern day footballing fairy-tale.

Twenty-five years previously, Dundee United had finished 35th out of Scotland's 37 senior clubs; now, unbelievably, they had scaled unprecedented heights to become Champions of Scotland.

Little wonder then, that Dens Park was a sea of tangerine and black scarves as ecstatic supporters in the stand and crammed terracings, not to mention those who had bolted onto the pitch to congratulate their heroes, let free their pent-up emotions. They had just witnessed Dundee United hailed as League Champions for the first time in their history – and become only the twelfth club – and perhaps last – to collect the top title north of the border.

United's day of destiny had dawned with one simple objective from their final fixture – beat Dundee. Achieve that, and no matter if Celtic emerged victorious from their Old Firm meeting with Rangers at Ibrox, nor how Aberdeen fared at home to Hibernian, and the title was theirs.

The final hurdles in the 1982-83 campaign had seen the closest race in Scottish history – never before or since would the top three be separated by just one point. Before the start of play, United were in pole position, a point ahead of Celtic and Aberdeen. Remember, it was still only two points for a win back then. Putting it simply, for either of the other protagonists to succeed, Dundee had to take something from the derby to end all derbies. In racing parlance, it was a three-horse race with the Tangerines the hot favourites. Were Jim McLean's side to drop a point, then it would be down to the wire of goal difference, in which case it would depend by how many Celtic defeated Rangers.

There was even one scenario whereby if United drew 0-0 and Celtic won 2-0, then the two clubs would finish with identical records and have to play off for the title – it was that tight.

Aberdeen, fresh from their glorious European Cup-Winners' Cup triumph over Real Madrid, were very much the outsiders. They would have to rattle in eight without reply against Hibs to pip United if the scores at Dens Park finished level. This was the table on the eve of the last games:

|           | P  | W  | D | L | F  | A  | Pts |
|-----------|----|----|---|---|----|----|-----|
| Dundee U  | 35 | 23 | 8 | 4 | 88 | 34 | 54  |
| Celtic    | 35 | 24 | 5 | 6 | 86 | 34 | 53  |
| Aberdeen  | 35 | 24 | 5 | 6 | 71 | 24 | 53  |

As for the likelihood of a Dundee win, given the style with which the Tangerines had won their last three games, no one was even suggesting that eventuality.

Obviously, there was a huge burden of expectation resting on skipper Paul Hegarty and his colleagues. However, had they been offered any venue, other than Tannadice, for this fixture, then Dens Park would have been the unanimous choice. Not only was it the scene of the club's only two previous trophy wins – annexing the League Cup there in 1979 against Aberdeen and retaining it the following year against Dundee – but it was a ground on which Jim McLean's men boasted a daunting recent league record. Having cantered to two comfortable two-goal wins the previous season, they then first-footed their neighbours at the start of 1983, United's 2-0 victory in no way reflecting their superiority.

Indeed, almost unthinkably, had the option been available to the players to play either at Tannadice or the one hundred and odd yards up the road, then Dens Park might well have got the nod! Results of the two Tannadice derbies that season would have undoubtedly influenced their thinking. Only a Davie Dodds goal in the October meeting had separated the sides and although United had won the second encounter a couple of months earlier 5-3, they had been 2-3 down at one stage.

Equally pertinently, Dark Blues' boss Donald Mackay, who'd served United for a decade in goal during the 1960s and early 70s, had presided over eight local derbies, but had yet to savour a victory. That was something he was at pains to make in his programme notes for the momentous day:

'I make no secret of the fact that the biggest disappointment I have had since taking over here at Dens Park as manager is that we have never beaten Dundee United. I applaud Dundee United in getting into the position of being able to win the championship through their own efforts but it won't require me to advise them that they can't expect any favours from us to help them on the way,' he wrote.

Indeed, Mackay went into print amid all the furore leading up to this day of days, bemoaning the Dark Blues' luck in those two Tannadice games, having conceded the decisive goal on their first visit with just four minutes remaining, and having to play with a rookie keeper for all but six minutes of the March meeting, when they had come from two behind to lead United 3-2. As he said, 'I feel this sort of thing can't go on for ever. We're bound to get at least our fair share of the breaks some time.' The question was, would it come on a day when it could cost United the championship?

Across the road, Jim McLean was leaving the United players more to their own thoughts than usual, given that no one needed to tell them that this was 'the big one'. As the United manager explained on the eve of the match: 'With what the players are going out to play for, there is no talking I can do now. They know that they will achieve near immortality if they win the league championship, and if that doesn't make them play, then nothing will. They have handled the pressure really well so far and there has been a chirpiness about the place this week which is difficult to have at this time of the season normally. That has made it very easy for myself and Walter [Smith, his assistant] recently.

Having said that, McLean was quick to point out that he was in no way complacent about the match. 'We have always said that the time to be at the top of the league is after the last game of the season. That is where we hope to be after playing Dundee.'

Whatever the outcome of this make-or-break final fixture, United had already set several club records. Their total of 54 points was their best ever, beating the 51 gained in 1928-29, when United won the old style Second Division title. The 1982-83 season's competitive aggregate of 125 goals overtook the previous best of 121, which had only been established the previous season. The league tally of 88 was the best ever in the Premier League and the best by any United side at the top level of Scottish football. An unbeaten run at the start of the season of nineteen games was the best ever opening to any campaign by a Tannadice side.

One further record was in sight, and it was the only one United supporters cared about. Two points against Dundee would equal the Premier Division record established by Celtic in 1979-80. Far more importantly, United would be champions.

Quite incredibly by modern standards, the game wasn't all-ticket. As local journalist, the late Tommy Gallacher, commented in the *Courier* on the morning of the match, 'Judging by the number of people I have met this week who told me they planned to be there, some of whom have not been at a football game for years, I would suggest that it could be a packed house.' Mind you, Gallacher also pointed out that the way all the stand tickets for the match had been snapped up was a pretty fair barometer. So the advice to all was come early. Given that only two decades have elapsed since, the admission prices are a bit of an eye-opener – £3 for adults and £1 for juveniles and OAPs.

Those who think that football is over-priced these days have a good case, if the economic rule of thumb that inflation doubles every ten years is applied, because that would mean going to a match nowadays should cost around £12.

Tannadice preparations for the game had been remarkably low key. Two of the injury doubts from the previous week's win over Motherwell – goalkeeper Hamish McAlpine and striker Davie Dodds – trained on their own as they recovered from a thigh strain and a badly bruised knee respectively. Biggest doubt for the big day surrounded John Reilly who, although scoring several important goals that season, couldn't command a regular place in United's star-studded line-up. The nippy striker injured his back in the reserves' derby at Tannadice four days before D-Day. Fortunately, by the time three o'clock on Saturday came round, all three were ready for the fray.

Long before the big kick-off, queues had formed around the ground. The United support was allocated the TC Keay end, which is the one nearest to Tannadice, whilst they also had the whole of the enclosure in front of the stand that was equally divided. The home support occupied the Provost Road end, plus the Dens Road side of the ground, more familiarly known as 'The Derry'. The capacity of Dens Park was to be tested to the limit and beyond.

Thousands of fans were in their places an hour before kick-off despite drenching rain. And as the turnstiles ticked round and round, both sets of fans waiting patiently outside were praised by a senior police officer who said, 'I am very pleased at their behaviour and that they took our advice to come early.'

Initially, the crowd was reported at an estimated 25,000. When the two sides had met in the League Cup final two and a half years previously, the crowd limit had been set at 24,700. Later it became known that almost four and a half thousand more had been shoehorned into the stadium.

If the fans behaved themselves, the weather definitely did not, with frequent heavy squally showers. So much so, that referee George Smith checked the pitch and requested the groundsmen to fork several areas where puddles of water had accumulated, so that they would drain away. So full was the ground that some supporters took up vantage points on roofs of buildings adjacent to the TC Keay end. Banners were waving and confetti flying all over the place as the United team emerged to a deafening reception.

Team news was that John Holt dropped out of the side that had beaten Motherwell the previous week, so that Richard Gough, returning from suspension, could be accommodated. Both sides won corner-kicks in a lively start, but nerves in the massed Tannadice support, which were to be tested to the limit later, were eased by their favourites' two-goal opening salvo.

It was fitting that the opener should come from the man who throughout the season had fashioned important goals out of seemingly nothing. This latest instalment in Ralph Milne's portfolio was as good as any of the other twenty. Paul Sturrock collected a Narey pass almost on the halfway line, turned neatly and slipped the ball to Milne, who conjured up an outrageous and sublime fourth-minute opener. Whipping the ball past future Scotland international full-back Stewart McKimmie, he took nine more stride and, having spotted Dundee keeper Colin Kelly well off his line, lofted a left-foot chip into the empty net.

Interviewed immediately after the game, the winger, who had celebrated his 22nd birthday the previous day, said, 'It's probably the best goal I've ever scored. Undoubtedly, it's the most important.'

There were few more exciting sights in football than Ralph hurtling down the wing at full pelt, leaving defenders in his slipstream. Initially a central striker with a prodigious scoring record for Celtic Boys Club in Dundee, he was brought to Tannadice by Dundee legend Doug Cowie who was in those days United's only scout. Unquestionably, Milne had a real eye for goal, losing none of his deadly ability in front of the posts by his move to the flanks, and he could finish lethally with either foot.

Then, just seven minutes after Milne's magic, United scored again. Richard Gough's move from right-back into central defence had released Dave Narey into midfield. The Scottish internationalist charged into the penalty box and went down under a challenge from Iain MacDonald. Dundee protested vociferously that it wasn't a penalty, but Bobby Glennie's remonstrations only earned him a booking.

Next it was Kelly's turn to be admonished by the referee for dancing about on the line as Eamonn Bannon waited to take the kick. Whether it was the tension of the occasion or the long wait, or possibly both, the normally reliable Bannon placed his kick too near the keeper who dived to his left and beat the ball out. Unfortunately for Dundee, the ball broke back into Eamonn's path and he steered it inside the right-hand post. Two up after eleven minutes; it was the start all United supporters had dreamed about.

The flow of play was very much down the slope at Dens Park towards Kelly's goal at the TC Keay end. The keeper was relieved to see Glennie clear after he had touched a speculative Sturrock lob on to the bar. The woodwork again came to Dundee's rescue halfway through the first half when Davie Dodds side-footed a Bannon pass against the underside of the bar. The ball bounced down, up and out, but there was no signal from the linesman, nor any appeals from the United camp as the referee waved play on.

That was the pivotal moment of the match. Instead of being three goals down, Dundee raced up the park to halve the deficit when Iain Ferguson – later to cross the great divide and score his fair share of goals for United – gave Hamish McAlpine no chance with a drive from eighteen yards.

You could almost see the confidence drain from the men in tangerine. It wasn't that Dundee were now in command but, worryingly, as the teams left the field at half-time, United were no longer dictating play.

However, those worries were cast aside when news arrived from Ibrox that Celtic were losing 0-2. There was further reassurance from events at Pittodrie, where Aberdeen were only two goals up against Hibs. That meant that even if Dundee did square the game, Alex Ferguson's side would have to score an unlikely six more goals.

Into the second half, and it was now a more even contest. Too even from a Tannadice stance, with as much time being spent looking at watches as the field of play. As the tension ratcheted up, Davie Dodds was booked for a foul on Fraser. United's raids were now more spasmodic, although Sturrock did force Kelly to tip a shot over.

Concerned by the shifting tide of play, Jim McLean switched things about. Narey stepped back beside Paul Hegarty in central defence, with Gough moving to right-back, whilst Derek Stark – one of the lesser sung heroes of the side – brought his energy in the tackle to the midfield.

There was more bad news for United fans when it became obvious that Paul Sturrock was limping. Both John Holt and John Reilly warmed up, but it was Holt, a defensive midfielder, who took the place of the injured striker.

Hearts were in Tannadice mouths when a Fraser free-kick was headed back across the goal to Albert Kidd, who headed over from point-blank range. Mercifully, Kidd put his talent for title-wrecking on hold for three years, because it was his two goals for Dundee that would rob Hearts of the title on the same ground three years later.

Beforehand, Jim McLean had been low key, but now the United boss was constantly bobbing up and down from the dug-out and bellowing instructions as Dundee continued to threaten. Kelly palmed a Bannon free-kick round the post and then had to dash from his charge to boot clear from the onrushing Milne. To the relief of the nerve-jangled United support, the dying embers of this game were fought out well away from Hamish McAlpine's goal.

When those fans were finally put out of their agony, Dens Park was transformed into a sea of tangerine and black scarves and bunnets on the realisation that dreams of the title had become reality. Even many fans of dark blue persuasion stayed to applaud United, maybe out of respect for emulating their own club's achievement of 21 years previously.

That final whistle sparked a race between Reilly and Sturrock from the dug-out to see who would be first to share in the spoils of victory with their team-mates out on the pitch. The normally taciturn McLean managed a nervous smile and wave to the exhilarated United support in the enclosure to his left, but being the disciplinarian that he was, still had time to remonstrate with a young fan invading the pitch and usher him back into the crowd.

Although the United heroes had left the field, the fans refused to budge. In response to the almighty din the players re-emerged and hoisted Jim McLean, now looking more relaxed, shoulder high. The only sour note was when a group of young Dundee fans ran from the terracing to boo, jostle and spit on the United players, but they were quickly dispersed to let the celebrations continue in earnest. Indeed, as the champagne corks popped around him, McLean confessed: 'We had to send out for this at time up. It's not our style to pre-judge anything.'

The man who had masterminded the club's finest hour revealed: 'For the first time in twelve and a half years as manager I couldn't speak to the players in the dressing room. I was shaking with emotion after dying a thousand deaths in the Dens dug-out. I am sure that very few people will grudge us the championship. Even although we froze against Dundee after our dream start.'

Scenes of jubilation went on well into the night as supporters sang and danced in the streets. The pubs and clubs in the city did a roaring trade in more ways than one.

For the players, officials, manager and coaching staff and their wives, it was a casual stroll down the road to Tannadice for a quick celebratory drink in the boardroom and then off to the Dundee United Supporters Association Player of the Year Dance, staged at the Enverdale Hotel, Coupar Angus.

There, Richard Gough was presented with the main trophy, John Clark who figured in one game on the road to the title was the 'reserve player of the year', Dave Beaumont the young player, and top scorer Davie Dodds, the player's player. The partying went into the wee sma' hours, finishing up with a private party at the house of Frank Kopel who had left the club fifteen months earlier to go to Arbroath after a decade as the regular left-back at Tannadice.

Not that there was much time for sleep, because United honoured a prior commitment by fulfilling a fixture at Forfar, attracting over 1,200 fans to the benefit match for Forfar skipper Billy Bennett and stalwart John Clark.

Whilst their appearance at Station Park fourteen miles up the road, less than 24 hours after making history, was appreciated by Forfar officials, players and fans, United's players took the field with the majority looking decidedly green about the gills after celebrating long into the night. The introduction of five substitutes at half-time seemed to affirm this.

Suffice to say that United lost 1-2 to the Second Division outfit and when it was suggested that, given the circumstances, the team might be forgiven for losing, Chairman Johnston Grant quipped: 'I'm bloody sure Jim won't forgive them.'

Sadly, Grant died less than fifteen months later, and he and vice-chairman George Fox must have savoured the title win more than most because their association extended as far back as 1955 when the club's fortunes were at an all-time low. Their shrewd guidance had lain the financial footings from which the club would grow and prosper beyond their or anybody's wildest dreams. Grant always maintained that the best job he did at Tannadice was to persuade Jim McLean to stay put, when Motherwell, Wolves and Hearts all tried to lure him away. What Grant didn't know was that he would experience the same scenario less than six months after celebrating his club's title success.

From Forfar, it was straight back to Tannadice to board an open-top bus, which wound its way to the city centre, allowing the players to parade the newly acquired trophy. It was 'newly acquired' because it had three possible destinations – Dundee, Glasgow or Aberdeen – and this was before the time when costly helicopter charters were laid on by the League's sponsors. Although it had recently become the practice of the Scottish Football League to present the trophy after the defining fixture, the League was not sponsored at that time.

Instead, a Glasgow photographer conveyed the trophy on Sunday and killed two birds with one stone, dropping off St Johnstone's First Division silverware on the way before heading to Tannadice with the Premier Trophy and snapping the happy recipients at both grounds. That meant there were only the seagulls present at an eerily empty Tannadice to see captain Paul Hegarty hold the championship trophy aloft for the first time.

Not that the lack of ceremony, nor the torrential rain, dampened the spirits of the thousands of Dundee United supporters who turned up in the city square to acclaim their heroes. Monsoon conditions and even thunder and lightning were ignored as they awaited the arrival of the bus at 6.15pm with club-coloured umbrellas plus the banners and flags turning the City square into a sea of tangerine and black. It was a reprise of the spectacle that Aberdeen had witnessed earlier in the week after the Dons had won the Cup-Winners' Cup, bringing the Granite City to a standstill.

Long before the arrival of the United players, the thousands who had gathered behind the crush barriers were chanting, singing and dancing. The cheering reached a crescendo when the open top bus arrived and United fans saw the coveted league trophy bedecked in tangerine and black for the very first time. Conditions were so wet that a microphone could not be used on the outside balcony, but messages of thanks for turning out in such numbers were delivered by chairman Johnston Grant from the microphone of a police car. Then it was off inside to a civic reception.

When the dust had settled, manager Jim McLean, reflecting on the heights scaled by his side, remarked: 'It's a miracle that we have won this title. At the start of the season, I certainly didn't believe we'd be champs. Simply because we have no depth of pool. Twelve players, the twelve who played against Dundee at Dens, have achieved this tremendous success. I'm always confident of winning a cup, but I honestly believed that the league was beyond us. Not that we're not good enough. Obviously we are. But we really should have a much bigger pool. Some of the players have been asked to play 66 matches. The league is the most difficult competition of all to win. I believe we can get better, but there is a need for more players. I'll definitely be trying to strengthen the pool.'

However, a major obstacle to his aims was finance, as he freely acknowledged: 'I feel that there are no players available in the price bracket in which we have to operate that will improve the team, so I intend to channel our resources into a furtherance of the policy that has stood us in such good stead in the past.'

No fewer than ten of the thirteen stripped for duty at Dens – McAlpine, Malpas, Holt, Kirkwood, Stark, Narey, Sturrock, Milne, Dodds and Reilly – had come through the youth ranks. Even more remarkably, six were born and bred in the city.

Indeed, you could legitimately call it eleven, because although Richard Gough came from South Africa and arrived at Tannadice after being rejected by Rangers, he did briefly figure in United's youth team before his swift elevation to the first team. In fact, seven of the championship side had lived through the 1978-79 campaign when United first threatened to intrude at the top table of Scottish football, only to run out of steam at the tail end of the season.

Another to serve an apprenticeship that season was Paul Hegarty, who had been signed from Hamilton for £27,000 in 1974. From average centre-forward, he was converted to a central defender of international standing. The quartet of Gough, Malpas, Milne and Reilly had all broken through to the first team, which left one piece in the championship jigsaw to be filled. The man in question was Eamonn Bannon, who was brought from Chelsea in October 1979 for a then sizeable club record fee of £165,000, and he proved to be worth every penny.

Even winning the league would not swell the Tannadice coffers to a huge degree. The financial spin-offs in the early 1980s for winning the league were modest. Sure, there was money from the Scottish League, but that was for distribution amongst the players. Everything else, other than qualification for the European Champions Cup, was less tangible. There was the possibility of greater cash returns from challenge matches and the chance of more lucrative sponsorship deals, but at that time the club had no jersey sponsor, nor for that matter even a commercial manager. Adidas were the shirt supplier, but the notion of selling replica strips was still to get off the ground.

Consequently, the range of souvenirs was limited to scarves and bonnets and a few fancy-goods items such as pens and lapel badges. The only outlets were a small souvenir shop on the stairs of the main stand and a rickety old wooden shed behind the North Enclosure.

Given the hordes of United supporters who were at Dens that day, it is hard to believe that the core United support numbered only 5,000. On paper, the average gate of 11,137 might not look impressive, but it was the club's best ever, just topping the figure for 1925-26, the club's first campaign in the top flight of Scottish football. Additionally, it must be remembered that the population of Dundee at that time was only around 172,000 and shrinking – the latest census shows that it is down to around 147,000. At that time it was roughly the same size as Portsmouth, but with a vastly smaller catchment area. Then you have to consider the existence of another club in a relatively small city.

It was a remarkable season for Dundee United – and not just in terms of winning the league. Consistency was the keynote of all Tannadice performances, reserves included. Indeed, in the final analysis, only sixteen of the 131 games played by the club at any level were lost – eight each by the first team and the reserves. In the process they scored a grand total of 285 goals, whilst only 114 were conceded.

As the ink dried on the most momentous campaign in United's history, another one was about to commence with the club about to dine at the same table as Europe's finest in the European Cup.

However, it is sobering to reflect on just how close this race for the title had been. Indeed, in modern times, on no other occasion since the War have three teams being in contention for the title at the death. Even more scarily, had Dundee managed to grind out an equaliser during that nail-biting second half, with Celtic having come back from the dead at Ibrox to win 4-2, it would have meant a play-off for the title with Billy McNeill's side.

It was that close!

Chapter 1

# ~ FOUNDATIONS ~

### (DECEMBER 1971 – JULY 1982)

That Dundee United should have triumphed once again on the home of their arch rivals was indeed ironic, for winning the League Championship was now added to United's two earlier League Cup triumphs at Dens Park. This only served to rub salt in the wounds of older Dundee supporters. Those who had first-hand recollections of United's humbler days could hardly have envisaged that the little team from across the road could ever equal their feat of having been league champions, which they were, 21 years previously.

To be honest, back in 1962 when Dundee took the title for the one and only time in their history, neither could I. The fact that Jim McLean – a former Dundee player and coach – would be the driving force behind United's new-found success only further embittered those Dundee fans old enough to recall their own side's championship success.

I was a pupil at Harris Academy in 1960 and can well recall being one of the few United supporters in the class. In fact, as far as I can recollect, Dundee outnumbered United supporters by something like twenty to one. Apart from Ally Dailly, father of Christian – who went on to play for United and who now plays for West Ham – I struggle to recall any other of my classmates who had Tannadice leanings, so outnumbered were we 'Arabs'.

Not that United had yet had that nickname ascribed to them when Dundee won the league; that only came into use a year later. In the spring of 1963, Tannadice resembled a desert, following a particular severe winter. The pitch was more suitable for ice-hockey than football. It was somehow made 'playable' for a cup-tie against Albion Rovers, but only by methods that would have today's pitch specialists cringeing. Tar burners from Messrs Wm Briggs (now part of the Nynas group) of Dock Street, were hired to burn off the thick layer of ice covering the pitch. As it melted, a thick layer of sand was spread and the game remarkably went ahead. When the mini ice-age finally relented at the end of February, Tannadice resembled Broughty Ferry beach and would have been ideal as the film set for 'Lawrence of Arabia'. Throw in the fact that United occasionally played in an all-black ensemble at that time, and the nickname of 'The

Arabs' was born. Or so legend has it, because no one has come up with a more plausible explanation.

A flavour of the rivalry between the sides can be found in the Dens Diary article in the programme for that do-or-die derby in May 1983:

'My attitude to Dundee United has never been quite the same since I received a "deepest sympathy" card from a friend on the occasion of Dundee being relegated from the first ever Premier League on goal difference. To tell you the truth, I quite liked my Tannadice-orientated friend's sense of humour although I did promise myself I would return the gesture at the first available opportunity. So, with any luck, I might be giggling my way up the road to the Post Office on Monday morning. Now, if there are any strangers to these parts already wondering what kind of nut this is, then I would congratulate them on their perception and speedy grasp of the situation. I *am* a nut, a Dens Park nut and I'm old enough to decide such matters for myself. Even a dyed-in-the-wool Dark Blue type such as myself could find excuses to cross the great divide to the other side of the road. After all, I like tangerines – especially at Christmas time; I admire Tannadice boss Jim McLean; Iain Phillip was a mate of mine at school; and ... I almost forgot ... my Uncle Fred is United daft. Possibly because of these mind-bending influences I bear United no *real* grudge and if they win the Championship then good luck to them. But if they don't, I'll be an extremely happy man as this day draws to a close. Or to put it another way, I'll be as happy as a newt. There is one over-riding reason for this form of thinking and I am certain it applies to the vast majority of those wearing Dundee colours this afternoon. It's United we are playing and we want to beat them – no matter the consequences. The same theory I'm sure would apply to the Tannadice ranks if today's situation was in reverse. After all, these fans did tend to make the most of our troubles when we were twice relegated to the First Division. I didn't enjoy hearing them sing – 'You're going down again' – but I did accept that this was football rivalry in action ... and long may that continue. That's why I'll be shouting myself hoarse this afternoon as Dundee go about doing the dirty on the Tannadice Championship hopes.'

And that pretty well sums up the largely healthy rivalry that exists between the two clubs. It compares more with the competition on Merseyside between Everton and Liverpool, which is full of divided families who can live in harmony, than the acrid antithesis which exists between Old Firm factions.

In the same feature in that match programme, Jim Henry, then my opposite counterpart as Dundee's programme editor, poured scorn on the Celtic chip on the shoulder which was obviously as prevalent then as it is today:

'Working in the west, as I do, it's been something of a frustration of late when talking to people firmly convinced that Dundee will "lie down" to United for "the honour of the city". Those folk just aren't aware of the facts – and the amount of pride at stake – as the teams take the field this afternoon. I just wish these Doubting Thomas types could have the opportunity to put across such a view in the vicinity of a Dens player! I can assure any Dundee fan who shares this worry that this type of talk is sheer bunkum – each and every Dens player is determined to give his all to try to get a result at last over our great rivals.'

~~~~~~~~~~

Dundee United's early existence was far removed from being a title-win-ning outfit. Formed in the spring of 1909 by the Irish community in Dundee, following the demise of Dundee Harp three years earlier, Dundee Hibs took over Clepington Park, the home of Dundee Wanderers, thus displacing the previous occupants of the past eighteen years, and immediately renamed the ground situated on the north of the city – Tannadice Park.

Dens Park, on the other hand, was originally farmland, with Dundee moving there in 1899 from Caroline Port, so it was Dundee's decision to relocate that was to eventually bring about the curiosity of the two clos-est senior football grounds in Britain – separated by less than the lengths of two football pitches.

As Mike Watson explains in his book, *The Tannadice Encyclopedia*, the newly formed Dundee Hibs had plenty of work on their hands before a ball could be kicked. 'The ground had literally been stripped bare by its disgruntled former occupants, Dundee Wanderers. Even the wooden boundary fence had been dismantled but the Hibs committee at least had the benefit that they could start from scratch and develop the ground as they wanted it.'

As was the tradition in those days, the dressing rooms were not built under the grandstand, not that there would have been any room under the modest wooden stand which seated 1,200 and ran less than half the length of the pitch. The dressing rooms were described in the local *Evening Telegraph* of 21 July 1909 thus: 'The pavilion is a splendid two-storey structure built of brick, containing two large dressing rooms, two committee rooms, press box and referee's room.' Such structures were common in their day and this one was similar to those that existed at the grounds of Airdrieonians and Fulham.

Whilst it was claimed that the new ground had a capacity of 15,000, it was probably nearer 10,000. That is supported by the fact that a reported 15,000 crowd for a Qualifying Cup-tie with Forfar could be accommodated only by extending the terracing and installing temporary seating.

Promotion to the First Division in 1925 heralded alterations, with the terracing being expanded, using the time-honoured railway sleepers, taking the capacity to 25,000. Until the advent of Taypools in August 1955, the ground was to change very little indeed.

The club's early venture into fund-raising was a great success. The pool, similar to the one that Nottingham Forest had launched, at its peak had over 100,000 members. It soon started providing the financial backing for a covered enclosure to be erected behind the goal at the Dens Park end, as well as the first concrete terracing.

Again it was promotion that was to be the catalyst to further, and this time, much more dramatic improvements being made. In August 1962 a new cantilever stand was opened, straddling the corner of the Tannadice Street side and the Arklay Street end. With the rest of the ground now fully concreted, and expanded terracing on the north side, the capacity increased to 25,000, although somehow 28,000 spectators squeezed inside the tight confines for Barcelona's visit in 1966 to establish the club's record attendance.

Given that Tannadice is now all-covered and all-seated, holding only half of its record capacity, younger supporters might find it surprising to learn that it wasn't until 1980 that any further cover was erected. The trigger to the North Enclosure being erected was the transfer of Raymond Stewart to West Ham for £400,000 in 1979. Indeed, the joke was that his right leg funded the arrival of Eamonn Bannon, whilst his left paid for the first major ground improvements for eighteen years.

It wasn't only the shadow of the Law Hill, the extinct volcano which dominates the Dundee skyline, that United had to live under, because for most the first 70 years of their existence, it was also Dundee Football Club whose achievements dwarfed anything United could boast. When Dundee Hibs had been formed, many felt that the decision to locate on their rivals' doorstep was foolhardy, motivated possibly by the fact that neighbours Dundee topped the First Division table. An article in the *Dundee Advertiser* on 12 April 1909 opined, 'It would have been better if the Hibs had gone to another quarter of the city where they might have gathered together a following of their own.'

The fact that they didn't probably accounts for geography playing no part in deciding which city team to follow, but initially there was no doubting that the newly formed club aimed to satisfy the demands of the Irish and Roman Catholic population of the city, but it wasn't long before that was to change.

Around 7,000 saw the first ever game at Tannadice Park when Edinburgh Hibs provided the opposition for a friendly match which finished 1-1. However, after fourteen turbulent seasons, a new management team confronted with an average gate of under 4,000 (Dundee were playing to average audiences three times that number) decided to broaden the club's appeal by dropping the overt Irish connection. An application to change the name to Dundee City met with fierce opposition from Dundee. A name change to Dundee United was sanctioned just before a game at Dumbarton in October 1923. Significantly, though, Dundee Hibs had begun that season in a new black and white strip, the green having been dropped at the end of season 1922-23.

Despite those early tribulations, the club stood the test of time and, as we have already seen, prospered beyond anyone's wildest dreams. United's promotion in 1960 fuelled the rivalry between the clubs and for this Jerry Kerr takes all the credit. What he achieved as manager should in no way be underestimated. When he took over in the summer of 1959, United had finished 35th out of Scotland's 37 senior clubs, with Dundee 31 places higher. But by the time he was ready to pass over the reins, United were fully-fledged members of Scotland's top flight, having just enjoyed their third sortie into Europe and closed the gap on their neighbours to the extent that United regularly finished above them, not to mention having for the first time had a better average gate.

However, a horrendous start to season 1971-72 saw the loss of sixteen goals in three consecutive matches – among them a 4-6 defeat at Dens. With age catching up on him, Jerry Kerr – then the longest serving manager in Britain – announced his resignation.

Another legacy left by Kerr was the adoption of tangerine and black as the club's colours. The idea was spawned from playing in tangerine and blue when representing Dallas Tornadoes in the North American Soccer League in 1967. It was decided to adopt an all-tangerine strip with black trimmings to give the club a more modern image. The new ensemble had its first airing in a pre-season friendly against Everton at Goodison Park on 2 August 1969, ending 46 years in black and white.

The only thing Kerr had failed to deliver was a major honour to adorn the Tannadice trophy cabinet. True, he had come close to glory with his Scandinavian-inspired side of the mid-1960s, reaching the final of the

Summer Cup in 1965, only to lose out to Motherwell. However, you could plausibly argue that this wasn't a truly national competition as neither Rangers nor Celtic bothered to enter that ill-fated and short-lived immediate post-season tournament.

November 11, 1971 saw Kerr's twelve-and-a-half-year tenure as manager come to an end as he stepped out of the limelight to assume the post of general manager and club secretary, a role that he would hold for only eighteen months, cutting his ties with the club at the end of the following season. Indeed, it was only after present chairman Eddie Thompson took over that Kerr's achievements were honoured. The Main Stand which, being a clerk of works to trade, he literally helped build, was in the summer of 2003 named after him.

The man appointed to succeed Kerr was to rewrite Dundee United's history. Yet, Jim McLean wasn't a written applicant for the vacant managerial post. Instead, he responded to an invite from Tannadice to be considered for the job. Writing in the club's official programme for Jim McLean's valedictory game in charge, against Aberdeen in May 1993, director George Fox paid tribute to McLean's 22½ years in charge and alluded to the motives behind his appointment: 'It is well documented that the fitness of the Dundee players who were coached by Jim McLean had impressed me and the rest of the board. When we interviewed him, he seemed very genuine, and we decided to give him a go!'

Little did anyone realise just how much of a 'go' McLean was to make of it, especially as his coaching CV consisted of having spent only eighteen months up the road at Dens.

Born in Asghill, Lanarkshire, McLean's tentative steps into a lifetime career in football were taken with his local Junior club, Larkhall Thistle. He stepped up to the senior ranks with nearby Second Division Hamilton Accies during season 1955-56. At Douglas Park, he acquired a reputation as a goalscorer, averaging something close to a goal every second game.

Clyde were attracted to his scoring potential and, early in 1961, snapped him up. Following his prolific partnership with John Divers at Hamilton, McLean then formed a prodigious left-wing scoring association with Sam Hastings at Shawfield. This prompted a further move and one for which Dundee United were ultimately to be grateful, because it brought Jim McLean to Tayside.

Not that Tannadice was his destination, because in September 1965 manager Bobby Ancell secured the inside-forward's services for neighbours Dundee for a fee of £10,000. So, at the ripe age of 28, Jim McLean became a full-time footballer for the first time, having previously combined playing with his other career as a joiner.

His debut as a Dark Blue could not have got off to a worse start, marred by Dundee's heaviest ever derby defeat, losing 0-5 to United at Dens Park. He might have feared that Dundee fans would never forgive him, but things could only get better after that, and they did – at least on the field of play.

In October 1967, Dundee reached the final of the League Cup, losing 3-5 to Celtic at Hampden, with McLean scoring one of the goals. In addition, he assisted Dundee in their passage to the semi-final of the Fairs Cup, where Leeds United only narrowly eliminated them.

However, his playing days at Dens were troubled ones and he has never made a secret of the fact that he wasn't exactly a crowd favourite. Commenting on them in his book, *Jousting with Giants*, McLean stated bluntly, 'Not to put too fine a point on it, the fans hated me.'

He and Sammy Wilson – an Irish international centre-forward from Falkirk – had been signed in the wake of Alan Gilzean's departure to Spurs. With another big name, Charlie Cooke, heading for Chelsea shortly afterwards, unfair comparisons were inevitably drawn with these two big names. McLean confessed in his book, 'I don't think either of us stood a chance, because the fans went along to the games looking for the star players and instead of finding them, found us – two bargain buys who were never judged on our own merits.'

Little wonder that McLean didn't need much persuasion to join Kilmarnock in August 1968 when the offer to team up with his younger brother Tommy at Rugby Park came along. Significantly, given how his future career was to pan out, McLean continued to live in Dundee and even trained a couple of days a week with his former colleagues at Dens. Shortly before his 33rd birthday, after two seasons with Kilmarnock, persistent ligament problems brought the curtain down on Jim McLean's fourteen years in the senior ranks.

After the harsh treatment meted out to him during his three years at Dens Park, you'd have thought that the city of Dundee would be the last place that Jim McLean would cut his coaching teeth. The fact that he did was down to the efforts of one man – John Prentice. McLean's former manager at Clyde now became his mentor, having moved from Clyde to take over from Bobby Ancell as manager of Dundee. Prentice had to work hard to persuade McLean to take the job as coach Only an assurance that he would be answerable only to Prentice, and that all his dealings at the club would be with the players and his manager, finally convinced him to accept the offer. 'Only the presence of John Prentice as a buffer between me and the board kept life sweet for me,' revealed McLean in his book.

Indeed, it was rumours that Prentice might quit Dens that first brought Jim McLean into contact with Dundee United. Again in his book McLean stated: 'There was a strong rumour going about that Prentice was leaving Scotland for Canada. I knew that if he left I would not stay.'

Indeed, the news prompted him to contact United boss Jerry Kerr to ask if there was any chance of a job as coach at Tannadice. That enquiry was to have long-lasting implications because shortly afterwards Kerr resigned. McLean was approached to see if he was still interested in a job at Tannadice, but this time as manager.

Duly appointed, at 34 he became the youngest manager in Dundee United's history. He was officially due to take up his duties on Monday, 6 December, but typically was in the dug-out for United's trip to Tynecastle the previous Saturday and saw his new charges lose 2-3.

Clearly not overly impressed, and with United sitting just four places off the bottom, McLean went into the transfer market. First, he got full-back Frank Kopel, who had recently been released by Blackburn Rovers. Kopel cost nothing but, with the modest sums made available to him, McLean prudently purchased midfielder George Fleming from Hearts, and strikers Paddy Gardner from Dunfermline and Archie Knox from St Mirren.

One of McLean's most influential early changes proved his tactical awareness. He converted Jackie Copland, a centre-forward struggling to cope with the demands of the higher division, after being signed by Kerr from Stranraer, into a top-notch central defender. As the newcomers settled in and the players adapted to his demands on the training ground, results picked up to the extent that the team just edged into the top half of the league come the end of April.

On taking over at Tannadice, McLean did not find an abundance of young, nor local players. Indeed, midfielder Jim Henry was one of only two who qualified on both counts. The other was goalkeeper Hamish McAlpine and he turned out to be the only player McLean inherited who would be part of the league title winning side eleven and a half years later.

However, there was one other player on the books who would also play a major part in that title triumph. Walter 'Wattie' Smith, a wing-half of modest ability, aspired to be McLean's ideal foil as coach, somewhat similar to McLean's own relationship with John Prentice. Certainly, Smith gained first-hand knowledge of what was expected of the players in the first pre-season under McLean as the new manager began his first full season in charge. Wattie joked that he would present his new boss with a bill for having his clothes taken in after preparations for the new season had caused him to lose a stone in weight. It was worth it, though, because in 1972-73, the young defender was to win a regular first-team place for the first time.

Satisfied that things were heading in the right direction, McLean set about putting in place the youth policy for which he, and Dundee United, would become famed. In the six months since taking over, nine players had been signed on Schoolboy terms. One of the first of that batch was a name that was to become synonymous with Dundee United.

David Narey was one of two youngsters to join United's groundstaff from the St Columba Youth Club side that lost to Celtic Boys Club in the national Under-16 youth cup. The other was Graeme Payne, and both were to feature in the title-winning team. Even more remarkable was how they landed up at Tannadice on the recommendation of a then member of the Dundee playing staff. As Gordon Wallace, later to play and coach at Tannadice, relates: 'In addition to playing for Dundee, I took St Columba's Under-16s for training and when Jim asked me if there were any players whom he should sign, I recommended Dave Narey and Graeme Payne.'

After McLean's first full season, during which the team made steady if unspectacular progress, the first buds of the youth policy were beginning to break through, with one young defender showing particular promise. Experienced campaigner Kenny Cameron, a prolific centre-forward of his day, was quoted as saying that he always found young David Narey a difficult opponent in training, commenting: 'He never seems flustered and reads the game wonderfully.' He added, without the benefit of hindsight, 'you will hear much more of him.' Indeed, we would.

Beating Narey into the first team, though, were two other exciting 17-year-olds. McLean blooded Graeme Payne alongside Andy Gray in a League Cup-tie against East Fife at the start of the 1973-74 campaign. During that season, Narey made the expected breakthrough and a fourth teenager, John Holt, was given a few outings as the class of '83 began to take shape.

The mix of youth and experience in the side saw United reach the semi-final of the Texaco Cup, eliminating Sheffield United and Leicester City, only losing out to a late Malcolm MacDonald goal for Newcastle in extra-time of the second leg at St James' Park. That season also saw the club make its first real mark in the Scottish Cup, reaching the final for the first time in its history. However, the fans still needed to be convinced that United were on the upward trail with only 3,800 of them watching the last home league game before their Hampden date.

The odds were stacked against United in the final, where they faced Jock Stein's Celtic, fresh from a ninth league title. There was to be no upset, with Celtic winning 3-0, but United acquitted themselves well enough and gleaned valuable experience from which both McLean and the club would eventually profit, not least because merely appearing in the final against the league champions secured a place in the European Cup-Winners' Cup.

The 1974-75 campaign was a crucial one in Scottish football because reconstruction at the end of the season meant that finishing in the top ten meant qualifying for the new Premier Division. That United would qualify was rarely in doubt. Indeed, by finishing fourth, the club achieved its highest ever league placing. Even more encouragingly, that landmark was reached in tandem with the introduction of two more of the future championship winners.

Towards the end of Jim McLean's first taste of the European stage, a straggly, long-haired striker came off the bench against Jiul Petrosani. Few then had heard of Paul Sturrock. He had only joined the groundstaff two months earlier after being called up from Bankfoot, but over the next fifteen years he was to become a United legend. The other youngster introduced that season was to become equally legendary, though Paul Hegarty's path to the top came via a very different route.

Along with Eamonn Bannon, Paul Hegarty was the only other member of the championship winning squad to cost a fee, with United paying Hamilton £27,000 for the 20-year-old. Then a striker, there was no indication then that United had just landed a future Scotland international centre-half and championship winning captain.

But as Hegarty struggled to make the transition from the Second Division, Andy Gray was blossoming at the top level. So much so that the 19-year-old finished the season with twenty league goals. This not only cast him as the club's leading scorer, but also as the joint-top scorer in Scotland – an honour shared with Willie Pettigrew of Motherwell. Pettigrew was himself to play his part in the later foundations towards the honing of a championship challenging side from Tannadice.

Despite an exciting campaign in securing a place in the top ten elite, manager Jim McLean had reservations, not only about the new set up, but also the ability of his young developing side to cope with its demands. He went on record as saying that the introduction of the Premier Division had come a year too early for his developing youngsters, which proved an all too accurate assessment as United fought for their Premier Division lives.

Matters weren't helped by the inevitable sale of top scorer Andy Gray a month into the rigours of the ultra-competitive top ten. Such a goal-haul by someone of such tender years had inevitably brought enquiries during the close season, with Ron Saunders of newly promoted Aston Villa leading the charge as he searched for a proven goalscorer to consolidate life in the English top flight.

After repelling initial bids, financial pressure eventually saw United relent and Andy Gray was sold for a club record fee of £110,000. Given that four years later Gray was transferred to Wolves for almost £1.5 million, he had left Tannadice at a giveaway price. That only strengthened the resolve of Jim McLean never to allow such an eventuality again.

He was as good as his word because the only other young player to leave Tannadice before the title was won was Ray Stewart, four years after Gray. The £400,000 that West Ham paid for a 20-year-old full-back who had played fewer than 50 league games can only be described as good business, especially as it very soon funded another piece of the championship jigsaw.

However, the trials and tribulations of that first Premier Division campaign had to be endured before such heady thoughts could be contemplated. Indicative of just how bad things had become, some United fans were even calling for the manager's head, following a 1-4 home defeat in January 1976 by Motherwell – managed by McLean's brother, Willie – which put United's Premier future in serious doubt. But United survived by the skin of their teeth, getting the point they needed from their final match at Ibrox to edge above rivals Dundee on goal difference.

Judging by the way future campaigns were to go, Jim McLean and his players were none the worse for this close call. The pressure of staving off relegation, however, meant there was no room for experimentation, though John Holt did establish himself as a regular member of the squad. No such worries the following season, though, with back-to-back wins in their opening five fixtures ensuring there was no repeat of the previous season's problems. Although United lost their unbeaten record to Celtic, going down to a seemingly emphatic 1-5 defeat, that result proved to be an aberration, and this campaign saw the first signs of a team capable of mounting a serious championship challenge. Only a 0-2 defeat by Celtic at Parkhead at the end of March finally put paid to title aspirations, but it was another very important step on the championship learning curve.

From the start of the McLean era, the influence of senior players on the emerging youngsters was very much a feature, and that trend was continued by the acquisition of Gordon Wallace from Dundee. A prolific scorer all his days, Wallace not only continued scoring at a rate of a goal every second game, but acted as a mentor for Paul Sturrock, who bagged fifteen league goals that season – a figure he never exceeded over the following twelve years.

The seemingly never-ending conveyor belt of young talent delivered again before the end of the campaign, when Billy Kirkwood made a scoring debut against Hearts and figured in all the last four matches of the season.

Around the same time, another milestone was reached – or should it be that a stigma was removed – when David Narey appeared as a substitute for Scotland against Sweden at Hampden. Incredibly, after 67 years, Narey was the first United player to play for Scotland.

Three days later, McLean made a momentous decision by pairing Dave Narey and Paul Hegarty in defence for the first time in a competitive match, after Hegarty had showed good defensive qualities earlier in the season during a friendly at Goodison Park. Paul had done an excellent job in keeping Bob Latchford in check as United held Everton to a goalless draw. For the next eleven years, he and David Narey formed the defensive cornerstone on which so much of United's success at home and abroad was to be built.

Towards the end of 1977-78, Davie Dodds was promoted from the youth ranks. Even more encouragingly – with Derek Addison, John Holt and Billy Kirkwood all holding down regular first-team berths – United finished third. That was the highest position in their history and another pointer to the increasing potential of the squad.

Accomplishment in the league was accompanied by a good run in the Scottish Cup with the semi-finals being reached for only the fourth time in the club's history. Rangers at Hampden stood in the way of United and a second final appearance under McLean. The manner of the 0-2 defeat, in which United promised much but failed to deliver, was the subject of Jim McLean's post-match frustration: 'We were guilty of lapses in concentration; we had chances, but snatched at them. Experience is vital in such situations and we just don't have it yet.'

His youngsters were going to take that lesson on board quickly because the club was only eighteen months away from landing a long-awaited first trophy. Before then, the quality within the squad was recognised by the naming of three Dundee United players in Ally MacLeod's squad of 40 for the World Cup in Argentina.

Equally significant was the appointment of Wattie Smith as assistant to Scotland youth-team manager Andy Roxburgh. Roxburgh had been greatly impressed by Smith's coaching, something he had been doing for most of that season at Tannadice after being sidelined by a badly strained stomach muscle.

Of course, the growing reputation of the side had its drawbacks. Determined bids by unspecified English clubs to prise David Narey and

Paul Hegarty away prompted worries that another Andy Gray saga was in store. However, the steps taken now, during the 1978 close season, probably played a significant part in keeping the club on course for the title by preventing an exodus of the best players. Long-serving players would be rewarded by a pension scheme, and on the back of this Dave Narey and Paul Hegarty signed long-term deals. Others were promised inclusion in the scheme, should they become the subject of similar bids.

Yet, season 1978-79 didn't start at all well. There were some misgivings amongst the support that the side might have peaked, but it is not beyond the bounds of credibility to say that this campaign was a dress rehearsal for the title win four years later. In the event, United buckled under the pressure of leading from the front for so long, added to which the Old Firm had games in hand. The Tannadice youngsters cracked in the run in, but the experience was to prove invaluable. No fewer than eight of the championship winning side featured regularly. Excluding keeper Hamish McAlpine, Paul Hegarty – voted the SPFA's Player's Player of the Year – was the oldest at 25. Even the normally pessimistic manager offered a note of optimism after the league had slipped away, saying, 'We just aren't good enough yet to win the league.'

Prophetically, during the summer of 1979, McLean stated that the addition of two players to his squad would enable Dundee United to mount a challenge to the Old Firm. In need of an experienced and proven goalscorer, McLean smashed the club's record transfer fee, which had stood at £60,000 for striker John Bourke from Dumbarton two years previously. He now splashed out £100,000 for Motherwell's international striker Willie Pettigrew, who would act as catalyst in the hunt for major honours. His arrival was immediately followed by the departure of Ray Stewart to West Ham for £400,000 – a figure twice the value placed on the player by McLean himself.

Speculation grew as to who might be McLean's next transfer target. In late October a fee of £165,000 brought Eamonn Bannon to Tannadice from Chelsea. The dividend from Bannon's signature was harvested early as United won the League Cup and ended the 70-year Tannadice trophy drought by beating Aberdeen in a replayed final at Dens Park. Reflecting on that triumph, McLean prophesised that this was only the beginning: 'These players have it in them to come back and be winners in the future. It's never going to be easy challenging Celtic and Rangers regularly, but we have that chance now. Everyone at the club will take tremendous encouragement from this victory, and we must cash in on that.'

That inaugural triumph would shortly lead to United and Aberdeen being tagged the 'New Firm'. After years of total Old Firm domination,

Aberdeen went on to take the championship that season – the first time that Glasgow's big two had been brushed aside since Kilmarnock did so fifteen years earlier. Furthermore, not since 1959-60, when Hearts added the championship to the League Cup they had won earlier in the season, had the Old Firm not claimed at least two of the three domestic trophies on offer.

Over the next six years, Aberdeen and United would demolish that Old Firm monopoly. Defeating Aberdeen at Dens Park in that final also shifted the perception of Dundee United in the eyes of the Pittodrie fans. Life-long Aberdeen fan Kevin Stirling, who began contributing to the Dons' match programme that season – and still does – explains:

'The rivalry between Aberdeen and Dundee United became one of great intensity. I suppose it never really materialised until AFC lost the League Cup to United in 1979. Up until then, we took the view that United had won nothing and subsequently were no threat. We would also take great pride in the fact that we were a far "bigger" club with lengthy traditions and varied success. Up until the introduction of the Premier Division in 1975, our traditional "derby" rivals had always been Dundee. The general belief was that United were viewed as the poor relations in that respect. That changed as Dundee went down in 1976 and so we lost our traditional derby-day fixture. United took on that mantle and I suppose the rivalry was born around 1977 before it escalated to what it became in 1983.

'That, of course, heightened in 1979 after the League Cup win. We felt badly done by after the first game, as we should have won it. The AFC fans would also scoff at the poor United support [at Hampden]. By moving the replay to Dens, that was different. Alex Ferguson, by his own admission, stated that he made an error by not changing his side and tactics for the replay and it cost AFC dear. From our point of view, it was a really hard one to take as we had lost the 1978 Scottish Cup and 1979 League Cup finals to Rangers. We also took the view that United won the cup by having an easy route – both of the Old Firm having been eliminated by the Dons along the way. The feeling was that United would only be judged as credible winners if they actually won at Hampden, not on their own doorstep, and against the Old Firm. That was still the case in 1983 after United clinched the title in Dundee.'

Having waited 70 years for the first trophy, supporters of the Tangerines had a mere twelve months before performing another victory dance at Dens after seeing their heroes retain the League Cup after a 3-0 win over Dundee. There could easily have been a second trophy to boast, but after also making it to the Scottish Cup final and letting

Rangers off the hook in the first game, United's inexperience of the big occasion reared itself in the Hampden replay, the team going down 1-4 in extremely disappointing fashion.

Between those finals, a young defender whom Rangers must have rued rejecting – given how much they would pay to buy him back seven years later – arrived at Tannadice after failing a trial at Ibrox. He impressed McLean sufficiently to be taken on. The player in question was Richard Gough.

In addition, Davie Dodds, who scored the opener in the League Cup final win over Dundee, took over Willie Pettigrew's mantle as top scorer with fourteen, four more than the former Motherwell striker. As a result, Pettigrew was soon on his way, moving in a double deal which also involved midfielder Derek Addison less than two months into season 1981-82.

Although United had become a team to be feared in Scotland, the fact remained that despite having qualified for Europe for the past four seasons, their greatest claim to fame abroad still remained the double victory over Barcelona in 1966. This was the season in which that was to change, thanks to some magnificent performances. Drawn against AS Monaco in the first round of the UEFA Cup, United gave a regal display in front of Prince Rainier and Princess Grace in the principality, beating the hosts 5-2. Indeed, so taken were the royals by United's performance, they accompanied Monaco for the return leg in Dundee. Testimony to the quality of the opposition can be gleaned by the fact that Monaco won the return leg 2-1 and ended that season as champions of France.

The man who scored the goal that quelled fears of a famous French fight-back was Ralph Milne, who had made the breakthrough two years previously. That was the first of his sixteen European goals, which to this day leaves him as United's top European marksman.

It was United's next tie that became a part of Tannadice folklore. Two down to Borussia Moenchengladbach after the away leg, McLean's men swamped the German outfit 5-0. There was another five-goal extravaganza at home to Winterslag in the third round, paving the way into the quarter-finals of a European competition for the first time, but there was disappointment in store with the unknown Radnicki Nis from Yugoslavia edging United out 3-2 on aggregate.

Maintaining McLean's earlier assertion that this team could challenge the Old Firm on a regular basis, in November 1981 United had reached their third consecutive League Cup final. Unfortunately, they let a winning position slip from their grasp as Rangers came from behind. A virtuoso goal from Ralph Milne seemed to have put United on their way to victory, especially when Paul Sturrock crashed in a second. However, the referee spotted an upraised linesman's flag and Sturrock's effort was chalked off. From a position of dominance, Jim McLean's side unaccountably crumbled and United lost 1-2. Davie Cooper equalised and Ian Redford, who would switch camps four years later, chipped in the winner. So United had lost their third final at Hampden in seven years and it was the manner of this one which really made fans begin to wonder if there was such a thing as a Hampden Hoodoo.

Though he didn't play in that final, Maurice Malpas had made his debut the previous week against Airdrie, and the last piece of this well-oiled Tannadice machine was now in place. United may have only finished fourth in the league, but they served notice of their intent to challenge Celtic for their crown the following season. The Parkhead side came to Tannadice for United's last home game looking for the two points that would guarantee them the title. Instead, the champagne was left on ice after Celtic were thrashed 3-0. Twelve months later United were to beat Celtic again, but this time it would be for the title itself.

Chapter 2

# ~ Sharp out of the Blocks ~

Before United ventured abroad in preparation for what was to be a momentous season, the 1982 World Cup in Spain provided a platform upon which the club's growing reputation was further enhanced.

Scotland didn't have much to celebrate, going out of the tournament at the first stage – not for the first or last time – but one Tannadice star succeeded in writing himself into Scottish footballing posterity. Dave Narey – already the first United player to ever play for Scotland – now became the first to appear in the World Cup finals. He came on as a substitute in the 5-2 win over New Zealand, but it was his second appearance which was to provide a snap-shot of historical importance, capping his first start against Brazil with a stunning goal. Famously dismissed as a 'toe-poke' by Jimmy Hill, his South American-style finish briefly gave Jock Stein's troops the lead before Scotland succumbed 1-4 to the Samba boys.

This really thrust Narey into the limelight, where he would remain throughout his playing career. The man himself always shies clear of publicity, however, but it is easy to find others quick to sing his praises. Team-mate and defensive colleague Paul Hegarty is one, and he has no doubts how beneficial it was to play alongside Narey in the heart of the Tannadice defence for over a decade: 'Our relationship seemed to be telepathic. He knew my strengths and weaknesses and Dave instinctively covered for me whenever I made a mistake. Unfortunately, I couldn't return the compliment, but Dave just didn't have any flaws in his game,' commented his admiring partner.

The esteem with which Narey is held as a player is equally high on the part of supporters. If anyone visits the unofficial Dundee United website of 'Arabland', they will find this tribute from 'Shedboy' to the player most people regard as the most gifted footballer ever to don a Dundee United jersey:

'The simple truth is you had to see him play. I am biased but I honestly feel he was one of the best defenders I have ever seen and compare him alongside Beckenbauer in his ability to read the game and timing of the tackle. He was a joy to watch. Luggy, Dodds, Milne and Bannon etc may have got the headlines for scoring the goals but without Mr Consistency at the back it would have been for nothing. I have at this point to mention Paul Hegarty because the Hegarty-Narey partnership was at least the equal of Miller-McLeish. I would have liked to have seen Dave playing for United when we finally won the Scottish Cup, as he had played in earlier rounds that season [Author's note: Narey starred in the 1-0 quarter-final replay win at Motherwell after being out of the side for five months] and had come away from Hampden in the past many times the loser.

'He was at Hampden the day we won and when I watch the video when he lifts up the cup to the fans it just about brings a tear to my eye. The ironic thing is that the mark of the man was shown most when he had left United and played in Raith's great win over Celtic in the League Cup final. The Raith defence, particularly Shaun Dennis, played superbly that day, but so noticeable was the way their defence stepped out to use offside just the way United's did when Narey was at the back.

'After that game big Dave refused to be interviewed by Chick Young on the park and went home for a cuppa to celebrate. If the world was a fairer place, Sacha Distel would be nicknamed Big Dave, for the French singer's resemblance to Dave Narey, instead of the other way around.'

Amazingly, given the career which lay ahead of 'Sash' (his nickname due to that striking similarity to the French crooner), as a schoolboy he failed to even make the Dundee Schools side. But as former United coach Gordon Wallace, who recommended him to United, recalls, Jim McLean demanded to know about Narey's ability to tackle, pass the ball, or run. Wallace's answer to each question was the same – 'if he has to'.

Wallace continued: 'I thought he would become a reasonable defender, but I don't think anyone realised just how good a player he would turn out to be and at the very top level.' You couldn't pay the man who has played more games for Dundee United than any other a higher compliment than that by Jim McLean: 'Dave Narey wouldn't look out of place in Brazil's team.'

In his book *Jousting with Giants*, Jim McLean also gave an insight to Narey's laid-back approach: 'If he were running against the slowest man in the club at training then he will beat him by a yard or two. If he runs against one of the fastest men in the club then he will probably beat him by the same margin!'

When mention is made of Dave Narey, it is almost impossible not to bracket him with Paul Hegarty. After all, the pair were the cornerstone of

United's central defence for five seasons before and five seasons after they helped bring the title to Tannadice, but their paths to the top took very different routes. Whereas Narey was star material in the making, Paul Hegarty had to literally take a step backwards for his career to go forward.

Indeed, had it not been for a humiliating Scottish Cup defeat at Love Street in 1977, Paul Hegarty's career could have taken a very different route. Paul was one of only two players of the championship twelve – Eamonn Bannon was the other – to cost money. Paul had been bought as a centre-forward for £27,500 from Hamilton Accies in November 1974 with the intention of partnering Andy Gray up front. Then just twenty, Hegarty had been a promising striker with a decent goalscoring record for the Second Division side. Repeating that at the top level was more difficult, as he freely admits: 'I lacked that wee bit extra pace you needed to be a top striker. It was only a half-yard, but it was the difference between getting to the ball in front of the defender or just after him.'

Early in November 1976, manager Jim McLean experimented in a hastily arranged friendly with Everton after international calls had left both sides idle. Ironically, Dave Narey was one of the players missing, so Paul Hegarty's first public airing as a defender was beside Alex Rennie in a United defence which kept Everton at bay as the sides drew 0-0.

At the start of that season Paul had played up front but, after the arrival of Gordon Wallace, McLean operated a three-man attack with Paul Sturrock and Tom McAdam alongside the veteran striker. As a result, Hegarty made the first of two steps back in the team, moving into midfield alongside Graeme Payne and George Fleming. However, as Paul recalls, it was an embarrassing Cup defeat at Love Street that was to open the door for him: 'Few players can look back and say that they were glad to have lost a cup tie, but the 1-4 defeat by St Mirren opened the door for me in defence and, from that day forth, I stepped back to play in defence and never looked back.'

Hegarty was endearingly referred to as 'Flipper' because of his big feet – he wore size nines – large by professional footballer's standards. Starting out in attack, and with subsequent switches to midfield, he did well to remain an ever-present through that campaign. Other than the odd injury, for the next ten years he was to be equally as permanent fixture in defence.

Standing only 5' 10½", Hegarty was remarkably good in the air. In addition to being spring-heeled, he had an ability to hang and out-jump opposition forwards with a height advantage of two or three inches. So quickly did he develop as an outstanding centre-half that Paul was named, along with his defensive partner Dave Narey, plus Graeme Payne, in Ally McLeod's initial 40-man squad for the 1978 World Cup. Four years later, although he had by then six caps under his belt, Hegarty's name wasn't in Jock Stein's final squad of 22 for the 1982 tournament in Spain.

Further evidence of the club's increasing stature came in that tournament, with Tannadice boss Jim McLean acting as Jock Stein's assistant, whilst striker Paul Sturrock was also in the squad. Though he didn't make an entrance, Sturrock was on the bench for the games against both Brazil and Russia.

Back home, the build up to the 1982-83 campaign consisted of a pre-season trip to Scandinavia, plus visits to Tayside by English First Division sides West Ham and Southampton. Over in Scandinavia, the hectic schedule of five games in six days saw United lose only once – 1-3 to Malmo in the opening game played in hot and humid conditions. That reverse, however, was to be one of the few suffered by the side throughout the whole of the coming campaign. A 3-3 draw with West Ham and a stylish 2-0 win over Southampton – Kevin Keegan and Alan Ball and all – put the finishing touches to the preparations for this never to be forgotten season. Saints' veteran Alan Ball not only found favour with the velvet green Tannadice pitch, but also his opponents. 'United were impressive, especially in the speed with which they broke from defence,' he observed afterwards and that was to be very much United's trademark during the first half of the 1980s.

In terms of transfer activity, it had been an uneventful summer, limited to the acquisition of striker Ally McLeod who'd been freed by Hibs. However, a severe knee injury, picked up during a Largs coaching course, meant not only was McLeod precluded from any pre-season involvement, but that he was also destined never to appear in the Tannadice first team.

Jim McLean did make one notable addition to his squad on the eve of the season because turning out in a tangerine jersey for the first time against Southampton was one-time Chelsea favourite Ian Britton. After 272 league appearances for the Stamford Bridge club, whom he had joined from school, the small but industrious midfielder had been released. He signed for his hometown club just in time to play against Southampton. The fact that he only played cameo roles in the championship chase was another gauge of the strength of the squad already on board.

Even before the campaign proper got under way, United landed silverware. No prizes for guessing where – Dens Park – as United beat

Dundee 2-1 to win the Forfarshire Cup, contested annually by the six teams in Angus. Few of the 9,027 crowd who witnessed United collect the cup could have envisaged that nine months later the same score against the same opponents on the same ground would land a trophy of so much greater significance.

Despite finishing the previous season fourth, and being runners-up in the League Cup, McLean viewed that campaign's achievements as far from satisfactory. This he admitted when interviewed by Dixon Blackstock in the *Sunday Mail* on the eve of the new season. 'We are one of the top five teams in Scotland. We must be there all the time when the prizes are being handed out. We have shown that we can beat the best teams in the country, but we must strive to do it more often.'

After he had seen his side comprehensively beaten twice in the League Cup opening section, St Johnstone manager Alex Rennie, a former Tannadice employee, lent his weight to United's potential: 'There is no doubt that Dundee United are equipped to win the Premier League title. They have the quality, they have the pool of players now, and they only have to lose the wee bit of inconsistency that shows now and again.'

Certainly there were no signs of that in the six sectional League Cup-ties, which were all won with a bit to spare, but given that Falkirk, Raith Rovers and St Johnstone were lower division sides, any other outcome would have been regarded as something of a shock. Indeed, apart from having a 100 per cent points tally, the goal difference of plus-twenty tells you all you need to know.

The first Saturday in September sparked the quest for the Premier League title, but even the hard-to-please Jim McLean was more than happy with his charges' start: 'It has been, in many ways, the perfect build up … as long as we realise it isn't the end product,' but he also warned, 'I believe that we are as good as Aberdeen and Celtic, but the record books prove they are better because both have recently won the league title. We have scored goals against lesser opponents, which is a thing we didn't always do in the past and we have, with the addition of Ian Britton and the improving form of Graeme Payne, plus the addition of Alex Taylor, extended our pool of players.'

As it transpired, none of that trio was to play a significant role in the title win. That was no slight on their ability, but more of an accolade to the quality of the players picked before them. Indeed, that trio between them were to make only fifteen appearances in total.

Testimony to the stability of the team can be found by comparing the side who opened the season to that which finished it – Bannon for mid-fielder Ian Britton being the only change in the starting eleven. No fewer than six of Scotland's World Cup Squad appeared in that league opener, with Dave Narey and Paul Sturrock in United's tangerine, whilst Jim Leighton, Alex McLeish, Willie Miller and Gordon Strachan were in the Dons' line-up.

Being the perfectionist that he is, even a hugely important win in this opening day fixture failed to satisfy the Tannadice supremo, to such an extent that McLean finished the match hoarse, croakily commenting, 'I lost my voice shouting my players forward in the second half. We played very well in the first half, during which we scored our two goals, but tried to sit safe second half. All against my instructions. It's a fine achievement to beat a team like Aberdeen. But I was looking for much more, especially from my front players.'

With that in mind, on the eve of the following week's game against Rangers, it was announced that Charlie George was joining the club on a short-term contract. George was one of the stars of Arsenal's double winning side of eleven years previously, and had later played for Derby and Southampton. Because George had a slight injury, his debut was put on ice until the following week at Easter Road. Some of his inspirational qualities wouldn't have gone amiss at Ibrox, where neither side could find the net, leaving Jim McLean again bemoaning his side's lack of conviction in the Govan area of Glasgow: 'We still don't believe enough in ourselves here – though we now believe a lot more than we have done in the past.'

Before tackling Hibs the following Saturday, United put their growing European reputation to the test against PSV Eindhoven at Tannadice. Winners of the UEFA Cup in 1978, the Dutch masters' standards might have slipped a little, but they still represented a formidable hurdle, and proved it in a first leg that ended – in light of the away goal – in an unsatisfactory 1-1 draw. Not that United, who were never at their most fluent, could have any complaints over the outcome. In the aftermath of a somewhat disappointing European night, Jim McLean, unprepared to accept that the tie was over, prophetically postulated, 'It might be easier for us in Holland, just as it was easier for them to plan their game here.' How those words were to come back to haunt the Dutch side.

Beforehand, there were two important league games and although Charlie George reported for training with a view to taking the field at Easter Road, a pulled calf muscle saw him pull out of training and, as it transpired, never to return.

For the second league game running, United failed to find the net, which left McLean labelling the League Cup quarter-final clash at Pittodrie the following Wednesday as 'a day of reckoning' for his strikers if they failed to deliver. Well, deliver they did, and for the second time in less than three weeks, United accounted for Aberdeen. They established an invaluable two-goal first-leg lead and took a huge stride towards their objective of a fourth consecutive final appearance in this competition. Equally as important, the side played well for the whole 90 minutes in what was widely accepted as the best performance of the season to date. Given that Aberdeen were regarded by many as the greatest threat to the 'Old Firm' in the title race, to beat them twice in such a short space of time really did augur well.

Perhaps not surprisingly, the men who won at Pittodrie were entrusted with the task of taking on St Mirren at Tannadice. Apart from the two points, the most pleasing aspect was the return to scoring form of Paul Sturrock, who bagged his first league goals of the season, getting a late brace to make the final score 3-0. Another shut-out left United as the only side in Britain yet to concede a goal in the league.

Not that McLean was resting on his laurels. Thwarted from utilising either McLeod or George, both of whom were bedevilled by fitness problems, his next target was reportedly Morton's Andy Ritchie. But all that was temporarily forgotten as United travelled to Holland for the second leg of their UEFA Cup-tie with PSV Eindhoven, where the Dutch league leaders were humbled. It might have only finished 2-0 in United's favour (3-1 on aggregate), but the home side just never got into the game. Just as McLean had hinted after the first leg, United did find it easier away from home, turning in almost equally as regal a performance as had left Monaco stunned twelve months previously. It drew this unusually fulsome praise from the taciturn boss: 'This was one of our finest European performances. I cannot fault any of my players. They did everything right and went at the opposition from the first whistle.'

The Tangerines weren't the only ones performing heroics on Dutch soil that evening. Celtic also gave a boost to the game in Scotland by beating Dutch Champions Ajax in the European Cup. The draw for the next rounds, made on the eve of the two sides' league clash at Tannadice, pitched Celtic against Spain's Real Sociedad, whilst United's next UEFA Cup opponents would be Viking Stavanger of Norway.

The packed house crammed into Tannadice saw United concede their first goals of the season, falling two behind shortly after the break with Paul McStay and Roy Aitken having given the reigning champions a seemingly invincible lead. Sandwiched between these goals came a double blow. Eamonn Bannon limped off before the half hour and John Holt, his replacement, hurt himself in his first tackle four minutes later. Holt had to be subbed by Ian Britton, all of which made a comeback look

unlikely. Fifteen minutes from time, to the dejection of the home support, the score was unchanged. Perhaps Celtic had been lulled into a false
sense of security because, in an astonishing late rally, United picked themselves off the canvas to scrape a precious point. Dodds poached the first
after a Sturrock shot had been parried by Pat Bonner, and with the crowd
reaching fever pitch, Ralph Milne hammered in a last-minute leveller.

If some of United's top-rated players didn't do themselves justice
against Celtic, there was no doubt that Ralph Milne did. Not only was
Milne showing greater confidence, he also added goal threat, and his
equaliser and first goal of the league campaign sparked a series of glori-
ously great and key goals.

The sequence of heavyweight contests continued with the quarter-
final League Cup home clash against Aberdeen. With a two-goal cushion
from the first leg, McLean hoped to introduce new strikers Charlie
George and Ally McLeod, but as was to be the case during the whole of
their time at Tannadice, both were sidelined through injury and destined
never to appear.

Alex Ferguson's Aberdeen still weren't firing on all cylinders, although
a 0-0 draw away to Dinamo Tirana and a 2-1 win over Motherwell suggested they had turned the corner. Indeed, the Dons' boss viewed the
task of trying to claw back two goals at Tannadice as 'the most difficult
task we've ever faced'. Too hard, in fact. Aberdeen could find no way
through, and a Paul Sturrock penalty sealed the tie. Remarkably, it was the
fourth season on the trot that Aberdeen had exited the League Cup at the
hands of a side from Dundee. Defeated by United in the 1979 final,
Dundee ousted them the following season at the quarter-final stage, and
the previous term they had been surprised by United who travelled to
Pittodrie a goal down, but returned with a 3-0 win to book their place in
a third consecutive final. Now a fourth successive final was just one step
away, but it was Celtic who stood in their path.

After the results against PSV Eindhoven, Celtic and Aberdeen, perhaps a touch of complacency had crept in. Certainly, it looked that way
as bottom of the table Kilmarnock took a point off United in a tousey
league clash. If a measure of a good side is to take points when not playing well, then United passed that test with flying colours at Rugby Park.
Ralph Milne had sent over enough inviting crosses to win half-a-dozen
games but, fittingly, Ralphie grabbed another vital goal, this time from the
penalty spot. In fact, both goals in the 1-1 draw were shrouded in controversy. Three Killie men looked offside as Gallacher got the final touch
to McDicken's lob. As the *Sunday Post* reporter opined, 'United were too
flabbergasted even to protest.'

Referee Robertson didn't cover himself in glory with the decision that led to the Tangerines' leveller. Chasing a high ball, Derek Stark appeared to be more sinner than sinned against by Derrick McDicken, but the official deemed otherwise and awarded a penalty. In football, they say the breaks even themselves out over the season: at Rugby Park they did so rather concisely in 90 minutes. More worryingly for United and their fans, the only two goals in 180 minutes of play had been penalties.

Mid-October might have brought a welcome break in terms of club commitments, but there was no relaxation for Messrs McAlpine and Gough, Narey and Sturrock. The first-named pair were in action for Scotland Under-21s against East Germany at Tynecastle, with goalkeeper Hamish McAlpine earning his first international recognition since his days of boys club football. Included as an over-age player, Hamish was in his seventeenth season at the club, but at 34 still very much in his prime as a goalkeeper. Explaining his decision to give McAlpine the captaincy, Jock Stein said: 'He is a great organiser with his club and that is one of the reasons that United have such a good defensive record.'

Hamish led the side to a 2-0 win over the East Germans and, whilst it was his first cap, skippering a side was nothing new to the extrovert goalkeeper who, until Paul Hegarty took over, captained United for a couple of seasons.

Twenty-four hours later, the full Scotland side emulated their Under-21 counterparts with a win by the same score, also against East Germany. Dave Narey was in the starting line up and Paul Sturrock came on to score Scotland's second goal within two minutes of stripping off. For Sturrock, the brief airing in Scotland's dark blue was most welcome. As he revealed afterwards: 'The fifteen minutes or so I was on was the best that I have played this season. I'd lost a lot of confidence this year. It had nothing to do with not getting a World Cup game in Spain. It was a combination of things – missing a lot of pre-season training; a few niggly injuries and illness; and bother with a house extension. I had also been doing too many things off the field with personal appearances and the like. It's sorted now, though,' he promised.

In previewing the following Saturday's league fixture, McLean stated, 'It's high time we saw two of our front players on form on the same day and I'm hoping that we will get closer to that position against Morton.' And they did that and a bit more, five ahead by the break they ran out six-goal winners against a demoralised Morton side with a display of fast flowing football.

Waxing lyrically about the Tannadice performance, the late Bob Wilson, writing under the guise of Don John in Monday's *Courier*, commented, 'Any complimentary adjective you can think of hardly does justice to the sheer quality of some of the first half play,' and later added, 'I haven't seen a better spell in years as the Tangerines scored four times between the fifteenth and 21st minutes.' Davie Dodds led the charge with a hat-trick, Billy Kirkwood notched his first league counter from midfield, whilst David Narey not only scored twice, but was a whisker away from matching Dodds with a treble.

The only pity was that the massacre was watched by United's smallest crowd of the season – 5,986 – which was the exact same figure as would turn out for Morton's second visit of the season.

Ralph Milne's vital goals this season weren't all confined to the title run, because his brace in Stavanger were hugely responsible for United negotiating yet another European hurdle. It wasn't until seventeen minutes from the end that Ralph Milne finally broke the deadlock, only for Per Henriksen to equalise three minutes later. Undeterred, Milne and Sturrock struck twice in the last ten minutes to secure a two-goal platform for eventual progress.

But just when everything appeared rosy, a freak accident in training laid Paul Sturrock low. Struck in the face by a ball, bruising behind an eye ruled the striker out for almost three weeks and five important games. Fortunately, an injury of such duration was the exception rather than the rule this season, another factor that helped the Tannadice cause.

Ian Britton came into the side for the injured Sturrock at Fir Park with the other ten all replying in the affirmative when asked by the manager if they were up to playing the full 90 minutes after Wednesday's exertions in Norway. Great results in Europe are notoriously followed by poor league results and for much of the game at bottom-placed Motherwell this looked another case in point. At no time did United show any kind of form, but David Narey popped up with a precious goal two minutes from time and Billy Kirkwood added another for an improbable two-goal victory. Without his striking partner, Sturrock, Davie Dodds was left with too much to do, despite a plentiful supply of ammunition from Richard Gough and Ralph Milne on the right.

The availability of either Charlie George or Ally McLeod would have eased the burden on Dodds. In the wake of the Motherwell match, Jim McLean confirmed that he had had a £40,000 bid for an unnamed player turned down, but that the search would go on, especially as Dodds had been soldiering on with a niggly injury and really could do with being rested.

There was, however, no let up in the punishing schedule. The first leg of the League Cup semi-final at Parkhead now loomed. With Eamonn

Bannon joining Paul Sturrock on the sidelines, there was no chance of Davie Dodds being given a breather for a tie which Jim McLean likened to a European one.

Fielding a 4-3-3 formation, with John Holt and Iain Phillip bolstering the midfield, United contained Celtic for 39 minutes. Not only that, but United might well have been ahead, with Davie Dodds holding his head in anguish after drilling a shot against Bonner's post. However, five fateful minutes turned this tie in Celtic's favour. A disputed penalty gave Celtic the lead when Glasgow referee Kenny Hope decreed that Derek Stark's tackle on Davie Provan was illegal, to the unavailing fury of the whole United side.

Having gone behind to Charlie Nicholas's conversion, worse followed on the stroke of the interval when Frank McGarvey scored a second. Although United were not out of the competition, that game signalled the end of the club's unbeaten record that had stretched to twenty games.

Frustrated in his efforts to strengthen the squad, Jim McLean spread the net, contacting former European opponents Lokeren over the availability of former Morton striker Jim Tolmie. However, the quoted fee of £100,000 for a player whom had cost the Belgian club just £70,000 two years previously soon ended that line of enquiry.

So United went into the first derby of the season with the same squad, but McLean blooded youngster Alex Taylor, a midfielder of cultured creativity, in a league game for the first time, despite the fact that Taylor had been transfer-listed earlier in the season.

As he promised to do so often, Ralph Milne looked like the man who could break the deadlock in the rarity of an uneventful derby as Dundee defended dourly in dank and damp conditions.

'A classic example of the irresistible force meeting the immovable object,' was the damning summary of the *Sunday Post*. A late error allowed Davie Dodds to sneak a goal as United won a game in the dying minutes for the second week running, clearly demonstrating the sheer tenacity of the Tangerines – another vital ingredient for a championship challenging side.

Having again missed the services of Bannon and Sturrock, McLean planned some minor shocks for the return leg against Viking Stavanger. Of course, the two-goal first-leg advantage obviously influenced his thinking, but defender Dave Beaumont and striker John Clark were drafted in, which meant that seven of the 17-man squad were aged 21 or under.

Not that many questions were posed by the reigning Norwegian champions, who adopted a defensive approach, despite being two goals in arrears. In consequence, it was all a bit of a stroll for the home side as the game petered out to a tame goalless draw. It is a match that John Clark will remember though: the big, burly 18-year-old striker came off the bench to make his first-team debut four minutes from the end. Even as a teenager, the blond-haired striker had boasted a powerful physique, but he now added a physical presence that was not a feature in the rest of the squad. For a big man, Clark had a good touch, too, but like Paul Hegarty before him, 'Clarkie's' future was to lie in defence.

United's reward for nudging out the Norwegians was a third round tie with Werder Bremen, but it was trying to bag two vital points from Aberdeen that was back in focus following Friday's Euro draw. At least Eamonn Bannon was back for the Pittodrie date, and when Richard Gough opened the scoring, hopes a fourth successive win over Fergie's troops were raised. However, backed by a gale straight off the nearby North Sea, the home side blew United off course. McLean's men suffered not only the first league defeat of the season, but their heaviest ever in the Premier League – 1-5. It was over six years since Celtic had inflicted a defeat by the same score at Parkhead. In addition, the result brought the then longest ever undefeated run in the Premier league of eleven games to an abrupt halt.

Incensed at his side's woeful performance, Jim McLean's post-match comments tellingly dwelt more on Aberdeen's strengths than his own side's weaknesses on the day. 'Aberdeen were magnificent. They had the players who wanted to win most. You cannot take credit away from them.'

What turned out to be United's worst afternoon of the season, only heaped further misery on season ticket holder and life-long United fan Tom Cairns. His planned family day out turned out to be a complete disaster, as Tom describes:

'My wife, Helen, and I picked up our nephew Andrew Sievwright and his pal Craig Rattray at Tay Bridge Station before setting to Aberdeen, where my wife was going shopping whilst the guys were looking forward to United continuing their great start to the season. We ought to have known it wasn't going to be our day because on the journey up the coast to Aberdeen my not so trusty Austin Allegro completely lost power. I called the AA out and we got going again, but this scenario was to be repeated again just outside Stonehaven. The temporary repairs enabled us to crawl the remaining fifteen miles up to the Granite City, where we barely slowed down to deposit Helen in the city centre just ten minutes before the big kick-off.

'The day began bright as we made it into the stadium to see Richard Gough putting United ahead after twenty minutes. Unfortunately, that was the only bright spot of a very dull and damp afternoon. The rest of the match is best forgotten as Aberdeen went on to net five in reply. But our tale of woe was far from over! On returning to our car, it did start but was shuddering violently. We managed to crawl into Aberdeen after the match traffic had subsided and picked up Helen from the shops.

'The journey home only added insult to the injury of seeing United slump to their biggest defeat of the season. The first pit stop on the way home came just outside of Inverbervie where the family ended up push-ing the car towards the hill so that we could free-wheel into the town. This time we called the AA and they called out a local garage who an hour later had us mobile. Before reaching Arbroath, it was back to square one with the car playing up again. Not wishing to risk further breakdowns, I headed for my workplace at Monifieth Ambulance station and borrowed a car to take the lads to the bus station, as by this time they had missed their train. The saga continued when I returned to Monifieth, where I collected my own car and took the low road rather than risk a repeat per-formance on an unlit road.

'And just when I thought things couldn't get any worse, the complete exhaust system fell off. The only saving grace was that my pal, Tom Crawford, lived round the corner and I was able to get the car there and was chauffeured home in a sports car.'

Little wonder that that day, calamitous as it was for us Arabs, sticks so vividly in the memory of Tom Cairns.

A defeat of such magnitude was hardly the ideal platform for the next assignment, given that it was the second leg of their League Cup semi-final with Celtic, with the added burden of having to try and retrieve a two-goal deficit. However, 24 hours ahead of the all-ticket match there was a boost for all concerned when a specialist gave Paul Sturrock the green light to play again. A hastily arranged closed-doors game was arranged at Stirling Albion to give 'Luggy' some badly needed match practice after the reserves' scheduled game at Forfar had been called off. And how his return helped regenerate the side.

If, the previous Saturday, it had been difficult to give credit to one United player, against Celtic it was almost impossible to find anyone who didn't merit praise, but the contributions of Gough, Hegarty, Narey, Milne and Sturrock were all that little bit worthier of special mention.

In fact, Paul Sturrock played as though he had never been away, rather than just returning from a three-week absence. His presence saw Roy

Aitken get the last touch before the ball crossed the line as the gap was halved, and Sturrock's persistence was wholly responsible for squeezing in the equaliser after 64 minutes. However, having outplayed Celtic, the key to the eventual outcome rested on John Holt's sending off twelve minutes from the end for a foul on Burns, after the United player had already been booked.

For almost the first time in the match, Celtic came into the contest and, with just a minute left, Tommy Burns sent away Charlie Nicholas and the youngster steered the ball home. It certainly didn't help assuage United's disappointment that Tommy Burns handled the ball not once, but twice before setting up the Celtic goal that denied United extra-time and that possible fourth successive League Cup final.

One neutral in the crowd that evening was Manchester City fan Bob Stafford. Bob was so taken with the match that he was driven to put pen to paper, writing the following letter to the club: 'As an ardent follower of English football, I was pleasantly surprised with my first taste of Scottish football at Tannadice last Wednesday. Not only was the game played with a skill and commitment rarely seen in England, but the supporters from both sides gave a perfect example of how the game should be watched and enjoyed without a hint of trouble.'

Rarely can what was, in effect, a defeat have been so encouraging. In praising his players for the tremendous pride and character they showed against Celtic, Jim McLean also pointed out, 'As far as I am concerned that was the most one-sided game we have ever played against either of the Old Firm since we beat Rangers 4-1 at Ibrox a couple of years ago.'

Chapter 3

# ~ CONSOLIDATING THE CHALLENGE ~

## (NOVEMBER 1982 – JANUARY 1983)

By the time Rangers arrived at Tannadice on the second Saturday in November, it marked the conclusion of one of the most intensive spells of vital fixtures ever undertaken by the club – Viking Stavanger in the UEFA Cup, Aberdeen in the league, and Celtic in the League Cup semi-final. The climax of this testing ten-day spell was a league meeting with Rangers, breathing down third-placed United's necks in the table.

|          | P  | W | D | L | F  | A  | Pts |
|----------|----|---|---|---|----|----|-----|
| Celtic   | 10 | 8 | 1 | 1 | 26 | 12 | 17  |
| Aberdeen | 10 | 6 | 2 | 2 | 20 | 10 | 14  |
| Dundee U | 10 | 5 | 4 | 1 | 18 | 8  | 14  |
| Rangers  | 10 | 4 | 5 | 1 | 21 | 11 | 13  |

Not that there were any complaints about this punishing schedule: it is the price every club willingly pays for success. However, the air of disappointment hung heavily over Tannadice in the aftermath of the exit from the League Cup, and particularly at the manner of it.

Jim McLean refuted any thoughts that the game against Rangers might be something of an anti-climax, confirming the single-mindedness and resolve within the club to stay in the championship race: 'The League title is still the one, and a game against Rangers is a major game no matter in what competition. It's a great game for us to recover from the disappointment of Wednesday.'

Equally as pertinently, with just over a quarter of the league campaign gone, Rangers, despite a poor start by their standards, only trailed United by a point.

Although Ralph Milne gave United the lead with a rare headed goal, John Greig's men hit back through Davie Cooper just before the interval and Derek Johnstone, who was to briefly wear tangerine twelve months later. Adversity, however, only fuelled the fire in United's hearts as they pounded Rangers during the last quarter of the game. That brought the reward of an equaliser from Davie Dodds and two late lightning strikes by Richard Gough and Ralph Milne to win the game.

That Richard Gough should score the goal that was instrumental in Rangers' downfall was indeed ironic. Joe Gilroy, once a striker with Clyde and Dundee, and who had emigrated to South Africa, had recommended the tall, sandy-haired teenager to Rangers. However, after taking a look at him on trial they cast him aside – an error of judgment that was to cost the Ibrox side a whopping £1.1 million when the lithe, athletic defender joined them from Spurs seven years later. It would be interesting to know who at Ibrox should take the blame for failing to recognise a prodigious talent, particularly as Gough was the sort of player who seldom had a bad game. It is hard to imagine him failing to impress, during a trial or anywhere else.

To say the least, Gough's background was cosmopolitan. His father was Scottish and had played football for Scotland at amateur international level. Although born in Stockholm, Richard was brought up in South Africa and inherited the single-minded approach to sport that is so prevalent in sportsman from the southern hemisphere. In other words, he was a winner.

Although Gough carved out a distinguished career in central defence at the highest level with Spurs, Rangers, and Scotland, he spent almost the whole of his five seasons at Tannadice at right-back. Perhaps it would be more accurate to describe him as a wing-back before his time, because he spent almost as much time charging forward as he did defending, even although he played in a flat back four. Whilst Rangers and Spurs fans might disagree, there is a school of thought that 'Bish' was at his most effective in his role at Tannadice, and the full-back's total of 37 goals from 252 appearances in tangerine bears testimony to that.

Gough's strike against Rangers was one of eight league goals he scored that term, and helped earn two precious points. These, combined with Aberdeen drawing at Morton, enabled United to leap-frog the Dons into second place.

Midweek inactivity brought respite to some of the United squad but, as it was an international week, not for all. Hamish McAlpine again led the Under-21s to victory – 4-3 against Switzerland in Aarau – with Richard Gough showing that he didn't just reserve his goals for the domestic arena. His first at international level was a trademark header, which proved to be the winning goal, ten minutes from time. There was no joy in Berne the following evening, when the full Scotland side went down 0-2 in their European Championship qualifier. That disappointment was doubled in Tannadice terms because Paul Sturrock suffered a pulled muscle and had to be substituted at half-time. The other Tannadice representative, Dave Narey, came through unscathed.

Of course, the worry was that with Paul Sturrock's recent return help-ing the side to victories over the Old Firm, the last thing that was need-ed was for him to miss out again. Fortunately, 'Luggy' passed a late fit-ness test for the visit of struggling Hibs. He showed just how important he was to the side by setting up Eamonn Bannon's first-half opener, but it was substitute John Reilly's goal that provided the only lasting memory from a competent rather than brilliant 3-0 win.

At least there were no more injuries before having to face Werder Bremen in midweek. Any West German side had to be respected and McLean's assistant, Walter Smith, had been sent to spy on them. After watching them in action against Karlsruhe he reported back that Werder Bremen were very similar to United!

Conversely, Werder coach Otto Rehhagel was under no illusions about the task facing his men. 'I watched Dundee United play Celtic and was very impressed the way both sides attacked for 90 minutes. We will have to be very careful in defence.' So concerned was he, that Rehhagel also contacted Borussia Moenchengladbach, who had been badly mauled by United twelve months earlier, and received a similar warning.

United took European centre-stage not only in Scotland, but through-out Britain, as they were the last UEFA Cup survivors from these shores. Clubs like Manchester United, Arsenal, Ipswich and Southampton had all fallen by the wayside. Having done the hard work in the away legs to secure victories over PSV and Viking in previous rounds, United were determined to give themselves a helping hand by winning the home leg, but given the quality of the German opposition, it is fair to say that this was borne of necessity. The importance of the home leg was something that Jim McLean fully appreciated. 'We want goals and we must be posi-tive from the first whistle. If we score one, we must immediately look for another, with no letting up. Equally, it should be remembered, it's also vital to prevent the opposition from scoring,' he warned, before what was the club's 43rd European tie.

Well, United achieved the advantage they sought, but it was only by the minimum of margins, and only after a titanic struggle. Following Ralph Milne's early opener, a barrage of United pressure produced fre-quent openings. In the end, however, only a marvellous goal from David Narey seven minutes from time – when goalkeeper Burdenski could only paw his lob into the roof of the net – gave United a slender advantage for the second leg.

Indeed, when the Germans had equalised through Norbert Meier sev-enteen minutes earlier, it had come as no great surprise, because United were going through a decidedly rocky spell. So, it was another feather in the cap when United responded by coming back strongly to win the game.

Those endeavours, combined with the strength-sapping mud, had already convinced Jim McLean that he had to make changes for the visit to St Mirren in the league three days later. Injuries, however, were to further force his hand.

John Reilly had already been earmarked for promotion, so that the overworked Davie Dodds wouldn't be in the starting line up for the first time that season. Even being relegated to the bench wouldn't prevent him making his mark, though. In addition, Derek Stark, who had put in a power of work in midfield in recent weeks, hadn't recovered from the bruised thigh that forced him out of the Bremen tie at half-time. John Holt, who had replaced him, retained his place at Love Street.

Confidence in the Paisley camp was low after the Saints had conceded nine goals without reply in their previous two matches – albeit against Celtic and Aberdeen. But United made an uncertain start before eventually stepping up a gear. Only the barrier of Billy Thomson in the home goal kept them at bay. The Scottish international keeper's performance that day helped shape his future career, because less than two years later he was a United player. He was finally beaten twenty minutes from the end when Eamonn Bannon blasted home. Davie Dodds had entered the fray four minutes earlier and his presence was a telling factor in making the breakthrough. Dodds scored a simple second from a Bannon assist to ease the nerves. If the hallmark of champions is to win games when turning in indifferent performances, then, at Paisley, United passed that test with flying colours.

Given that this was the 36th fixture in a little over four months since first-team proceedings got under way in Malmo in July, a week off in early December was welcome and gave a chance to draw breath. The break came about because of defeat by Celtic in the semi-final of the League Cup. The two clubs had a league date at Parkhead on the first Saturday in December. This was also the date for the League Cup final, so a crucial championship contest was put on ice. Remarkably, it was the only fixture of the season not to be played on its allotted date, but fate was to determine that it would be some four months before United made their first visit of the season to Celtic Park.

Celtic's opponents in the Hampden final were Rangers, who had been due to meet Dundee in the league. The Dens Park club had suggested bringing the Dens derby – due on New Year's Day – forward. But given United's near non-stop programme, not to mention the forthcoming second leg with Werder Bremen, it was a switch that was wisely rejected.

Consequently, Jim McLean celebrated eleven highly successful years in the Tannadice hot seat spying on Werder Bremen. He was cautiously impressed by the Germans as they defeated Eintracht Frankfurt 3-0 in the Weserstadion, venue for the second leg four days later.

Back home, striker Ally McLeod's ill-fated stay on Tayside was terminated without his kicking a ball in anger for the first team. It was mutually agreed that he would part company with the club. This, combined with the Charlie George fiasco, brought further frustration in the attempts to strengthen the team's strike-force.

With a ten-day break before the European return leg, you'd have thought it safe to assume there would be few injury worries, but as luck would have it, Davie Dodds and Iain Phillip were sent home from training on the Friday, suffering from heavy colds, joining a similarly afflicted Paul Sturrock on the sidelines. Fortunately, they had all recovered by the time the chartered flight to Bremen took off, though it left without Billy Kirkwood, who was the latest to suffer flu-like symptoms. However, 24 hours later the midfielder was on his way, having recovered sufficiently to enter the lion's den of the Weserstadion. Here, United were to be subjected to probably the most torrid European tie in which they have ever been involved, having to survive a blitz from the German side to hang on by their finger-tips to take another notable continental scalp.

Paul Hegarty proved to be Captain Courageous – and not just in defence. McLean confused the Germans by fielding Milne, Gough and Kirkwood all on the left, rather than the right. The United skipper sent a downward header past Burdenski after Ralph Milne switched flanks to send over a corner with just three minutes on the clock and register a vital away goal. Bremen now needed three goals to win outright, or two to force extra-time.

Although Hamish McAlpine made a couple of vital saves in the first half, the tie could well have been all over two minutes from the interval. Hegarty headed down a cross from Eamonn Bannon and the ball fell to Davie Dodds six yards out. The spread legs of Burdenski denied Dodds, kept the Germans in the tie, and acted as a catalyst to an incredible second half onslaught. Rudi Voller, the current German national team coach, waged his own personal war of attrition. Within three minutes of the re-start he levelled the scores on the night to bring his side within a goal of equality.

Time after time the German attacks were thwarted. True, Hegarty and Co enjoyed a little help from the woodwork, with Voller incredibly striking it three times. Voller threatened to snatch the goal that would take the tie into extra-time when he lobbed over the onrushing McAlpine, but

Hegarty came to the rescue, sprinting back to hook the ball to safety from under the shadow of the crossbar.

The United skipper remembers the incident and the game only too vividly: 'I saw Hamish coming out and just instinctively knew that he wasn't going to cut out Voller's lob and hared back to goal and was lucky enough to just reach the ball as it was about to cross the line, whilst I landed up entangled in the back of the net,' he recalled, adding, 'It was a real backs-to-the-wall job during that second half as we were forced to defend in our own penalty box. Curiously, it was a good night for me personally, and I had what I would consider one of my best ever games, though probably because I was always in the thick of the action.'

So United survived the siege of Bremen to qualify for the quarter-finals of the UEFA Cup for the second successive season. The competition would now hibernate through the winter until March. The draw in Zurich paired Jim McLean's heroes with Bohemians Prague, but with the championship challenge very much preoccupying them, thoughts of that tie three months hence were put on the back burner.

Next up were Kilmarnock. Having ceded a point to the bottom-markers at Rugby Park, the title protagonists went out to ensure that there was no repetition. From the word 'go', Killie were under the cosh, much as United had been in Germany 72 hours earlier. Milne, Stark, Kirkwood and Bannon all went close, but it was one of the lesser sung heroes of the class of '83 who came up with the vital opener. John Reilly's ratio of seven goals from eight starts that term was pretty impressive, and when he poached the first after keeper Alan McCulloch spilled a Sturrock shot with half-time approaching it opened the second-half floodgates as United ran in six more without reply.

Reilly got another, whilst central defender Dave Narey crashed in his eighth goal of the season. A superlative Ralph Milne strike made it five, and a double from Davie Dodds completed the scoring. The 7-0 tally was a repeat of the scoreline on the Rugby Park men's previous visit to Tannadice almost exactly two years earlier, and equalled United's best ever Premier League win.

So scintillating was United's performance, that even the handful of fans who had travelled from Ayrshire showed their appreciation, as Arab Eamonn Malone, then 22, remembers: 'The Killie supporters were singing and clapping United as they ran rings round their own team. I had never seen anything like it, nor since, in all my years of attending matches involving United.'

Before the following week's match at Morton, there was another interlude for all but four of the United staffmen. Under-21 regulars Hamish

McAlpine and Richard Gough were in action for Scotland in their 2-1 win over Belgium at Gent, whilst Maurice Malpas showed his mettle in his first start at that level, after having had little opportunity to shine in his debut from the bench against Switzerland the previous month. Despite two goals by Kenny Dalglish, Scotland went down 2-3 in the full international at the Heysel Stadium. King Kenny's presence, as was so often the case, meant only a seat on the subs bench for Paul Sturrock, although Dave Narey again featured.

Fortunately, all four players involved on international duty reported fit for the trip to Cappielow, which was hazardous enough, given that since the advent of the Premier League, United had only won one and drawn two of their eight visits to Greenock. Throw in a snow-covered and icy surface and you had the proverbial potential banana-skin. In fact, were that wintry scene to have confronted a referee these days, when players' safety is paramount, the game most certainly would not have been played. But in true championship commitment, if not style, United forsook their normal passing game on the skating rink lottery that Cappielow present-ed, as Jim McLean affirmed afterwards: 'We just had to batter the ball up the park.' Whilst it may not have been pretty, it was effective and the end product of two points justified the means. Even falling behind to an early goal by Eddie McNab proved surmountable. For the second week run-ning, John Reilly scored an all-important opener with a scissor-kick, and Sturrock sealed victory when he converted an Eamonn Bannon cross.

Despite Sturrock's excellent overall performance, whilst his team-mates enjoyed a long lie the following Monday, bizarrely he had to report to Tannadice for a spot of pre-season training in a bleak mid-winter set-ting. As McLean explained before the Morton game: 'Paul missed our pre-season preparation. After being involved in the World Cup finals, he went on to Largs for the SFA Coaching School before going straight to Denmark for our pre-season matches. So, as he isn't as fit or as sharp as he should be, and as Paul's game is based on sharpness, he has got to be super fit. He isn't, and as a result his confidence has dipped. Hence the reason he has only scored two goals in eleven league games.'

Not that the player was complaining about a rigorous training sched-ule, which would see him report back on at least two afternoons a week, plus any days his colleagues were given off. 'I'll never ever miss pre-sea-son training,' he resolved, adding, 'My preparation was all wrong.'

Cappielow may have housed only a meagre assembly – the 1,887 being the second lowest to watch any of United's title winning games – but interest in United was growing at home and abroad. As secretary Helen Lindsay recalls, the sale of half-price season tickets had been brisk with many from outside Dundee. 'We have had fans with addresses from places as diverse as Glasgow, Edinburgh, Aberdeen, Stirling and Kirkcaldy, whilst others came from smaller population centres as Scone, Pittenweem and Stenhousemuir to name but three.'

And the boundaries of United's increasing support weren't confined to Scotland. A party regularly travelled up from England, and two Dundee lads, Steve Smith and Dave Mann, who worked in Alkmaar, had formed a Dutch branch of the Supporters' Association. Such growing support from so many out-of-town supporters was a measure of the Tangerines' success.

And the United bandwagon showed no signs of stalling on the field of play. The visit of Motherwell made it six back-to-back league wins as United kept up the pressure on leaders Celtic. The Tannadice goal-machine swung into action in the final fixture of 1983, banging another five goals without reply as the gulf between top and bottom was only too clearly indicated. The visitors held out for over half an hour, but the second period was nothing less than a rout.

It had nothing to do with the season of goodwill, but even the demanding Jim McLean, not prone to dishing out plaudits lightly, praised the side in no uncertain terms: 'To say I am pleased at the way they are playing would be an understatement. Counting our pre-season friendlies, and including our UEFA Cup-ties, we have now played 40 matches, and we have had shut-outs in twenty of them. The present team is the most positive I have had in eleven years,' he reflected by way of a half-term report, continuing, 'We have fellows like Paul Sturrock, Ralph Milne, Eamonn Bannon, Davie Dodds and John Reilly, whilst the back four is immense with Dave Narey in a different class.'

One of the lesser-sung heroes also attracted special mention. 'Derek Stark is the player I am most pleased about. It isn't so long ago that he was threatening to join the police. But since he changed his mind and decided to become a full-time player, he has improved beyond measure. In my time with the club, I can safely say that I have never seen a player who puts so much effort into the game.' Originally a full-back, Derek occasionally filled in at centre-half on the rare occasions that Paul Hegarty was absent. But the championship season saw him operating in midfield to telling effect.

Before the traditional New Year's Day derby, there was a bit of trans-fer activity involving some of the fringe players at Tannadice. Full-back Derek Murray, midfielders Graeme Payne and Ian Gibson, and goal-keeper Andy Graham were offered on loan to other clubs. The emer-gence of John Clark and Alex Taylor in the first-team squad was cited by

McLean as the reason for this. The manager tied up a deal with Morton, that saw midfielders Ian Gibson and Graeme Payne switch to Cappielow until the end of the season, with striker John McNeil coming to Tannadice. At that time clubs were allowed to loan only one player, the identity of whichever one was being transferred kept secret by the clubs at the time. Later it was ascertained that Graeme Payne had played his last game for United.

John McNeil arrived at Tannadice with a fine reputation and capped an impressive performance with a goal on his debut against Dundee reserves. He was included in the squad for the first-team derby two days later, but little was seen of the 23-year old striker. Indeed, he was to see just twelve minutes of first-team action and they didn't come at Dens Park, where Ralph Milne helped United extend their domination of this fixture to ten games without defeat. In the process, United extended their league winning ways to seven.

A large crowd of just over 18,000 delayed the kick-off by ten minutes, but United soon made short work of their hosts with a Ralph Milne double. His first was a header; the second a deflection by unwitting Dundee defender Iain McDonald from Richard Gough's cross. The scribe from the *Sunday Post* wrote: 'Next-door neighbours called the tune with their original party piece; they were different class. The score flattered the hosts. In fact, if United hadn't been in such benevolent mood, the result would have been embarrassing … it's difficult to make comparisons. Although United squandered numerous opportunities, Dundee didn't create any to miss.'

By this time, Rangers had dropped out of the title hunt, leaving it a three-horse race:

|          | P  | W  | D | L | F  | A  | Pts |
|----------|----|----|---|---|----|----|-----|
| Celtic   | 17 | 15 | 1 | 1 | 50 | 18 | 31  |
| Dundee U | 17 | 12 | 4 | 2 | 43 | 11 | 28  |
| Aberdeen | 18 | 12 | 3 | 3 | 35 | 13 | 27  |
| Rangers  | 17 | 5  | 8 | 4 | 25 | 19 | 18  |

Two days later, Tannadice housed the second of the festive holiday fixtures. The visit of Aberdeen to Tannadice was undoubtedly the game of the day, and with Celtic three points ahead of United, and four ahead of the Dons, who had played a game more, it really was one which neither team could afford to lose.

Unfortunately, Aberdeen proved highly embarrassing visitors, bursting United's previously unblemished home record and inflicting the first league defeat since the fateful 1-5 reversal at Pittodrie two months earlier. Conscious of how important victory was to them, Ferguson's troops hustled and bustled United out of their stride. Although in terms of possession, United had more of the ball, they rarely threatened Jim Leighton, whereas Aberdeen always looked dangerous on the break. But for the heroics of Hamish McAlpine, the 0-3 final scoreline could have been doubled. Almost unbelievably, Aberdeen had now plundered eight goals in the last two meetings with United – two more than the Tannadice rearguard had lost in their other sixteen matches.

Unpalatable as it may have been to United supporters, the only saving grace that day was Dundee's result. Two down to Celtic at Celtic Park, Eric Sinclair scored twice as Donald Mackay's side fought back to hold the champions. Nevertheless, United now trailed the leaders by four points and had slipped to third place after the Dons leap-frogged above them.

Paul Sturrock's fitness regime left its mark in an unwanted way, for the player failed to recover from a foot injury for the trip to Ibrox five days later. Jim McLean had omitted John Reilly from the team to play Aberdeen in preference for the strength of Davie Dodds up front, but the youngster had come on and impressed for the final few minutes. The unavailability of Sturrock to play Rangers secured 'Boney' a starting slot and the young striker didn't let anyone down, poaching an opener, but unusually casual play let Rangers back into it just before the interval. Sadly, goals by Swedish international Robert Prytz and Andy Kennedy's first strike for the Light Blues cost United a second consecutive league defeat – half of their total for the whole season. A late United rally saw a neat piece of skill from substitute John McNeil, who came off the bench to make his debut, but it was to be the first and last taste of first-team action in tangerine for the man from Morton.

As candid as ever, manager Jim McLean curtly summed up proceedings in the Govan area of Glasgow: 'We got exactly what we deserved – Nothing.'

With Celtic and Aberdeen both winning, the gap between United and the top two had widened to a worrying three points behind Aberdeen in second place and a daunting six points behind the reigning champions.

Despite those double dunts, no one was pushing the panic buttons, least of all the manager – well not in public anyway. Following the Ibrox defeat, Jim McLean's verdict was: 'Only Hamish McAlpine [who had little to do] and Paul Hegarty were worthy of praise,' but he added: 'How can I slate the players who have done so much for the club already this season.'

In fact, the two recent reversals had galvanised the resolve of their championship challenge. Given that there were still seventeen games to go, and 34 points at stake, it would have been foolish to assume that all had been lost, just because of two defeats.

Nevertheless, the repercussions of that Ibrox defeat were that changes were made for the league trip to Easter Road. Youngster Maurice Malpas was omitted from the squad stripped for duty, Iain Phillip taking his place. John Holt replaced Derek Stark, Ian Britton took over from Milne, whilst fit-again Paul Sturrock returned to the attack instead of Kirkwood.

Those changes did not work the expected magic. Indeed, it was another sub-par performance by United against what was proving to be a bit of a bogey side – Easter Road was the only ground on which United failed to find the net that term. However, unlike the previous visit in September, when neither side had many chances, this time United had to ride their luck. During a contest in which play was reduced to near farce because of a swirling wind, Hibs' Gary Murray shrugged off the attentions of Dave Narey to 'score' before referee Alan Ferguson from Giffnock incurred the wrath of the home side by calling play back for a foul by the United defender. Hibs also failed to capitalise from a penalty awarded against Eamonn Bannon. In spite of this, United almost snatched a late winner. Ralph Milne's follow up, after a Sturrock 30-yarder rebounded off the post, was thrillingly foiled by Scotland keeper Alan Rough.

Hero of that game was undoubtedly goalkeeper Hamish McAlpine, by saving Gordon Rae's spot-kick. The enduring custodian had been a huge favourite with the Arabs for many a year. He was equally popular with his team-mates, and the regard in which he was held was epitomised after the 1980 League Cup final triumph over Dundee at Dens when skipper Paul Hegarty stepped aside to push Hamish forward to go up and collect the trophy.

Hamish's nickname 'The Goalie' tells you how much of a commanding figure he was. After vying with Donald Mackay and Sandy Davie briefly for the goalkeeping jersey, in 1974 he made the position his own to the extent that for the next decade he missed a mere ten league games. One thing nobody could accuse Hamish of being was orthodox. He had his own individual style and during the 1970s captained the side – the only post-war keeper to do so – and also for a spell was the recognised penalty taker, scoring three times from the spot.

As Jim McLean revealed in his book *Jousting with Giants*, Hamish was a maverick when it came to training: 'He was the one player who was able to destroy single-handedly everything I have ever believed in about the game of football,' he wrote, and continued, 'If you did force him to do specialist goalkeeping work, then he was murder.' However, McLean also went on to concede, 'What Hamish had was an eye. He was unbelievable and that eye made him a top goalkeeper.' That was further endorsed by the fact that McAlpine was a very good cricketer, not to mention an excellent golfer.

More often than not, Hamish insisted on playing outfield in training matches, which explains why he was so comfortable on the ball. He put that to good use, too, because on many an occasion he would effectively act as an auxiliary sweeper, often rushing from his box to mop up dangerous situations. In addition, his distribution of the ball, whether from hand or foot, was of uncanny accuracy, often creating scoring opportunities at the other end. Truly a character, little wonder he was revered by the United support.

'Hamish, Hamish, give us a wave,' they used to chant, and when he responded, they followed up with 'Hamish, Hamish, give us a dance,' and again he would duly oblige.

Yet, he had to survive two major injuries. Back in 1969, just after he had made his debut, Hamish severely tore knee ligaments which kept him out for almost a year. The second injury, in 1980, was a burst blood vessel in his leg which not only threatened his career, but the limb itself. Thankfully, he recovered quickly and was soon back between the sticks. At 35 years he was by far the granddad of the championship side, but an inspiring, if unorthodox keeper.

His team had now gone three games without a win. This was hardly championship form, but United weren't blown off course because Celtic found the wild weather even more to their dislike, surprisingly losing 1-2 at second-bottom Motherwell, whilst Aberdeen were held to a draw at St Mirren.

Two games remained in January. This was described by McLean as 'the crunch time of the season', as the club's fate in not one, but two competitions hung in the balance. And the fact that St Mirren were to be the opponents two weeks running – the first at Tannadice in the league, followed by a Scottish Cup-tie at Love Street – was not to the liking of Jim McLean. The previous season, United had a similar experience with Hibs. Having won 1-0 at Easter Road in the league, the Cup-tie then went to a third game before United finally prevailed, only to be eliminated at the quarter-final stages by St Mirren at Love Street.

History, unfortunately, was about to repeat itself. In any normal season, United fans would have gladly traded a league defeat for cup progress, but this could never be described as a normal campaign. Already without Eamonn Bannon, injured in training ahead of the first meeting with Saints, there was a further shock in store for the home support with Paul Sturrock's name missing. Instead, 18-year-old John Clark was handed his league debut.

United stormed into a three-goal lead and the absence of Bannon and Sturrock appeared to be hardly noticed. However, Saints pulled one back, whereupon United strangely resorted to a long-ball game. It finished a bit too close for comfort, though Saints' second goal was too little too late.

Although Paul Sturrock returned for the second instalment of this double-header – recovering from his virus infection – Eamonn Bannon failed a fitness test on his leg strain and so missed the Cup-tie at Paisley the following Saturday.

Jim McLean's misgivings about playing the same opponents in consecutive weeks proved justified and United crashed out of the cup thanks to a Doug Somner goal after 28 minutes. It was only in the latter stages that United really came into the tie, leaving Jim McLean bemoaning, 'We must be braver.'

It wasn't quite the cliché of 'now we can concentrate on the league' because United, of course, still had the UEFA Cup on their plate, but at least the breathing space brought about by that premature Scottish Cup exit wasn't to hinder the championship cause.

History was also on United's side. Twenty-one years earlier neighbours Dundee had gone out of the Cup at the first hurdle at St Mirren's hands. They they went on to lift the title.

Jim McLean, hoisted high, and the players join in the celebrations after taking the
Scottish League title at Dens Park in May 1983

No goal this time for Derek Johnstone, far left, but the striker did hit the target twice in
his United debut against Morton in October 1983

Davie Dodds acrobatically fires a shot on target against PSV Eindhoven, despite the close attention of Ernie Brandts

More action from the PSV Eindhoven UEFA Cup-tie as Richard Gough tangles with team-mate Paul Hegarty, watched by Willi van der Kerkhof

Ralph Milne, right, hits a typically rasping late goal to salvage a draw
from Celtic's visit in October 1982

Kilmarnock's Derek McDicken does his best to block Eamonn Bannon's path to goal
during United's 7-0 thrashing of the Rugby Park side at Tannadice in December 1982

Ralph Milne leap-frogs Alloa keeper Donald Hunter during
the League Cup encounter at Tannadice in August 1983

Paul Sturrock, right, in his comeback match against Hamrun Spartans of Malta in
September 1983. Sadly, it was a sight too rarely seen in the first half of that season

Paul Goddard of West Ham is denied by a trade-mark Derek Stark tackle
in this pre-season friendly at Tannadice in August 1982

Richard Gough clears from a Czech forward in the drab Bohemians stadium
in Prague during the UEFA Cup quarter-final tie in March 1983

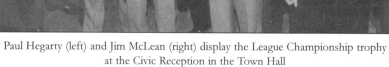

Paul Hegarty (left) and Jim McLean (right) display the League Championship trophy
at the Civic Reception in the Town Hall

Davie Dodds relishes the task of a simple finish to score the third goal
against Celtic in March 1984

Local derby action in April 1984 as Paul Hegarty shields the ball from Dundee's Walker McCall. Also in the picture are United's John Reilly and Dundee keeper Bobby Geddes

All four of John Holt's goals during the title campaign were against Kilmarnock. Here he slides in the last of them, in April 1983, under pressure from Killie's Jim Simpson

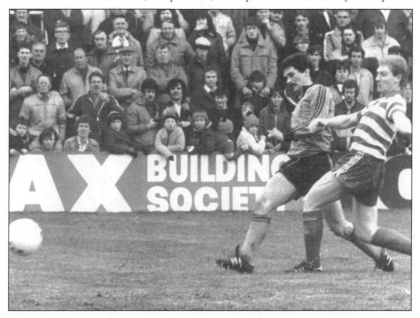

No goal this time, but Ralph Milne (right) was on target twice in the 4-0 home win over Standard Liege of Belgium in March 1983

Three of the title winners – Sturrock, Hegarty and Kirkwood – prepare to defend their crown. Here they take a breather during pre-season training in the summer of 1983

John Reilly slips past Dundee's Tosh McKinlay in this local derby
at Dens Park in September 1983

United's proud Championship-winning squad line up for the cameras
at the start of the 1983-84 season

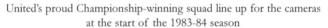

Alex Taylor shows a clean pair of heels to a Dunfermline defender
in this League Cup clash in August 1983

Singing in the rain in the City Square
the day after winning the League title

Davie Dodds celebrates one of his two
goals against Motherwell in May 1983

Derek Stark heads the vital opening goal in this 4-0 thrashing of Kilmarnock
in April 1983

Richard Gough rises high to head the winning goal against Celtic at Tannadice
in October 1983

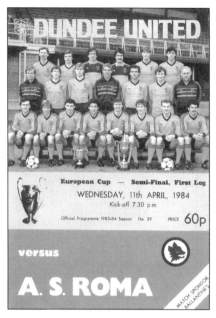

This glossy programme marked the great occasion of a European Cup semi-final

Ralph Milne was respected by friend and foe – even by Alex Ferguson

Spring-heeled Paul Hegarty outjumps Aberdeen's John Hewitt in the opening league meeting of the 1982-83 campaign

This Ralph Milne rocket beats Aberdeen keeper Jim Leighton at Pittodrie in March 1983, with Doug Rougvie looking on. Milne scored twice in United's 2-1 win

Eamonn Bannon (rear, centre) sees his cross evade everyone when Falkirk visited Tannadice in the League Cup in August 1982

Sturrock (far left) and Dodds watch John Reilly (out of picture) beat rookie Dundee keeper Brian Scrimgeour in March 1983 as United came from behind to win 5-3

Paul Sturrock heads high into the net against Morton in March 1982.
He scored a hat-trick in United's 5-0 victory

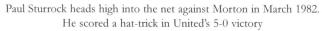

Davie Dodds wears a silly hat, Sturrock sits looking exhausted, while Ralph Milne summons the energy to raise a scarf as the realisation of becoming Scottish champions sinks in

Time to celebrate after the final whistle at Dens Park in May 1983. Ralph Milne and Paul Hegarty hug each other, while David Narey rushes to join in

The headline says it all. The now defunct *Sporting Post* proclaims Dundee United as Champions of Scotland

The reception committee that awaited the teams in the Olympic Stadium in Rome, before they took the field for the European Cup semi-final second leg in April 1984

Standard Sport – the Liege club's issue for Dundee United's European Cup visit to Belgium in October 1983

A timely tackle by David Narey denies Graham Harvey of Hibernian at Tannadice in March 1983

St Mirren's Mark Fulton, left, cannot prevent Davie Dodds from scoring the second of United's three goals in January 1983. United won 3-2

Dundee's Bobby Glennie protects himself from a crashing shot by John Clark which earned United a 1-1 draw immediately prior to their European Cup semi-final in Rome

Midfielder Billy Kirkwood, right, hammers in the opener in United's 2-1
Tannadice triumph over Celtic in October 1983

Paul Sturrock celebrates David Narey's late winner in the first leg of
United's UEFA Cup-tie against Werder Bremen at Tannadice

The new Champions of Scotland relax in the communal bath at Dens Park
after defeating the hosts 2-1

Rapid Vienna keeper Herbert Feurer dives to deny Eamonn Bannon in the
European Cup quarter-final second leg.

The Dundee programme for United's day of destiny at Dens Park, on the final day of the 1982-83 season

Royalty at Tannadice. Prince Rainier and Princess Grace see the UEFA Cup-tie between United and Monaco from the office which used to overlook the Tannadice pitch

The hard-to-obtain Roma Mia isue for United's historic day in Rome, when they were defeated in the semi-final of the European Cup

Dundee keeper Kelly parries Eamonn Bannon's spot-kick, but Bannon recovered to net the rebound for the goal that was destined to win the League

John Clark is tackled by St Mirren's Mark Fulton in what was Clark's only championship appearance, in January 1983

This was the magazine which was given away free when United visited Vienna for their quarter-final European Cup-tie in Austria.

Paul Sturrock, far right, scores United's opening goal against Hearts in February 1984. Jim Bone, with arms raised, appeals vainly for offside

A tired but elated home dressing room after United's superb 2-0 first-leg win over Roma at Tannadice in April 1984

A last-gasp goal from Davie Dodds seals this local derby win
when Dundee visited Tannadice in October 1982

Jim McLean – flanked by coaches Ian Campbell (left) and Gordon Wallace – against
Dundee in November 1983. McLean must decide whether to take the Rangers job

Chapter 4

# ~ Sprinting for the Title ~

There was no time for licking of wounds, because it was out of the Cup frying pan and into the fire of the league with a proverbial four-pointer against top of the table Celtic. The weather threatened to bring a new dimension into play. Tannadice was hard and flat, but playable for the crucial Celtic visit, although with overnight rain forecast, conditions were expected to soften up. Whilst that was the case, it left a tricky playing surface none the less.

On a mud-scarred pitch, Billy McNeill's men rode their luck. The 1-1 draw ostensibly tightened their grip at the top, opening up a three-point lead over Aberdeen with the same number of games played. Pat Bonner's save from a Bannon penalty kept United at almost arm's length from the leaders.

Yet it could have been worse, because Charlie Nicholas had steered Celtic in front after only four minutes for, incredibly, his 35th counter of the season. Bonner's penalty save followed Dodds' equaliser late in the first half. United's leading scorer, with nobody near him, also ended up on his backside, with nothing more to do than knock Derek Stark's lob into an empty net.

That United had enough of the game to have won it was freely conceded, even by Celtic, although it took great saves by Hamish McAlpine to deny Paul McStay and George McCluskey. In the end it was a case of having to make do with a point rather than being satisfied with one. As United trailed Celtic by five points, some newspapers suggested that the normally reliable Bannon's penalty miss might prove costly in the great scheme of things – especially as the two remaining fixtures against Celtic were due to be played at Parkhead.

At a time when other Scottish clubs were feeling the pinch at the turnstiles, United were bucking the trend. The bumper crowd of 17,000 for Celtic's visit on a cold February afternoon withstood competition in the form of Scotland's televised rugby international in Paris. In those days, live sporting events were the exception rather than the rule.

That assembly boosted Tannadice's average to 11,500 – not far off the average for the whole season – and was the prime reason that there was no exodus of star players from Tannadice. As Jim McLean explained at the time: 'With such a response from the public, I can safely say that it would take an unbelievable offer to make us consider transferring any of our top players. We owe that to our fans.' True to his word, it would be over three years before any of the championship side would leave Tannadice and then only when the club's hand was forced.

The following week's match could have hardly contrasted more with the last. Kilmarnock were entrenched at the foot of the table, prompting McLean to voice his concerns: 'It's easier for the players when the atmosphere is right and there will be a big drop in atmosphere and attendance from the 17,000 at the Celtic game.'

The manager's fears, however, were unfounded. Although only about a tenth of the previous week's crowd bothered to turn out, he could not have asked his players for a more professional performance than the one which saw them put five past a sorry Killie side without reply – equalling United's best ever Premier League result on opponents' soil, having posted the same score at Broomfield a little over three years earlier.

Richard Gough got married in the morning at Dundee registry office and his best man was Ralph Milne. But whilst Gough started the game, Milne was only on the bench, where he was joined by Derek Stark. Milne was replaced by Iain Phillip, making a rare appearance in the starting line up that season.

For once, it was one of the lesser Tangerine heroes in the Tannadice pack who came up trumps. More noted throughout his long and distinguished Tannadice career as an industrious defensive midfielder, at Rugby Park John Holt enjoyed his fifteen minutes of fame as a goalscorer. He notched the only hat-trick of his career. And it was a 'true' treble. The midfielder scored the opening three goals, followed by singles from Bannon and Dodds, who bagged his fourth goal in the last three league games.

For one Tannadice follower – Andy Crichton – that scintillating victory at Rugby Park was one which stood out. He recalls: 'Having been a season ticket holder for five years, season 1982-83 was the first one in which I travelled regularly to away games, missing only three of the 36 league games. I managed to see 89 of the 90 goals scored that term, with Ralph Milne's penalty in the first game at Rugby Park the one that I missed. Kilmarnock was the venue, however, for what was one of my favourite goals of the entire campaign. The fifth goal at Rugby Park that misty February afternoon shone through because it was so simple, yet so brilliant. Hamish McAlpine threw the ball out to Paul Sturrock who was standing on the halfway line. Luggy typically twisted and turned to leave his marker for dead and hoisted a long through ball to the onrushing Davie Dodds. In turn, Doddsie knocked the ball forward with his head, letting it drop and, as it bounced on the left-hand corner of the penalty area, he hit it on the drop with the outside of his right foot diagonally over the keeper into the postage-stamp corner. From defending to scoring at the other end only took a matter of seconds and for me summed up just what a class act this side was. I just feel very lucky to have seen so much of an unforgettable season and watched the greatest Dundee United side become Scotland's number one.'

However, that great day was still three months off. The blank Saturday left by that Scottish Cup exit was put to good use. The growing affinity between Jim McLean and West Ham boss John Lyall manifested itself in the clubs meeting each other in a friendly, after both sides found themselves at a loose end.

After the two teams' thrilling 3-3 draw at Tannadice in a pre-season friendly, the 'return' at Upton Park proved no less entertaining. Again it finished all square and the 6,500 crowd were treated to four goals of the highest order. Twice behind, United came back with Paul Sturrock cancelling out Frank van der Elst's opener and substitute Ralph Milne doing likewise after Warren Donald had put the Hammers back in front. Coincidentally, former United favourite Raymond Stewart returned to the Hammers' team for the first time in five weeks after breaking a toe. McLean's team was at full strength, apart from Dave Narey, who wouldn't miss any of the club's 55 competitive games that term.

One reason why McLean had been anxious for his charges not to be left twiddling their thumbs whilst Celtic were dumping Dunfermline from the Cup was that the re-scheduled Parkhead clash was booked for the following Wednesday.

Immediately on his return from London, McLean was piling up the air miles again with a trip to Prague, where he watched forthcoming UEFA Cup quarter-finalists Bohemians oust city rivals Sparta from the Czech Cup.

That was the night before United's game at Parkhead. McLean had left his assistant Walter Smith in charge of the team, but plans for the manager to meet up with the side in Glasgow were scuppered by the weather. One of the most crucial games of the season was literally put on ice, after frost left the Celtic Park playing surface rutted and dangerous. It was the only postponement of the season. With United's continued involvement in Europe and Celtic's Scottish Cup commitments, the two crucial Parkhead clashes would now be squeezed into a fortnight. But much water was to flow under the two Tay Bridges before those encounters.

More immediately, Morton had to be faced at Tannadice. In their side was John McNeil, recently returned to Cappielow after his two-month loan spell at Tannadice. It was not so much his inside knowledge of the Tannadice set up as United's own inadequacies which allowed ten-man Morton to poach a surprise point. A sloppy and casual performance led to Benny Rooney's men being well and truly let off the hook.

The visitors never looked like buckling under the first-half pressure, but when Jim Duffy, the current Dundee manager, took his marking role on Paul Sturrock too literally he was dismissed – having already been booked for an infringement on the elusive United striker. That should have given the green light for two points, especially when Richard Gough nodded home after keeper Roy Baines failed to hold on to Paul Hegarty's header across the face of the goal. Further chances were squandered and the price was paid when Morton snatched a late equaliser. McAlpine had previously had only one save of note all afternoon.

To say that Jim McLean was less than happy with his side's perform-ance would be an understatement. 'Our approach was all wrong. There was no zest or enthusiasm. Even allowing for the forthcoming game against Bohemians, there is no way that I can excuse our lethargic per-formance,' he bellowed afterwards. Adding salt to those wounds, both Celtic and Aberdeen recorded convincing home wins – over Kilmarnock and Dundee respectively – all of which meant United now trailed Aberdeen by four points.

That wasn't exactly the required confidence booster for the first leg of the UEFA Cup quarter-finals. Less than 24 hours after playing Morton the players were out on the Tannadice track loosening up in preparation for the trip to Czechoslovakia. A place in the semi-final of a European competition was at stake. There was good news concerning Ralph Milne, whose calf muscle injury sustained against Morton was less severe than at first feared. Milne was one of the twenty-strong pool which flew into a snow-covered Prague.

Fortunately, the snow was thawing and the match was in no danger. Jim McLean's assistant, Walter Smith, had watched United's opponents defeat Cheb 2-0 to top the Czech League on the same day that United had struggled against Morton. Bohemians' pitch had a soft surface, but was hard underneath, and the rising temperatures over the following two days had improved things further, though clearly the going was going to be very heavy.

Whilst the ankle injury that Derek Stark sustained against Morton was not going to keep him out of contention, Ralph Milne was still only rated as being a 50-50 shot to recover in time, so Jim McLean was keeping his fingers crossed: 'I know the line-up I want and it won't be far away from the last away tie in Bremen,' he revealed.

Not that the Tannadice boss saw this latest task in the same light as the drama-laden contest of the previous round: 'That was a triumph for guts. Tactically that night our defence was crazy and we were lucky to get away with it. If we have to defend against Bohemians, it has to be around the halfway line, not in our own penalty box.

McLean also admitted, and not with the immediate UEFA Cup task in mind, that he had another unfulfilled wish: 'We need a really tough guy in our side. Somebody to niggle and nark and keep the others on their toes. George Fleming was a good example for us. Hamish McAlpine can do it – but he isn't near enough to the action.'

However, like his hopes of augmenting his strike force, McLean would have to wait some three years before bringing that kind of player to the club, and then only as this championship winning side began to break up.

As the team prepared for the 90 minutes' action in Prague there was the boost of Ralph Milne being declared fit, so it was the same side who had performed heroics against Werder Bremen that took the pitch in the less than palatial Bohemians Stadium. The playing surface resembled a sea of mud and by the end it was more like a ploughed field, but with the players heeding their manager's call to give their best they trooped off covered in as much glory as mud.

The loss of a goal after just ten minutes made the final whistle seem very distant, but tireless running restricted the Czechs to that solitary strike. Therefore hopes of progress were high, with the late Bob Wilson, under the guise of Don John in the *Courier*, giving this verdict in his match report: 'Bohemians showed themselves to be a good side, but no better than the Tangerines, who must fancy their chances of turning the tables at Tannadice Park.' He added: 'Before and after the goal, the visitors gave more than they got in atrocious conditions.'

'Magnificent,' was manager Jim McLean's one-word description of his side's performance, though he did pragmatically warn, 'We are only at the halfway stage and there is still a job to be done back home.'

Spirits were high on the charter flight back to Glasgow and plastic cups were raised to toast the birth of Paul Sturrock's new baby daughter – Lisa – who had been delivered earlier that day. The toast could have been equally for Paul himself after his outstanding display.

The handling of the game by Belgian match official Marcel van Langenhove was labelled 'disgraceful' by Wallace Moore in the *Daily Record*. The decisions which earned him that accolade started as early as the third minute, when he booked Derek Stark for a foul on Chaloupka, after only issuing warnings to a couple of home players for tackles of equal measure.

The offence which led to the only goal was also dubious. Eamonn Bannon's challenge on Jakubel appeared legal. Marcik was rightly booked for a foul on Paul Sturrock, only to escape a sending off when he repeated the same foul on the same player seconds later. A long stud gash in Paul Sturrock's calf was testimony to the treatment meted out. The litany of refereeing indiscretions continued with free-kicks being awarded to the home side when no foul had been committed; and from one of these Paul Hegarty was forced to clear off the line. In addition, United were denied what looked a clear-cut penalty when Billy Kirkwood was barged off the ball by Prokos, but by then the visitors had learned not to expect fair play and would have been astonished had it been given.

A fixture with bottom of the table Motherwell three days later was a far cry from Prague, but it was no less vital a contest. Having contemplated making one or two changes to freshen up the side, McLean consulted his players, who each testified to his willingness to play. In the event, McLean's only voluntary change was to bring in Derek Murray for Maurice Malpas. Paul Sturrock failed a fitness test, so John Holt deputised.

Hamish McAlpine chalked up a notable landmark by keeping goal for the 400th league game, and was in the thick of the early action. United fell behind when Well's Andy Harrow intercepted Narey's slack back-pass and John Gahagan was left with a simple chance after Harrow's shot was deflected into his path. United hit back immediately thanks to Richard Gough, and the Under-21 internationalist scored a second on the half hour to give United an interval lead, revelling in a midfield role which gave him licence to maraud all over the park. In the second half United rattled in two more goals, with their skill and strength proving far too much for Jock Wallace's modest side. Even Jim McLean was smiling after this one-sided contest, remarking, 'I was very pleased with the way the lads performed. When Motherwell went ahead, I thought we might find it difficult. The trip to Prague took a lot out of the players. We began slowly, but came on to a good game. To win 4-1 away from home is always a great result in the Premier League.'

The two points, however, only saw United mark time with their title rivals, both of whom also won away from home. Already there were some who doubted the durability of United's championship challenge. As the *Sunday Mail* scribe admitted: 'United kept their slim Premier League Championship hopes alive with a fine victory at Fir Park.'

To be fair, Aberdeen were five points better off and Celtic four with just over a third of the season remaining, so clearly United's destiny was not in their own hands. Equally daunting, all three remaining games against their title rivals were away from home.

The build up to the penultimate city derby centred around the verbal gamesmanship of the two managers. Whilst Jim McLean scoffed at the suggestion that his side would be distracted by the imminent return leg against Bohemians, his opposite number, Donald Mackay, thought otherwise: McLean insisted: 'There is no way my players will be looking over their shoulders and thinking about next Wednesday when we play Dundee,' although he acknowledged that United's challenge was not as strong as it once was: 'We are in with an outside chance of winning the Premier League and we know only too well that we have to win every game to do so. Draws are no good to us in our situation.'

With ten minutes of this Tannadice derby remaining, most United followers would have gladly accepted a draw, had it been on offer. The Tangerines were at the time 2-3 down, despite Richard Gough repeating his feat of the previous week by scoring twice to put United 2-0 ahead. Moreover, Dundee keeper Bobby Geddes, only recently recalled, had to go off injured after just six minutes, with defender Brian Scrimgeour having taken over.

However, this was to prove a real ding-dong derby. John Reilly – as he had done on several occasions this season – pulled the irons out of the fire with an equaliser, which probably would have been saved had Geddes been in goal. Further goals from Paul Hegarty and Davie Dodds in the last six minutes snatched victory from the jaws of a defeat which would surely have snuffed out the championship dream. It had been more like a cup-tie than a league game, which was fitting given that elsewhere Aberdeen and Celtic were in action in the quarter-finals of the Scottish Cup. That in turn meant that United were able to rein in two points on their rivals in what was a defining week in the club's quest for honours.

Ahead of a crucial league meeting with Aberdeen the following Saturday, there was the little matter of the second leg UEFA Cup quarter-final against Bohemians of Prague. Those hopes appeared tainted by an injury to Paul Sturrock, but thankfully the striker had recovered from his strained thigh to take his place in the side trying to make history.

Chaloupka – the man who scored in Prague – was a supposed doubt for the Czech side, but perhaps it was all ideology, as he was in his usual place when the teams lined up. United hammered away at the Bohemians' defence for almost all the game but just couldn't find a way through. There were a string of missed chances and hard-luck stories. Suffice to say that their keeper, Hruska, was the man of a match that finished goalless, enabling the 'Kangeroos' – as the Czech side were curiously nicknamed – to inch, rather than bound, through to the semi-finals.

If it was all gloom and boom at Tannadice, the very opposite was the case at Pittodrie, where Alex Ferguson's side dismissed the redoubtable Bayern Munich to reach the last four of the Cup-Winners' Cup.

The mood in the two camps could scarcely have been more contrasting for a match which United couldn't afford to lose, and indeed the events of Saturday, 19 March 1983 – and not just at Pittodrie – were to impact hugely on United's title quest. One legacy of United's European exit was that Paul Sturrock – who only played against Bohemians with pain-killing injections – was now ruled out. With John Holt starting a two-match suspension, Iain Phillip and Ian Britton were added to the pool with the former replacing the absent Sturrock in what was the only change from the side in action the previous Wednesday.

Against Bayern Munich, Aberdeen had come from behind to snatch the tie in what remains the greatest night in Pittodrie's history. Against United, a repeat outcome appeared on the cards when Gordon Strachan netted from the penalty spot with 25 minutes left to halve the two-goal lead United had established. Worse, Jim McLean's side had to hang on with ten men.

Saint and sinner for United was Ralph Milne. His two fabulous long-range goals in the space of four first-half minutes had put the Tangerines in the driving seat. Yet they were deprived of his services for the last eighteen minutes after he was expelled for aiming a kick at Alex McLeish, having been fouled by the Dons' central defender. Mercifully, United's defence was resolute and hung on for the crucial two points.

Events back on Tayside made this a red-letter day. Whilst United were doing the business up north, Dundee did their neighbours a huge favour by beating Celtic 2-1, enabling United to move above Billy McNeill's side. Perhaps Dundee were just repaying a debt, because 21 years earlier a United victory against leaders Rangers at Ibrox had put Dundee's championship dream back on track. The top three now looked like this:

|          | P  | W  | D | L | F  | A  | Pts |
|----------|----|----|---|---|----|----|-----|
| Aberdeen | 27 | 19 | 4 | 4 | 57 | 20 | 42  |
| Dundee U | 27 | 17 | 7 | 3 | 65 | 25 | 41  |
| Celtic   | 26 | 19 | 3 | 4 | 68 | 29 | 41  |

With three-quarters of the season gone, and just nine games to play, United's title destiny wasn't quite in their own hands, but they were now only a point behind Aberdeen, and level with Celtic, who had a game in hand. But, of course, they still had Celtic to play twice at Parkhead.

This three-horse race still had twists and turns to take. Celtic were held at home by Rangers the following Wednesday – which was enough for the Celts to recapture second place above United – but the following weekend brought even greater intrigue. United welcomed Hibs to Tannadice. In addition to suspensions for Ralph Milne and John Holt, Paul Sturrock was still out, and Ian Britton was the shock selection in attack.

After three minutes Hibs netted their first goal of the season against United, in the fourth meeting, though Gordon Rae's 40-yarder took a deflection off the referee. Goals by Dodds, Britton and Gough turned the tables before half-time, but nerves took over in the second period. United's form nose-dived from championship quality to relegation fodder in the course of 90 nerve-jangling minutes. Irvine pulled a goal back for Hibs, but if United could hang on they might go top of the pile for the first time. Aberdeen were trailing at Morton, and Celtic to St Mirren at Parkhead. However, goals in the last ten minutes at all three venues swung the pendulum hard against United.

At Tannadice, Hibs deservedly equalised. Davie Provan prised a late leveller for Celtic, preserving the *status quo* between them and United. From Cappielow came bad news. Leaders Aberdeen went one better with goals from Andy Watson and Eric Black to bag a victory and extend their lead by another point.

Another international midweek saw more Scotland honours come United's way. Richard Gough won his first full cap in Scotland's 2-2 draw against Switzerland at Hampden. The previous evening Hamish McAlpine captained the Under-21s to a 2-1 win over the Swiss at Dens Park. Maurice Malpas was the other Tannadice colleague on duty. Elsewhere, Ian Gibson, who didn't figure in the championship season at all, was loaned to St Johnstone for the rest of the season, having completed two months on loan to Morton.

The arrival of April brought good news on the injury front. Dave Narey and Paul Sturrock, who had had to pull out of international duty, were declared fit. In addition, Ralph Milne and John Holt were back from suspension for a double-header with the Old Firm.

First up were Rangers at Tannadice. Having found the Ibrox side so hard to beat, despite being streets ahead of them in the league, United could take nothing for granted, and so it proved. Only a late brace by Paul Sturrock – his first goals since December – brought United victory. Everything had appeared to be going according to plan after Ralph

Milne's opening goal. But as so often happened, Rangers defied the odds to equalise midway through the second half. Sandy Clark claimed the goal, although television replays showed that Davie Dodds got the last touch. The two points guaranteed United a place in Europe next season, as they could not now finish below third place. Rangers, in fourth, could no longer make up the deficit. But the big news was Aberdeen's astonishing home defeat by St Mirren, which toppled them from first to third.

Jim McLean was quick to seize on the effect of that result. It meant that the Tannadice side's destiny was for the first time in their own hands, but only if they didn't lose either of their two upcoming visits to Parkhead.

The first was a hard-fought, physical encounter and, although United seemed to be holding their own, a rare error by skipper Paul Hegarty let Frank McGarvey in for a soft opener. A super Charlie Nicholas strike twelve minutes from the end left United three points in the wake of the leaders. Aberdeen were level on points with United, but with a game in hand. Four days after having their championship destiny in their own hands, United had allowed it to slip out of them again.

In the wake of that defeat, McLean told his player to relax or forget about winning the title. That was easier said than done, given that victory over St Mirren at Love Street was essential. Putting it candidly, United could afford no more slip-ups, and there were to be none.

Eamonn Bannon from the spot and Paul Sturrock with his third in two games kept the pot boiling, even if Doug Somner, who had applied the *coup de grace* in the Scottish Cup, pulled one back. United's crop of eighteen corner-kicks to Saints' four reflects the balance of the game.

Celtic's win at Easter Road didn't do the United cause any favours, but Aberdeen's 1-2 defeat at Ibrox – their third loss in four league games – certainly did. Celtic were due to meet Aberdeen on successive Saturdays, first in the semi-final of the Scottish Cup, then at Pittodrie in the league. In between lay United's second, re-scheduled trip to Parkhead.

Whilst Celtic were preoccupied with their Hampden date, United's preparations for that crucial Celtic clash were more relaxed. Following their win at Paisley, Jim McLean ordered his first-team players to stay away from Tannadice for at least two days. Not that it was a totally idle weekend because Everton supplied the opposition for a Friday evening game – the 60th of the season, taking into account friendlies. An equaliser by Eamonn Bannon saved United's unbeaten record from their four jousts against top-rated English sides that season, the game ending 1-1.

On the Monday, McLean couldn't have expressed United's task more succinctly: 'If we don't win, it will not be our title.' Celtic were three points better off and, with four games then remaining, the necessity for victory was obvious.

Billy Kirkwood was United's only doubt, and he failed to make it, whilst Charlie Nicholas's return strengthened the reigning champions. Nicholas's penalty cancelled out Paul Hegarty's 14th-minute opener to leave matters all square at the interval. With so much at stake, tempers overheated at times, and no sooner had Bannon restored United's advantage, also from the spot, than Richard Gough was sent off after indulging in a spot of wrestling with Celtic winger Davie Provan. Worse still, Tommy Burns equalised, but in this action-packed thriller there was a sting in the tale for the home side. Only six minutes were left when Ralph Milne pulled another rabbit from the hat to score another 'special'. Taking a cross from Bannon on his chest, Ralphie brought it down to simply belt the ball over Bonner to seal a 3-2 win for McLean's ten men.

United's manager was not in the mood for understatement: 'I think this was probably our best performance away from home since I became manager of Dundee United. I was proud of my players.'

For someone sitting in the Celtic Park stand, that defeat was to have huge implications for his future career in football. Looking on was Celtic scout Graeme Liveston. He recalls: 'Little did I know it but that win and United's eventual wresting of the trophy from Celtic was to cost me my job. That played a significant part in Billy McNeill being sacked and although I was still there at the start of the season, new manager Davie Hay showed me the exit door soon afterwards. But instead of one door closing and another one slamming me in the face, Jim McLean approached me to work for him just before the end of the year and, early the following year, I was appointed United's scout in the west of Scotland.' Twenty years on, Graeme can boast being the only member still connected on the playing side with continuous service, having started season 2003-04 as the club's Chief Scout.

Milne's goal had at a stroke blasted the title race wide open. United now sat only a point behind Celtic and four ahead of Aberdeen, who admittedly had two games in hand.

|  | P | W | D | L | F | A | Pts |
|---|---|---|---|---|---|---|---|
| Celtic | 32 | 22 | 5 | 5 | 79 | 33 | 49 |
| Dundee U | 32 | 20 | 8 | 4 | 76 | 34 | 48 |
| Aberdeen | 30 | 20 | 4 | 6 | 60 | 24 | 44 |

However, the run in favoured Jim McLean's men, not just because they had an easier programme, but because Celtic were due at Pittodrie less than 72 hours after losing to United. 'With only four games to go, we are in the best position we have ever been to win the championship. Either a win for Aberdeen over Celtic or a draw would be a great result for us,' calculated McLean. These were the remaining fixtures:

Celtic: – Aberdeen (a), Kilmarnock (a), Morton (h), Rangers (a).
United: – Kilmarnock (h), Morton (a), Motherwell (h), Dundee (a).
Aberdeen: – Celtic (h), Motherwell (a), Dundee (a), Hibs (a), Kilmarnock (h), Hibs (h).

Already the question was being asked, would it be a derby decider at Dens on 14 May. For that to happen, minds had to be concentrated as Jim McLean was at pains to point out: 'We have got to win all our four remaining games, that is the important thing. We mustn't be thinking about scoring a lot of goals to improve our goal difference. We have to first win the games – and then worry about our goal difference.' On that account, the players were certainly to deliver and more.

Having banged in twelve goals in the previous two meetings against Kilmarnock, there was an air of expectancy amongst the home crowd that gathered on the Tannadice terracings on 23 April. Billy Kirkwood returned in place of the suspended Richard Gough for the only change to the victorious Parkhead side, and United stormed into a four-goal lead by the interval. Although there were no more goals, it was a job well done, although for Kilmarnock it was curtains in their battle to stave off the drop.

As Ron Scott, then writing under the alias of Bill McFarlane, in the *Sunday Post* keenly observed: 'Dundee United's skill and ability has never been in doubt. Now they've allied self-confidence and belief to those attributes, they'll take some stopping in their challenge for the Premier League flag.'

Meanwhile, Aberdeen's 1-0 home win over Celtic made it a traumatic time for Billy McNeill's side. The Celtic legend was left shattered after seeing his side slump to a third defeat in eight days (to United and twice to Aberdeen, in league and cup): 'A week ago our horizons were bright. Now they are dark. Obviously we'll concede nothing until it's impossible. We almost need a miracle to retain the Premier League as we must depend on two teams slipping up.'

With three games remaining, United couldn't have hit the front at a better time. They now headed the table for the first time since the start of the season. Apart from being a point ahead, United now had the best goal difference, having turned round a four-goal disadvantage.

|         | P  | W  | D | L | F  | A  | Pts |
|---------|----|----|---|---|----|----|-----|
| Dundee U | 33 | 21 | 8 | 4 | 80 | 34 | 50  |
| Celtic   | 33 | 22 | 5 | 6 | 79 | 34 | 49  |
| Aberdeen | 31 | 21 | 4 | 6 | 61 | 24 | 46  |

United's destiny really was in their own hands. Three more wins and they would be champions, for Aberdeen had nine goals to make up, in addition to four points. Typically, Jim McLean wasn't satisfied with the Kilmarnock performance: 'If we play the way we did in the first half, we have a real chance of winning the league. However, if we play as we did in the second half, we don't! The great pity is we've to play Morton at Cappielow on Saturday. There will be little or no atmosphere. If we could transport the 7,500 fans who watched the Kilmarnock game, what a difference that would make.' He added, tongue in cheek: 'And I don't think Hal Stewart [the Morton chairman] would complain about the extra £1.50s.'

Flag-fever was reaching fever pitch. The club, prompted no doubt by Jim McLean's thoughts, came up with the unique idea of supplying vouchers worth £1.50 for adults and £1 for juveniles and OAPs, which would entitle them to get into Cappielow for nothing. The scheme was run in conjunction with British Rail, who would supply the vouchers when fans bought their travel tickets costing £5 for adults and £2.50 for juveniles. In addition, other vouchers were available from Tannadice for those making their own way through to the west.

The scheme ended up costing United around £6,000, with 5,000 vouchers issued. Morton supporters were hard to spot in a crowd that numbered over 8,000.

But the idea paid off handsomely. When Dave Narey put United two up shortly after half-time the partying began in earnest. Further strikes by Ralph Milne and Davie Dodds only served as icing on the cake. The only blemish on the day was an injury to Hamish McAlpine, which forced him to come off. Skipper Hegarty took over between the sticks but he was hardly troubled. The final score was 4-0 and Morton's only consolation was the cheque from Tannadice; for the second week running United condemned their opponents to the drop.

If Morton were despondent, then United fans were in ecstasy, knowing their heroes were only two games away from glory. Even before facing Motherwell in the final home game of the season, there was the boost of Hibs holding Aberdeen to a goalless draw at Easter Road, which meant that wins over Motherwell and Dundee would guarantee United the title without resorting to the slide-rule of mathematics.

Preparation for that penultimate game included the club's annual golf outing, which at least kept thoughts of the enormity of what lay in store temporarily at bay. McLean was worried that minds were drifting towards the Dens Park derby, and stressed that minds had to be focused on first taking on Motherwell. 'My players are well prepared. They are not being carried away by the excitement of the final fixture. They know where their priorities lie and that is to beat Motherwell.'

Remarkably, his side went out and chalked up their third consecutive 4-0 win, though it has to be said that they had an attack of the jitters in the early stages. A spectacular free-kick by Eamonn Bannon calmed the frayed nerves. Bannon was clearly the hero of the hour, scoring a second from the spot eight minutes into the second half and at last the crowd of almost 12,000 could begin to relax. Two goals from Davie Dodds brought unmitigated joy to the Tannadice terracings and the realisation that only seven sleepless nights and 90 nerve-racking minutes stood between United and the biggest domestic prize.

All United had to do now was go to Dens and win. And they did!

Chapter 5

# ~ HIGH HOPES ~

## (MAY – OCTOBER 1983)

Fruits of the championship success were almost instant. There was bare-ly time to celebrate the enormity of the club's achievements before four of the Tannadice squad were called up by Jock Stein for what was to be the last year of the Home International Championships. Scotland regu-lars Dave Narey, Richard Gough and Paul Sturrock were joined by club captain Paul Hegarty, whose reward for leading the team to the title was a recall to the Scotland squad for the first time in three years. Their ranks were swelled to five when Jim Bett's late withdrawal brought Eamonn Bannon a call up, thereby setting a record for the number of United play-ers in an international squad, and further testimony to the club's new-found status within the Scottish game.

Jock Stein paid the new Premier League champions the highest possi-ble compliment when he picked four of the five Tannadice men at his disposal for the side to meet Northern Ireland at Hampden. Sturrock was the omission, but he had only just made the squad after recovering from a hamstring strain. He was the only Tannadice representative not to fig-ure in any of the three internationals.

There was one other landmark in the Northern Ireland match. Paul Hegarty became the first Dundee United player to captain Scotland – something which has only happened once since, with Maurice Malpas emulating that feat when skippering Scotland to a 1-0 win over Bulgaria in Sofia in 1987.

Unfortunately, there was no win to celebrate as the goal famine afflict-ing the Scots at that time saw the game finish goalless. The *Courier* reporter Tommy Gallacher wrote: 'Although all of the Dundee United players came out of the game with a bit of credit and Eamonn Bannon, in the first half particularly, looked quite impressive, he faded in the sec-ond when he didn't get much of the ball.'

With Stein restoring Dons duo Miller and McLeish in the heart of the defence for the match against Wales at Ninian Park three days later, Paul Hegarty dropped down to the subs bench, but the other three kept their place in a Scotland side which started with no fewer that seven New Firm players – a tribute to the exploits of Aberdeen and United that season in winning the European Cup-Winners' Cup and Scottish Championship respectively. Former Dundee United striker Andy Gray scored the first and Alan Brazil the second as Scotland clinched their first win on Welsh soil for ten years.

The same New Firm seven were also picked to tackle England at Wembley to decide the destination of the championship, but England proved too strong and beat the Scots 2-0.

There was no time for the five internationalists in the United squad, nor for that matter Jim McLean, who was Jock Stein's assistant, to relax. Less than a week after the England game they were off for to Canada for Scotland's three-game trans-Atlantic tour. As he joined up with the party, the United boss wasn't basking in any new-found glory. Far from it, in fact. He was disappointed that, for the second summer running, he had been unable to add to his United squad. The only significant close-season acquisition was to the backroom staff, Gordon Wallace returning to the club he had served so well in the twilight of his career as a player. Wallace had been Paul Sturrock's mentor and after leaving Tannadice had played for, and then managed, Raith Rovers, the club with whom the Dundonian had made his name during the 1960s. Wallace had, in fact, been named Scottish Footballer of the Year in 1968.

When announcing the appointment of the Raith boss, Jim McLean made it clear that it carried no job description: 'He'll coach, he'll manage a bit when necessary, he'll be part of the backroom team.' On the playing front, despite McLean's commitment to doing so, the fact of the matter was that by the time the new season began, the hoped for big-name signing simply failed to materialise.

So, initially, it was a case of soldiering on, but there was a blow when the 31 players – only four of whom had cost any fees – reported for pre-season training in mid-July. Even at that early stage, McLean was expressing doubts about the fitness and stamina which he felt had eluded Paul Sturrock the previous term: 'At no time was he completely fit – and I've no doubt that some of his injuries stemmed from this,' observed the United boss. Instead of strengthening his squad, by the time the season started, McLean was to be shorn of one of his star players. Injury had sidelined Paul Sturrock.

Indeed, the only close-season acquisitions were the five 'S' Form signings who were called up. These included midfielder Gordon McLeod and striker Kevin Gallacher, and although it was Gallacher who made the bigger name for himself, going on to play for Coventry City, Blackburn Rovers and Newcastle United, McLeod beat him to first-team recognition at Tannadice, as was seen sooner rather than later.

The only departure over the summer, apart from a couple of youth-team players, was Ian Gibson, whose loan to St Johnstone during the latter stages of the previous season was put on a permanent footing.

One of the first 'rewards' for winning the Premier League title was an invitation to play in a four-club tournament in Spain in early August. Originally, it was to have included Kaiserlautern from West Germany, a Catalan XI comprising players drawn from Barcelona and Espanol, plus Brazilian champions America de Rio. As it transpired, the Germans' place was taken by Valencia – not as high a profile club as they later became – whilst Espanol from Barcelona alone represented Catalan.

Before heading to Spain, United opened the new season in the first round of the Forfarshire Cup. Davie Dodds and Ralph Milne both scored in the last five minutes and spared United's blushes against an Arbroath side which had finished 26 places lower down the league ladder than United the previous season. Some 3,339 turned up for that opening game, an indication of the trappings of success, because the vast majority were now season ticket holders. Season tickets had been selling furiously over the summer and broke the 3,000 barrier for the first time. This was a remarkable number, given that during Jim McLean's first full season in charge eleven years earlier, a mere 500 seasons had been sold. Mind you, just how much value they represented can be gleaned from the fact that an adult stand season ticket cost £65 and a ground one just £35, not to mention that they were valid for the club's first tilt at the European Cup.

Commercially, too, football was becoming big business. United were actively seeking a sponsor to cash in on their success and Pat Honeyman was appointed as commercial manager to fill the void after Graeme McLaren's departure three years earlier.

On the downside, Paul Sturrock missed that game with Arbroath, but there was the consolation of the display of his deputy – Alex Taylor. There was further disappointment at Station Park, where United lost on penalties to Forfar in the semi-final of the Forfarshire Cup, so it was hardly the kind of start you'd expect of champions.

Shortly afterwards, a 17-man squad jetted out to Barcelona from Edinburgh via Amsterdam to take part in the four-team Costa Dorada Tournament in Tarragona. United made a good start by beating Espanol 2-0 with late goals from Alex Taylor and Davie Dodds, thereby maintaining United's 100 per cent record against teams from Barcelona and booking themselves a place in the final.

Even if United did lose to America de Rio, they emerged with credit from a joust that would have done justice to more salubrious surroundings than the modest Camp Nou Gimnastico of Tarragona. McLean's men couldn't match the magic of the Brazilians, but after falling two behind, substitute John Clark came on to pull one back. Eamonn Bannon and Billy Kirkwood missed the game through injury.

By now it was clear that Sturrock's knee injury was more serious than was first thought. Whilst it might appear foolish to suggest that was fortunate, in terms of timing, it turned out to be so. Rumours had been rife that Celtic were trailing the Scotland striker and, after United returned from Spain, McLean confirmed that Celtic had indeed enquired about Sturrock: 'Davie Hay phoned me, stating his willingness to put in a written offer for the player. The fee, however, was far short of our valuation and less than half the sum Celtic received for Charlie Nicholas [who had just moved to Arsenal]. Paul Sturrock, in accordance with our usual policy, was immediately told of the development. My chairman [Johnston Grant] phoned the Celtic chairman rejecting the bid and there it rested.'

To show how highly regarded Luggy was, McLean also revealed that a letter from a season ticket holder had sought an assurance that Paul would remain a United player. McLean replied: 'I cannot give a promise. No manager can. There could come a time when financial considerations took priority. But I can remind that supporter, and all others, that no club directors have shown more determination than ours to hold on to our playing assets. That will always be our priority.' That policy, indeed, proved the very root of Dundee United's success for a decade from the late 1970s onwards.

The *entente* with West Ham continued when the East London club came to Tannadice for a pre-season friendly – the third meeting between the clubs in a year. Again it was an entertaining affair, but not if you were a Hammers fans as United turned on the championship style and over 6,000 saw John Lyall's side thrashed 4-0.

Completing United's preparations was a visit by Spurs in recognition of Hamish McAlpine's seventeen years of service. United's unbeaten run against top English sides was advanced to six, though this time United had to settle for a draw. Equally satisfying was the near 11,000 turnout for the testimonial for the loyal keeper who was as popular with his teammates as he was with the fans, though this season was to be his last as an automatic choice. The game against Spurs finished 1-1 with John Clark cancelling out Tony Galvin's opener. That was the young United striker's third goal in pre-season and McLean payed him the highest compliment, saying that he rated him the best finisher at Tannadice since Andy Gray.

Alex Taylor was the other youngster to impress in the build up to the new season, but the United manager's biggest fear for the coming campaign was that the supporters would expect too much: 'I only hope our fans don't think we should slaughter every team we meet because we won the title last season,' adding, 'Apart from that, I don't see any reason why we should not be better than we were.'

McLean's reasoning was sound. Only Hamish McAlpine, who was hardly a veteran in goalkeeping terms, and defender Iain Phillip, were over 30, whilst the rest of a relatively young squad had had another year of invaluable experience under their belts. McLean assessed the prospects thus. 'Along with Aberdeen, we have the best back four players in Scotland and you can say the same about our attack. But we will still need to get more from our midfield than we got from them last season. That is the one department that can be improved upon.'

When the new league campaign got under way, there were no grounds for complaint from manager or fans. Before the opening fixture against Motherwell, David Letham of Queen's Park had presented the League flag to United Chairman Johnston Grant and had officially handed over the trophy to skipper Paul Hegarty. Minutes later United were up and running, to the delight of a crowd not far short of five figures.

The team that lined up showed just two changes from the one that had started the final game. Alex Taylor came in for Sturrock, and John Holt was in for Derek Stark, who had been under the weather since the pre-season trip to Spain. For poor Motherwell, who had been the last visitors to Tannadice on league business, it was a case of *déjà vu*. Once again they were thrashed 4-0. The talented Taylor made a telling impact, crossing for the first goal, the architect of the second, scoring the third – his first goal for the club. The fourth was another Kirkwood header, but this time from a Milne cross.

So the season started as it had ended, with United, Aberdeen and Celtic occupying the top three places and left Motherwell boss Jock Wallace convinced that on the evidence of this display United could easily retain the trophy. 'Dundee United can win it again,' said Jock.

The fact that two of the goals that beat Motherwell were scored by Billy Kirkwood was ironic because he had made a scoring debut as a striker a little over six years earlier. Recruited from Cornbank Boys Club in 1976, 'Kirkie' had played beside two of his future team-mates. Derek Stark and Eamonn Bannon were also in the Scottish Under-18 Schoolboy team, when he won his two caps at that level.

Given that Kirkwood finished second top scorer in season 1978-79, as United staged their first credible assault on the league championship, his future as a forward seemed assured. Ironically, it was the sale of his good mate Raymond Stewart to West Ham that was to bring about a fundamental change in his career: 'I had played right-back a couple of times when Ray had been absent from the side the previous season and filled in for him after his departure when Paul Hegarty had been injured and there was a shortage of defenders. By the time he had recovered, Willie Pettigrew had established himself up front and the manager's thinking was that as I could get about the park for the full 90 minutes, my days as a striker were effectively over. Mind you, he still wanted me to score goals as well!'

Whilst in later years Kirkwood's man-marking jobs on Aberdeen's Jim Bett became almost legendary, in the seasons under review it was tracking the likes of Tommy Burns of Celtic and Gordon Strachan of Aberdeen which were his terms of engagement. However, being a defensive midfielder had its drawbacks in the Tannadice team of that era as Kirkie pointed out: 'More often than not, Derek Stark, John Holt and myself were all left to compete for two available places, which meant most weeks one of us was disappointed.' As a result, Billy made 26 starts during the championship season and a further five from the bench, but defensive duties curtailed his scoring to just three goals.

The two he bagged against Motherwell were the first of nine in 1983-84, and with one goal in Europe he reached double figures, thus proving the versatility of this lithe and athletic player, who in a United career which spanned more than a decade filled every outfield position.

The League Cup had been given a face-lift and a preliminary round was now necessary to decide the four sections of four, the four winners contesting the semi-finals. A 6-1 win over Second Division Dunfermline at Tannadice in the first leg rendered the second leg a formality. United added two more goals and entered a group comprising Alloa Athletic, Morton and Motherwell. United were huge favourites to qualify.

Unlike previous tournaments, the new format saw the six sectional games stretch over two months, all played in midweek. Alloa visited Tannadice for the first time for 24 years and goal-hungry United added another five to take the season's tally to seventeen in four games – but less than 5,000 were there to see them as the new and elongated format came in for increasing criticism.

It was a welcome relief when league action returned on the third Saturday. United passed their first major test with flying colours as Dundee failed to break the four-year hoodoo in derby matches. This latest gloomy instalment for the Dark Blues saw them capitulate as United embarked on a late romp to post another big win.

'In a bone-jangling affair of a rumbustious local derby, it was rather appropriate that a kid who goes by the nickname of "Boney" should have the ultimate say in the destination of the points,' was how Ron Scott of the *Sunday Post* summed up the latest instalment of United's derby dominance of their rivals.

Walker McCall's early opener had raised home hopes that Dundee's drought might be coming to an end, but John Reilly quickly levelled matters and his strong running through the middle upset Dundee's pedestrian defence all afternoon. United dominated the second half and the young striker hit the all-important second with twenty minutes left. Further goals from Milne and Derek Stark kept United's scoring average above the four-per-game mark.

United's first setback of the new term came at Cappielow, but only in the context that United's 100 per cent record was tarnished. There was no harm done with the 1-1 draw against gutsy Morton, in fact it was the only point dropped in the six group games in the League Cup. Readers won't be surprised to learn that McLean was less than enamoured over the complacency shown by his charges: 'Our approach to the game was wrong from the start. We got an early goal and too many players thought it was easy.'

Up to that point, Eamonn Bannon had been helping with the match programme by compiling the Player Profile, but he was now told to cease, so that he could concentrate on his football.

In the wake of that Morton draw, changes were promised by the manager, but for the league fixture against Hibs at Tannadice, Derek Stark's inclusion in place of Billy Kirkwood turned out to be the only change. Hibs wilted under a Tannadice onslaught as United hammered five past Scotland international goalkeeper Alan Rough without any retort. The paucity of the Hibs performance was summed up in the Edinburgh *Evening News*: 'While few teams may be successful at Tannadice in the course of the championship, this was a woeful performance from Hibs who never had any chance of improving their pointless status.'

If Hibs languished at the foot, United remained top of the pile with Celtic and newly promoted Hearts, the only three sides with an unblemished league record after three games. That set up the Tangerines nicely for the competition which would dominate United's season – the European Champions Cup. Today's Champions League was not introduce until the 1990s: in the '80s it was still a straight knock-out from start to finish. The draw, made back in July, had been kind to United, pairing them with Maltese opposition – Hamrun Spartans. The heat, plus the condition of the Ta'Quali pitch was of as much concern as the opposition, not to mention the travelling. Although Rangers, competing in the Cup-Winners' Cup, were also scheduled to play in Malta, they declined to share a charter, which would have made the trip to the Mediterranean island easier than having to take two scheduled flights. The only bonus was that Dundee Airport was the departure point before picking up a flight from Heathrow to Luga Airport. Rangers' decision not to double up was made even more bizarre when both parties found themselves on the same scheduled flights to and from London. Not only that, the two sides were even to share the same pot-holed, baked and bumpy pitch on the same day. In a double-header, Rangers' tie against Valletta kicked off at 3pm, whilst that involving United was played in the 'cool' of the early evening two hours later.

United followed on after Rangers' 8-0 whitewash, but there was to be no landslide against Hamrun. To John Reilly went the honour of scoring United's first European Cup goal, when he netted his fourth goal of the season after a mere two minutes. Eamonn Bannon headed the second and Derek Stark added a third. Though not a noted scorer, Stark was to show a healthy appetite for goals in this competition over the season.

All in all, it was a highly satisfactory start to the Euro campaign and another step in the footballing education of youngsters like Alex Taylor, John Clark and John Reilly, who all took part in the tie. Whilst Taylor's development lay elsewhere following a bitter dispute which saw him leave the club three years later, and Clark's best days were still ahead of him, Reilly was the only one of the trio to have made a notable contribution over the championship season.

On many occasions, then and since, manager Jim McLean insisted that twelve players took the title to Tannadice. That, however, is patently unfair to John Reilly who with seven goals in seventeen appearances – of which nine were from the bench – contributed significantly to the championship success. Whilst the small but nippy striker's scoring contribution couldn't be described as prolific, almost all of his haul were highly important. His build was so slight that he was nicknamed 'Boney', and his biggest problem, like others before and after him, was dislodging Milne, Sturrock or Dodds from the team. The absence of Paul Sturrock at the start of 1983-84 did allow him a run in the side but, although he would enjoy almost twice as many starts, he could only equal his tally of the previous season. No one could question the enthusiasm of the Dundee-born striker, who was capped many times at youth level, but he just couldn't establish himself as a first-team regular at Tannadice and less than two years after scoring that Euro opener John was sold to Motherwell for £50,000.

Having defeated Hamrun, the players now faced an unscheduled refuelling stop at Nice, which evoked memories of that fabulous win over

Monaco two years earlier. Three days later the same line up faced St Johnstone at Muirton, in what proved to be United's closest call so far. If United struggled against the plucky promoted Saints, then Davie Dodds certainly didn't. The previous season's top scorer kept rising from a series of hefty tackles to take the fight to the Saints. Having given his side the lead, he then saw Jim Morton equalise, but the introduction of Alex Taylor brought new dimensions of pace and skill to the Tannadice attacks. The youngster was involved in the build up which saw John Holt dive full length to head a fine winner.

Davie Dodds' early season form – eight goals in nine games – earned him a late summons from Jock Stein for Scotland's friendly with Uruguay after weekend withdrawals by Charlie Nicholas, Colin Walsh and Andy Gray. He joined Richard Gough and David Narey already in the squad. Although not expected to start, Davie did make his international debut. He became only the sixth United player to play for Scotland – replacing Frank McGarvey who was stretchered off – and scored one of the goals in his country's 2-0 triumph. Dave Narey missed out on adding to his cap tally though injury but he, along with Gough and Dodds, were all pronounced fit for what had to be the most important game of the season so far – the 'New Firm' derby at Pittodrie.

A trademark of so many of these clashes was the tactical battle between Aberdeen's Alex Ferguson and United's Jim McLean. The general trend was that Aberdeen did better at Tannadice, whilst United tended to do rather better at Pittodrie, and this latest instalment was no exception. Summing up just how tactical this game was, Ron Scott in the *Sunday Post* declared 'This game was more cat and mouse than a Tom and Jerry cartoon.' But the Dons found it no laughing matter as they yet again lost out to United in their own back garden, which was packed to the gunnels. Eamonn Bannon unleashed a 30-yarder past Leighton. John McMaster then blasted a penalty over the bar, although there appeared little wrong with David Narey's tackle on Mark McGhee. Billy Kirkwood touched home a cross from Ralph Milne to extend the visitors' advantage, but then Narey conceded his second penalty of the game and substitute Gordon Strachan netted. United survived a grandstand finish to preserve their 100 per cent league record and register a club record eleven consecutive Premier League wins. Not only that, but it had surpassed the club's previous best of nine during 1951-52.

Alex Ferguson immediately targeted United as the team to catch. 'We have an uphill struggle on our hands to catch United. They are a very good, competitive side and very solid in defence. Whoever wins the championship this season, United are the team they will have to beat.'

A legacy of that Pittodrie win was that three key players were struggling to be fit for the return leg with Hamrun Spartans. Narey, Gough and Stark all picked up knocks and struggled to shake off their injuries before the date with the Maltese. In the end, only Narey was absent. His ankle injury kept him out of the side for the first time in two years.

Not that, with a three-goal advantage, their services were crucial. McLean even elected to forsake naming a goalkeeper as one of his substitutes, allowing 16-year-old Gordon McLeod, who'd only been called up a couple of months earlier, to take a seat on the bench for the experience. McLean rated the former captain of Scotland schoolboys as good a signing as he had ever made, but the midfielder, although enjoying a good enough career with Airdrie, Dundee and Meadowbank after leaving Tannadice, never quite fulfilled the quality he had showed in his youth.

United celebrated the first European Champions Cup game to be held in the city for twenty years with another three goals. The Maltese side spent 85 of the 90 minutes trying to prevent United from scoring more. The only surprise was that it took 28 minutes for Ralph Milne to score the first European Cup goal at Tannadice. The eventual 6-0 aggregate win equalled United's best in European competition: they had accounted for Keflavik of Iceland by a similar score in 1975.

There was good and bad news regarding Paul Sturrock. He made his long-awaited first appearance of the season against the Maltese and looked sharp for the first 55 minutes before limping off after a series of sapping challenges took their toll. Graeme Payne replaced him in what was to be the small but skilled midfielder's last season at Tannadice. Jim McLean summed up the club's entry to the second round pragmatically: 'That is our holiday in Europe over for this year.'

The draw in Switzerland now handed United the chance of revenge because it paired them with Belgian Champions Standard Liege, who had defeated them 1-0 in the UEFA Cup five years earlier. But four important domestic games had to be played before any thoughts could turn to Liege.

There was disappointment for United before and after the game with Rangers. Paul Sturrock failed to make it, whilst Ralph Milne was ruled out with flu. United certainly missed their cutting edge in a fixture which was dominated and deservedly won by a Rangers team that hitherto had been in the doldrums. As McLean lamented afterwards: 'There can be no excuses. Rangers won the same way we beat Aberdeen the previous week. The first goal is always vital in matches against opposition such as Aberdeen, Celtic and Rangers. We got it at Pittodrie and Rangers got it at Tannadice.' The 0-2 defeat terminated United's incredible run of seventeen games unbeaten, all but one of which – at Morton – had been won. The result also saw Celtic depose United from the top slot for the first time in almost six months.

There was little time for McLean to dwell on that disappointment. McLean, with his assistant Wattie Smith and coach Gordon Wallace, plus Aberdeen duo Alex Ferguson and Archie Knox, took off on a spying mission abroad. Like United, the Dons had drawn Belgian opponents, and the clubs doubled up on a chartered flight to watch their respective adversaries. Standard lost 0-1 to city rivals FC Liege, whilst the Dons' Cup-Winners' Cup opposition, Beveren, drew 1-1 with Kortrijk. It proved a worthwhile exercise as both Scottish clubs were to progress.

Jim McLean gathered his thoughts on the Rangers game on the eve of a League Cup-tie with Motherwell. The United boss was concerned by the attitude of the players after the Rangers defeat: 'Having not spoken to them on Monday, I was very disappointed with their attitude in training today. This is not the time to give up. A reversal like the Rangers one should make us all the more determined to get our sleeves rolled up and fight harder than ever.'

Perhaps it was the growing injury list that prompted those remarks. So worried was the United boss that the whole playing staff was told to report to the ground on the morning of the Motherwell tie, and any misgivings were soon forgotten as United swept to a four-goal lead inside the first quarter of the game. Eventually running out 4-2 winners, United proved how dominant they were in this fixture. The Steelmen were buckling to their tenth successive defeat at United hands.

This intensive spell of fixtures continued when Celtic came to Tannadice on the second Saturday of October. The team that accounted for Motherwell – with the exception of Maurice Malpas replacing Derek Stark – defeated the league leaders in the style of champions to regain their place at the top. Doug Baillie, the *Sunday Post*'s chief football writer, declared after United's 2-1 win: 'Seven down and 29 to go in the Premier League and Baillie's Forecast is looking good. Yes, Dundee United are back on course to make it two league wins in a row.'

Indeed, this was the first defeat suffered by new Celtic boss Davie Hay. Tannadice was packed for the occasion and saw Billy Kirkwood's drive take a deflection off a Celtic defender. Richard Gough headed a second from a Bannon cross, but United had to hold out in the last ten minutes after a Jim Melrose goal had given the Celts hope. Overall though, this game never really quite lived up to expectations.

No Arab could have asked for a better start to the season. Top of the league, through to round two in Europe, and favourites to qualify for the semi-final of the League Cup, everything had gone just swimmingly, but there were choppy waters just around the corner.

| | P | W | D | L | F | A | Pts |
|---|---|---|---|---|---|---|---|
| Dundee U | 7 | 6 | 0 | 1 | 17 | 6 | 12 |
| Aberdeen | 7 | 5 | 1 | 1 | 19 | 3 | 11 |
| Celtic | 7 | 5 | 1 | 1 | 20 | 8 | 11 |
| Hearts | 7 | 5 | 1 | 1 | 10 | 6 | 11 |

Chapter 6

# ~ CHOPPY WATERS ~

### (OCTOBER 1983 – FEBRUARY 1984)

Mid-October brought an unscheduled hiatus. Following a near constant diet of two matches per week, the league match with St Mirren in Paisley was rained off. Even then there had been no midweek respite for Hamish McAlpine and Maurice Malpas, who had been joined by Ralph Milne in the Scotland Under-21 side that drew with Belgium.

There may have been no goals in the first ever Under-21 international to be played at Tannadice, but the result was sufficient for the Scots to qualify for the last eight of the Under-21 European Championships. The following evening the full international also ended in a draw. Belgium held a Scots team which included Richard Gough, but Dave Narey was restricted to a place on the bench.

A newcomer in the United squad for that aborted Love Street trip was Bobby Flavell. Recently released by Motherwell, the midfielder had previously served Hibs after a spell in Swedish football, but his arrival, like many others of that era, failed to have the desired impact. It again served to endorse how difficult it was to bring in players of superior ability than the ones already on the Tannadice playing staff. Frankly, this could only be achieved by shelling out serious amounts of money. Indeed, Flavell's arrival had nothing to do with the mystery player for whom the club had confirmed that they had made a £100,000 bid – in those days a very sizeable fee. Later that transpired to be Iain Ferguson of Dundee, but though McLean was eventually successful in acquiring the striker's services, he had to wait almost three years to do so.

Jim McLean indicated that signing Flavell had been prompted by the fringe players not putting enough pressure on the men holding down first-team places. The former Motherwell man had also had a decent game for Well on the opening day of the season.

That idle Saturday, on account of torrential rain in Paisley, at least meant no fresh injury worries. On hearing of the postponement, the team bus about-turned at Cumbernauld, allowing preparations for the first leg of their European Cup-tie against Standard Liege to begin.

Having decided on sixteen of his 18-man travelling party, McLean's dilemma centred on whether to take Paul Sturrock, who had only seen 45 first-team minutes all season, but who had just completed the full reserve game with St Mirren. Sadly, his delicate knee ligaments ruled Sturrock out. Bobby Flavell was chosen instead so that he could get to know his new team-mates, though that was to prove fruitless, given how little time he was to spend at Tannadice.

Unlike the previous round in Malta, this time the party only had to take a short flight from Leuchars to Liege. They arrived in the midst of a row between Standard's star German striker, Horst Hrubesch, and his manager Raymond Goethals. The 32-year-old ex-Hamburg player, out of action for a month with a host of injuries, had demanded to play against Lierse on the Saturday before the clash with United. He was instead only given a place on the bench, but then demanded a starting slot for the Euro tie. Player power may have won that battle, but it didn't help the Belgians establish any sort of advantage other than not conceding an away goal, as the first leg finished goalless.

How adept United had become in Europe was exemplified by their performance in the Stade de Sclessin. United played Standard at their own deep defensive game. In a close tie, the Tangerines had the better chances, but even though they didn't get an all-important away counter, McLean was more than happy with his side's performance. Not for the first time in recent years, the United boss labelled his side magnificent: 'Every player in the side worked very hard. I was never worried about losing and I thought we had the chances to win the game, both early on, and late in the second half.' Even Goethals paid this tribute to the Tangerines: 'They are not like any other British or Irish team that we have played against. They play like a continental team with great discipline and have many skilled players.' Goethals was spot on when he added: 'They will be hard to beat at Tannadice and it is the team who scores first that are likely to win.'

From meeting the champions of Belgium, United stepped off the plane to prepare for Saturday's top of the table clash at home to a newly promoted Hearts side that was going well. A shadow that had loomed over the game was removed when a dispute over money owed by Hearts to United following the sale of Derek Addison and Willie Pettigrew two years earlier was finally resolved, thereby lifting the threat of a boycott by Hearts fans.

Indeed, a healthy crowd of over 13,000 saw United – for whom striker John Reilly for Maurice Malpas was the only change from the heroes of Liege – eventually clinch both points. Davie Dodds ended his six-match goal-drought in a game which was more about brawn than brains, but after which United still topped the table.

Dundee United's ultra-bright start to the new term saw the following letter from Mr J Smith published in the *Sporting Post*:

'It amuses me how most Scottish football observers display their blatant wish-fulfilment that United can't possibly hold on to their position at the top because of their alleged lack of depth, whatever they mean by that. Umpteen hands-on-deck Rangers seem to be struggling against the sardines in the front of their tin, and Celtic, Nicholas gone, could do with an accomplished forward like Paul Sturrock, without whom United are okay. As for Aberdeen, their bubble will burst once the realisation of Scotland's international ineptitude [Author's note – some things never change] is laid at their door – rightly or not. The McLeish-Miller twosome are clearly less than world class in Scottish colours and are only preferred over Hegarty and Narey because of Jock Stein's, and any contemporary management's, predilections because they are employed by a club which has a more illustrious history. The greatest danger to Dundee United's future is that they will be damned by faint praise. But they must be used to it by now!'

While United were beating Hearts, events at Ibrox were to impact hugely on United's immediate fortunes. Storm clouds gathering over Govan started to precipitate after Rangers had slumped to their fifth league defeat of the campaign against a lowly Motherwell side, gaining their first win of the season. That reversal prompted a crowd congregating outside the Ibrox portals to give vent to their spleen and manager John Greig in particular. His days in charge were clearly numbered and he did the decent thing and fell on his sword, resigning at the end of the following week. The repercussions of Greig's departure would have a knock-on effect on Dundee United Football Club, not only in the short term, but also long term.

That same week also marked the most intensive spell of transfer activity at Tannadice for several seasons, with the arrival of *two* strikers. The prolonged absence of Paul Sturrock – his leg had been put in plaster, though purely as a precautionary measure – clearly perturbed McLean. Ex-Ranger Derek Johnstone was about to be fixed up on a month's loan from Chelsea, and the first member of the championship winning squad departed. As one Stamford Bridge player entered the Tannadice portals, another with Chelsea connections, Ian Britton, accepted the offer of a free transfer. A bit player during the championship campaign, 'Razor' had so far only figured as a substitute in one League Cup-tie this season, but nonetheless the terrier-type midfielder departed with this tribute to his abilities from his manager: 'He has done a good job with the young reserves, and deserves to find another club where his qualities fit in better.' Initially, that took him to Blackpool, but he also went on to play for Burnley.

On midweek duty in the League Cup, Derek Johnstone did well on his debut. McLean had wanted to sign him on a permanent basis, but United's offer to negotiate a fee was rejected by the London club. Not least because Johnstone, a boyhood United fan who once trained at Tannadice, scored two cracking goals to thrill the larger than expected audience of 6,645. Johnstone also took the weight off others, shielding the ball well and distributing neatly.

United fan Mr G Nicholson of Carnoustie was clearly impressed, waxing lyrically in the *Sporting Post*: 'I am writing to express my gratitude at having been at Derek Johnstone's debut game. Johnstone, who has always been a class striker, brightened up an otherwise drab night by sheer determination, dedication and, above all, the reason why he's worth his chance, brilliant goals. I sincerely hope that he stays at Tannadice. It's been more years than I care to remember seeing the way he led the attack.'

Was this answer to United fans' prayers. Sadly, no. Yet again, however, another newcomer's sojourn at Tannadice was to be of brief duration. The player returned to Chelsea at the end of his month's loan, eventually going back to Ibrox, but was never the same player that he had been during his first spell with Rangers.

Two days after Johnstone's cracking debut, United signed the country's current top marksman, Tommy Coyne, from Clydebank for £60,000. Unlike most of the players McLean brought to Tannadice, the manager had never actually seen Coyne in action, signing him on the back of highly favourable reports from his coaching staff. Although Coyne would enjoy a long and successful career, it only really took off after he left United two years later. Until then, he struggled like others before him to usurp the triumvirate of Milne, Sturrock and Dodds.

Not that Coyne didn't make an impressive enough start, coming on for Derek Johnstone at Motherwell. In fact, as preparation for the forthcoming home leg with Standard Liege, the game was ideal – except for the result. The 2-2 draw cost United pole position as Aberdeen took over, albeit on goal difference. Richard Gough recovered from a bruised knee to keep his place, and Euro specialist Ralph Milne – left out of the side against Motherwell – was recalled to hugely telling effect. Two brilliant first-half goals by the flying winger took his European tally for the Tangerines to eleven and built the platform from which the Belgians, shorn of the injured Hrubesch, were blitzed. Milne also laid on goals for Hegarty and Dodds.

The comprehensiveness of the victory could be summed up by one incident as recalled by coach Gordon Wallace: 'Standard's Walter Meeuws came to retrieve the ball from close to our dug-out to take a throw-in. At the same time [our] manager was berating one of the players, at which point the Belgians' skipper turned to Jim McLean and enquired, "Why are you getting so excited, you are winning 3-0 and the game is over?"'

Dismissing Europe's finest like Standard Liege was fast becoming the rule rather than the exception, so inevitably, one of the first questions posed to the man who masterminded this latest episode was whether this was his side's greatest ever European performance.

'You can't really compare one with another,' McLean observed. 'The circumstances are always different in some regards. So it is impossible to say if it was this game or that game. Mind you, at the moment, I would be tempted to say that this was the one which has given me most satisfaction because it has just happened.'

The dust had barely settled on that victory and indeed, because of it, speculation mounted that Rangers would try to lure McLean to Ibrox to fill the vacant managerial hot seat. In fact, ever since John Greig's resignation, three names had almost totally dominated the list of possibles – Aberdeen's Alex Ferguson, Motherwell's Jock Wallace, and Jim McLean.

When Ferguson signed a five-year deal to remain at Pittodrie after rebuffing Rangers, attention switched to the other two on the Ibrox shortlist. It hardly came as a bolt from the blue when, on the eve of the second local derby of the season, a statement was issued by the Tannadice board. Following their usual Friday meeting, they first confirmed that Rangers had indeed asked to approach their manager, but continued: 'Although Mr McLean is under contract, the directors in the interests of a good future relationship between the manager and the club, have reluctantly agreed this permission should be given. The directors sincerely hope that Mr McLean will decide to stay at Tannadice, where he has the whole-hearted support of both the players and directors.'

For once, supporters' thoughts were focused more on urging McLean to stay than on an impending city derby. 'Our first thought was to organise a petition,' said secretary Finlay Mackay of the Dundee United Supporters Association. 'But we soon realised that events were moving so fast there would be insufficient time for such a lengthy process. We therefore decided to make a public statement so that Mr McLean would know the feelings of our association.'

The office at Tannadice was inundated with phone calls pleading for McLean to stay. Against this backdrop, a Dundee derby was of almost secondary importance.

The distraction seemed to tell on everyone with Tannadice affiliations. There was a deafening echo of 'McLean Must Stay' from all tangerine quarters of the ground as he emerged from the tunnel to make his way to the dug-out after viewing an indifferent first-half performance from his office. By then, however, United were trailing to a Peter Mackie goal and although the manager's hands-on presence galvanised United, Dundee summoned up enough grit and determination to hold out for their first Tannadice derby win since 1975-76. It was manager Donald Mackay's first derby success at the twelfth time of asking.

The loss of two points to their fiercest rivals only exacerbated the trauma felt by all United fans that weekend, with the future of their manager apparently on a knife-edge. On Sunday, McLean was embroiled in discussions with Rangers' directors for three hours, but promised to let them have a decision as to whether he would be John Greig's successor within 24 hours.

True to his word he did, but his decision was not the one that Rangers chairman Rae Simpson wanted to hear, because McLean put his family first. 'Family is more important than money. Their happiness comes first. They are settled in Dundee, their friends are here,' he explained.

The announcement that Jim was staying was issued from the boardroom with this statement: 'Dundee United FC feel it is vitally important to retain the services of Jim McLean at Tannadice, and his deep feelings of loyalty to the club and staff have decided him to remain at Tannadice, and to complete the magnificent work he has done here over the last twelve years. In response to the demand from the supporters, and in grateful recognition of the sacrifices he is making in staying, the club will make arrangements for a testimonial game to be organised for Jim McLean.'

Having rejected Rangers, it was now unlikely any other club in the country could tempt him away. United were immediately involved in a League Cup-tie at Alloa, the 4-2 win easing them into the semi-finals, even though they had one sectional game, at Motherwell, still to play.

A week of furious activity ended with former defensive stalwart Doug Smith being appointed to the board of directors. At the same time, physiotherapist Andy Dickson, who had been with the club since its Second Division days, announced he was stepping down due to ill health, as soon as a successor was appointed.

After all the upheavals, the players made it seventh heaven on the park by equalling the club's record Premier League victory. They slammed seven past the Saints from Perth. New boy Tommy Coyne started for the first time, but although he didn't hit the target, he again impressed. That win still left United two points adrift of Aberdeen at the top, though the Dons had played a game more.

The demands on the club at international level continued. On a four-inch carpet of snow at Jena in East Germany, Maurice Malpas and Ralph Milne helped Scotland draw 1-1 with their Under-21 East German counterparts in a game which meant nothing as the Scots had already qualified from the group. That vividly contrasted with the full international side who lost 1-2 in Halle to finish wooden spoonists behind Belgium, Switzerland and East Germany. Richard Gough and Eamonn Bannon were in the side, with the latter having the consolation of scoring his first goal. Bannon candidly added, when I spoke to him recently, that it was his 'last' goal at international level.

United's next domestic game was away to Rangers, for whom it was Jock Wallace's first home game back in charge at Ibrox. Rangers had turned to the Motherwell boss to take charge for a second time, but Wallace was never to match those earlier achievements, when Rangers had achieved the treble. Although it ended goalless and United dropped three points behind leaders Aberdeen, McLean admitted to being satisfied with a draw given that Jock Wallace's return had doubled the home support of recent weeks.

If the United boss was pleased enough with the way things had gone at Ibrox, the same could hardly be said about the visit to Paisley six miles further along the M8 three days later. In the re-arranged league game, the champions slumped to their biggest defeat in over a year as St Mirren hustled and harried their way to a 4-0 triumph. Bobby Flavell made his debut as a substitute for what was his first and only United appearance.

Perhaps surprisingly, McLean did not read the riot act afterwards, preferring to concentrate on the lessons to be learned and offering the players the chance to redeem themselves in the top of the table home clash against Aberdeen.

Defender Gary McGinnis started a first-team match for the first time, replacing the suspended Billy Kirkwood, whilst Derek Murray took over from Derek Stark who was out with a strain. Paul Sturrock was back, even if it was only on the bench. Regrettably, that was the only good news for United fans at Tannadice on a dull November afternoon, made all the more gloomy by Aberdeen cantering to a 2-0 win to collect both points and open a five-point gap over their New Firm rivals. 'Dons stroll over shot-shy United', was the headline in the *Sunday Mail*, reflecting the poverty of the Tangerines' performance.

Although the season was only fourteen matches old, at odds of 5-4 against, Aberdeen had become the shortest-priced favourites in years to take the title. Celtic, trailing the Dons by three points, were 2-1, whilst United had slipped to 9-4, according to John Smith Bookmakers (Glasgow). Worryingly, this was the third consecutive match in which United had failed to find the net, with Jim McLean unable to offer any excuses.

After all the trials and tribulations of November, that month at least ended with a victory. Not an important one, given that the final League Cup-tie away to Motherwell was academic, but getting back on the goal standard was welcome, United scoring three without reply.

In the wake of that win, Bobby Flavell was released just six weeks after his arrival. The career of another United player was downgraded with the announcement that 32-year-old defender Iain Phillip was to take up a new career with the Department of Health and Social Security, but remain with the club on a part-time basis. That decision was no doubt heavily influenced by the player sustaining a double fracture of the lower fibula in a reserve match at Perth. Iain was destined never to play for the first team again, moving on to Raith Rovers after his recovery from the injury. Helping to nurse him back to fitness was Bill Ramsay, formerly with Airdrie, who was announced as the club's new physio.

December ushered in normal service when United headed to Easter Road and chalked up their first win in four outings, beating Hibs 2-0. Sturrock's tale of woe this season continued. Flu had ruled him out against Hibs, whereupon a pulled shoulder muscle deprived him of a starting slot at Hearts a week later. That game at Tynecastle proved to be a dull-as-dishwater draw. 'Just Ghosts of the Old United,' was the banner headline in the *Sunday Post*. Fortunately, with Aberdeen being held by Celtic at Parkhead, no further ground was lost in the championship race.

Ground was lost the following week, but through no fault of United's. Tannadice was waterlogged for the visit of St Mirren, which was proba- bly just as well as the club were going through a mounting injury crisis of the kind which had mercifully steered clear the previous season.

That postponement cost goalkeeper John Gardiner a league debut because Hamish McAlpine, originally expected to be out for a month, was declared fit for the trip to Parkhead a week later. There, Paul Sturrock started a league game for the first time this season. The game ended 1-1, a result from which only Aberdeen benefited. It was a result that McLean viewed as an opportunity lost. Indeed, a measure of the strides made by the club can be gauged by the headline in Monday morning's *Courier* – 'Point at Parkhead is not good enough.' It was also a result that could be ill-afforded as third-placed United were now eight points adrift of the Dons and their hold on the title was becoming ever more tenuous.

|          | P  | W  | D | L | F  | A  | Pts |
|----------|----|----|---|---|----|----|-----|
| Aberdeen | 18 | 14 | 2 | 2 | 46 | 9  | 30  |
| Celtic   | 18 | 11 | 4 | 3 | 42 | 20 | 26  |
| Dundee U | 17 | 9  | 4 | 4 | 32 | 16 | 22  |
| Rangers  | 18 | 8  | 2 | 8 | 27 | 25 | 18  |
| Hearts   | 18 | 6  | 6 | 6 | 19 | 23 | 18  |

Not that matters were helped by a bad winter, with home games being particularly badly hit. During December and January, Tannadice staged just one match. December also saw the draw for the quarter-finals of the European Cup, pairing United with Rapid Vienna, the first leg in Vienna. The ties were not due for three months, but already thoughts were turning to the return leg, but only because of reduced admission prices for regular supporters. Vouchers worth 50p were to be issued at two selected home games, which would mean a £1 reduction on match tickets. Remarkably, this didn't affect season ticket holders, because unlike almost any other club in Europe, United's covered all European ties.

One of these was the final game of a monumental year in the club's history and almost 7,000 paid to see the visit of bottom club Motherwell to Tannadice. There were even grounds for calling that one off, the entertainment ruined by gale-force winds.

Apart from picking up two points, thanks to Derek Stark scoring with a wind-assisted shot from twenty yards, and a Hegarty header, the good news was that Luggy was back. Whilst Sturrock's absence might not have been missed in the early part of the season, later on when injuries, suspension and loss of form kicked in, his unavailability was a big handicap. Writing in the programme for his testimonial match against Real Sociedad six years later, Jim McLean wrote: 'Of the many exceptional players I have had the pleasure of playing with during my playing career and coaching at Tannadice, I can't think of a singularly more important player to a side than Paul Sturrock.'

Luggy's absence for most of the first half of the season was a legacy of the previous campaign, as the player himself explained: 'I had a hamstring problem for the last ten weeks of the season and even although I played an hour or so of the title winning game against Dundee, it went after twelve minutes and I paid the price for it the following season.'

Whilst Sturrock was out, it wasn't so much his scoring that was missed as his creative flair. Always willing to take players on, he was an unselfish type and his ability to link the midfield and front players was invaluable.

No less a judge than Alex Ferguson opened the door for Paul to play in the World Cup finals in 1986, when Fergie was temporarily in charge of Scotland after Jock Stein's tragic death. Ferguson believed that, at his peak, Luggy was in the same mould as Kevin Keegan. As mentioned earlier, Celtic had been keen to sign him, as were West Ham. Fortunately, neither move materialised and Paul was a modern day rarity, playing his entire professional career with one club.

Signed in 1974 from Bankfoot, no forward has played more United games than Paul over a decade and a half, aggregating 576 appearances and scoring 171 goals – a total only surpassed by the club's record scorer Peter McKay. As Patrick Barclay, then with the *Independent*, now of the *Sunday Telegraph*, wrote in his contribution to Paul's testimonial programme: 'Paul was central to an era when the Old Firm's domination of the Scottish game was broken by United, under the enlightened guidance of Jim McLean, and Aberdeen. These clubs made the Premier Division a success by using increased revenue to keep their stars. Gone were the days when the likes of Paul and Dave Narey went to the highest English or Glaswegian bidder. It was demonstrated to Europe that Scottish football had a greater depth of strength than had hitherto been suspected, and few did more for this cause than Paul. So as a Scot and a Dundonian (albeit with a dark-blue heart) I was delighted he stayed at the right club. In many ways Paul has been the ideal player; loyal and sportsmanlike as well as exceptionally skilful, a virtuoso at a time when athleticism was always threatening to strangle the game He could turn with the ball under pressure, a rare gift, and showed a level of perception more readily associated with high-class midfield players than those who operate in a hurry at the hectic end. He was, in short, one for the aficionados to savour.'

Yet despite all his attributes, Luggy only won twenty caps, a figure that would have been far greater had he not been a contemporary of Kenny Dalglish.

In those days, strikers tended to hunt in pairs and if Luggy evoked comparisons with Kevin Keegan, then Davie Dodds was the John Toshack of the partnership. And if 'Doddsie' was less stylish than the Welshman, then there is no doubt that he was equally as effective. He might have scored a total of 21 fewer United goals than Paul Sturrock, but Doddsie figured in almost 200 fewer games. Tallish and gangly, he might have looked ungainly, and may not have been naturally gifted as a youngster but, like Sturrock, his willingness to learn from Jim McLean saw him become equally as big an asset as his attacking partner.

At one time Davie almost turned his back on a full-time career. Although he made his debut in August 1976, he remained part-time whilst he completed his apprenticeship as a painter and decorator and even went on loan to Arbroath before taking the plunge at Tannadice.

For five of seven seasons in which he was a first-team regular, his 22-goal tally during the championship season is the only one in which a United player has breached the twenty-goal barrier since the advent of the Premier set-up.

Dodds won two caps for his country, scoring on his debut against Uruguay in October 1983, and he and Paul Sturrock are the only two players to have achieved a century haul of Premier goals.

Two of those came in the second visit to Perth, where United repeated their earlier 2-1 win. Football, however, was soon in winter's icy grip and that was the only match United were able to fulfil during the whole of January. Home postponements against Hearts and Rangers impacted heavily on finances, particularly with the recent introduction of a ruling that clubs in Scotland could keep their home gate-money.

Indeed, the disruption of that winter was the principal reason why United decided to invest in undersoil heating. Although it wasn't installed until the summer of 1985 at a cost of £100,000, United were one of the pioneers of the system. They joined Hibs, Queen's Park and Rangers as the only clubs in Scotland having pitch protection.

When United did return to action, they could have done with some pitch protection because of a pre-match snowstorm for a Scottish Cup-tie against Ayr United. Looking rusty after so long without any competitive action, Paul Sturrock's only goal of the game finally shrugged off the First Division outfit's challenge.

And United were still in second gear when they met Hibs the following Saturday, never approaching their pre-freeze form. The performance was still good enough to see off a poor Hibs side and threw up a smoke-screen for the on-looking Rapid Vienna coach Otto Baric.

Before tackling the Austrian side, United had two other important cup dates. First up was the two-legged League Cup semi-final against Rangers. The Ibrox side's league form had picked up, but although they were only one place behind United in fourth, they were three points worse off, having played three more games. The elements continued to intrude during the first leg at Tannadice. The pitch was fine, but swirling mist and fog shrouded the ground for long periods of the second half.

However, it was clear as daylight when Aussie striker Dave Mitchell cancelled out United's opener with five minutes remaining to deny United a first ever cup win over Rangers. The Tangerines' goal midway through the second half, incidentally, is credited to Davie Dodds in the record books, despite newspaper reports giving the goal to Richard Gough.

Four days later, the Tangerines were again on Cup business, this time against Hearts at Tannadice, and a late goal – this time Davie Dodds was clearly the scorer – won the day. It had been a bruising Scottish Cup-tie in which Hearts' Jim Bone was sent off three minutes from the interval. United were 1-0 up at the time, but John Robertson had then levelled with a penalty.

If there was joy at reaching the quarter-finals of the Scottish Cup, Rangers were to inflict more cup misery on United at Ibrox. Hopes of a fourth League Cup final appearance in five years were scuppered in eleven fateful minutes as United slumped to their first defeat of 1984. Jim McLean's men afforded Sandy Clark the freedom of Ibrox to chest the ball down and fire home the first, three minutes from the interval. An Ian Redford lob brought a second early in the second half to make it an extremely disappointing evening for United fans who were still waiting to see their favourites beat Rangers in a cup-tie of any description.

Chapter 7

# ~ OLYMPIC FAILURE ~

### (FEBRUARY – APRIL 1984)

As the end of February approached, it was a case of 'one down, three to go'. That was the positive stance taken by the club following their exit from the League Cup. Championship chances may have bordered on the slender, but that didn't mean that the title would be given up easily. Uppermost on everyone's minds was the European Cup quarter-final tie against Rapid Vienna, which was only just around the corner.

Before negotiating that, however, hopes of retaining the title suffered a further blow at Love Street. Despite establishing a two-goal lead, St Mirren stormed back and not only equalised with half an hour remaining but might even have taken both points.

The last domestic outing before heading to Austria was a visit from second-placed Celtic and, in Jim McLean's book, nothing less than a win would suffice for either protagonist: 'Whoever loses, if there is a loser, can forget about any outside chance of winning the league.'

United's timing in re-discovering their top form was impeccable. After stuttering along for a couple of months – although they had only lost once in twelve games – they beat Celtic with ease, 3-1. However, Aberdeen were triumphant again and, even though United had two games in hand, the Dons' lead was a massive ten points. Celtic, four points better off than United, had played a game more than Aberdeen.

|          | P  | W  | D | L | F  | A  | Pts |
|----------|----|----|---|---|----|----|-----|
| Aberdeen | 24 | 19 | 3 | 2 | 61 | 12 | 41  |
| Celtic   | 25 | 15 | 5 | 5 | 68 | 29 | 35  |
| Dundee U | 22 | 13 | 5 | 4 | 43 | 21 | 31  |

The display against Celtic was almost universally accepted as the best since beating Standard Liege in the last round of the European Cup, but it was going to take two performances of a similar high standard to oust Rapid.

Austrian domestic football might not be all that strong these days, but the Vienna-based side boasted a host of international players, the best known of whom were the Czech midfielder Antonin Panenka and perhaps the most famous player produced by Austria in recent years, Hans Krankl. Having said that United's starting eleven would come from the thirteen on duty against Celtic, McLean did make one change, bringing in Ralph Milne for Tommy Coyne in the Hanappi Stadium. 'We've got to try and get at least one away goal to take back with us to Tannadice,' reasoned McLean on the eve of the trip to the Austrian champions. In the first round, Rapid had accounted for Bohemians of Prague, United's conquerors twelve months previously at the same stage of the UEFA Cup.

When the opening goal did come, it was from an unlikely source for a finish of such high quality. Dick Donnelly, a freelance journalist covering the game and one who has never tried to hide his allegiance to United, could hardly believe his eyes: 'When Paul Sturrock slipped the ball into his path, the last player I expected to see flashing the ball into the net from 25 yards was Derek Stark, though he certainly made me eat those words in the semi-final against Roma.' That goal was, indeed, fundamental to United reaching the last four.

For all the pressure Rapid exerted, it wasn't until fourteen minutes from time that they managed to find a chink in United's defensive wall with a goal by substitute Max Hagmayr – the first United had conceded in the campaign. A second goal from Yugoslavian midfielder Zlatko Kranjckar four minutes from the end gave Rapid coach Otto Baric the win he craved, but not by the margin he had hoped.

Not that Jim McLean was complaining, especially as he knew that his side had got out of jail: 'That was the poorest we have played in Europe since we lost to Radnicki Nis in Yugoslavia two years ago. Our players were nervous about the game and it showed. It was Hamish McAlpine's goalkeeping that got us a result. He was magnificent and he more than anyone kept us in the tie.' McLean finished on an optimistic note: 'They are a good side, but I am not concerned about them. If we play as we know we can, we can still make it to the semi-finals.

Writing in the Dundee *Courier*, Tommy Gallacher prophetically wrote, 'I have seen United play better in Europe away from home, but in the second half they had to withstand tremendous pressure from Rapid and in the end had to accept defeat. In my opinion, however, they are still good enough to overcome this in the second leg with the advantage of having scored away from home.'

Gallacher's assessment would be spot on, though the Austrian's cause wasn't helped by post-match comments from Otto Baric: 'Although Dundee United are a well-disciplined side, I thought they were very ordinary – in fact, one of the poorest sides we have played in Europe.' Those words were to come back to haunt him.

Before the return tie with the Austrian club, United had vital games to play in the two domestic competitions which remained open to them. Their slender title hopes were maintained when Hearts were beaten 3-1 in the first ever Sunday Premier Division match to be staged at Tannadice. Two goals from Tommy Coyne – his first goals since signing from Clydebank – did the damage.

That match used up one of United's games in hand, as Aberdeen lost a League Cup semi-final at Celtic the previous day. United were now two points behind Davie Hay's second-placed side with two games in hand.

The Dons now had to be faced in the Scottish Cup quarter-finals a week later than was originally scheduled. Indeed, with only seven weeks of the season remaining, the Arabs faced a minimum of fifteen fixtures, so the last thing they wanted was to be involved in a replay with the Cup holders. As luck would have it, that was what transpired after a dour goalless draw at Pittodrie.

Vital game followed vital game, but they didn't come more vital than the second leg of the European Cup-tie against Rapid four days later. Looking ahead, McLean was in a more confident frame of mind: 'The side are getting over their sticky spell, whilst our defence has turned the corner with important players like Richard Gough and Dave Narey back to their best.' He also acknowledged, 'I can't say the same thing about the forwards yet, though Eamonn Bannon's contribution has been great recently. But I look forward to the challenge – and the rewards – of the important spell ahead to bring the whole side to its peak. We have so much to play for we can't let the opportunity slip.'

Both Sturrock and Hegarty, who had missed the tie at Aberdeen, were back in harness. Twelve players had been receiving treatment, but the Tannadice boss reported a full squad fit and ready to try and overhaul the one-goal advantage held by the Austrian side. The stand was sold out and almost 17,500 fans filled the ground.

There was one newcomer to the European adventure. Striker Tommy Coyne made his debut, but Ralph Milne, United's top European marksman, had to make do with a place on the bench. That was the only change from the first leg. Top scorer on the domestic front, Davie Dodds, chose this game to hit his most important goal of the season – his eighth in Europe – and send Tannadice into raptures as a place in the last four of Europe's top competition was reached. Fans swarmed on to the pitch at full-time, but that was as much in relief as in celebration after a tension-filled 90 minutes.

Prior to kick-off, McLean had said that if the team played as well as they had against Standard Liege they would survive. Well, United did progress, but without coming within touching distance of that earlier performance, a fact acknowledged by McLean when interviewed immediately after the game: 'This is a magnificent result against a side I rate very highly, but in no way was it our best performance in Europe. We played our best in both legs when Rapid had the ball. When we had it, we treated it like a hot potato. But the whole team worked their hearts out and we can all be very proud of the achievement of reaching the semi-final of a European trophy for the first time.'

The tie had also swelled the Tannadice coffers by some £50,000, a figure boosted by television rights and advertising, with an even bigger bonanza lying ahead. Testimony to the quality of the beaten Austrian side arrived a year later when they contested the final of the European Cup-Winners' Cup, losing to Everton. As for United, they had now emulated Hibernian, Dundee and Celtic by reaching the last four of Europe's Premier tournament at the first attempt.

Indeed, it was a truly great night for Scottish football. Aberdeen overhauled a two-goal away deficit to defeat the Hungarians of Ujpest Dozsa after extra-time, to reach the last four of the Cup-Winners' Cup.

Incredibly, when the semi-final draws for all three European competitions was made the following Friday, all six ties involved a British club. And when Liverpool were drawn against Dinamo Bucharest and United paired with AS Roma, an all-British European Cup final loomed thrillingly on the horizon.

Pandemonium reigned at Tannadice when details of the draw emerged. An early caller asked for twenty tickets, only to politely be told that he had jumped the gun a bit. A further six names were taken for the charter flight to Rome for the second leg, although that was almost a month away.

But before any further contemplation could be given to the European high-life, there was important bread and butter of domestic trophies to be considered. Or, rather, there would have been had the weather not intervened to leave both United and Aberdeen in a fixture muddle of monstrous proportions. The pair were due to meet in the league and United were drinking in the last chance saloon as far as retaining their league title was concerned. Instead, the only fluid frequenting Tannadice were pools of water, torrential rain forcing a postponement. That left United and Aberdeen needing to fulfil thirteen and twelve league fixtures respectively before the end of the season, which had just seven weeks left to run.

In addition, each had to play at least two vital European encounters, plus the New Firm's Scottish Cup replay. Thankfully, that went ahead and

Roma's spies saw Aberdeen get the better of United as they usually do at Tannadice, and as they habitually had done in the Scottish Cup. Mark McGhee's second-minute goal extended the Dons' dominance over United in this competition. This was the eighth meeting between the pair and, remarkably, United had yet to register a victory. Being a typical blood and guts Scottish Cup-tie, neither AS Roma's assistant manager, Luciano Tessari, nor Joao Mota, his counterpart at Aberdeen's opponents Porto, would have learned much about their respective European adversaries.

The watching Roma spy, who had previously watched the same pair in league action at Tannadice in November, thought United unfortunate to exit the competition: 'Dundee United made one mistake and it cost them a goal and the match. They are a good side collectively, but they missed both Bannon and Gough, Bannon especially as he is the creator. An intelligent player with much vision, he was the player who most impressed me on my last visit. I thought that once Aberdeen scored they were quite happy to sit back and contain Dundee United, but I thought Dundee United were a bit unlucky to lose the game. They will be difficult opponents for us in the semi-finals.'

In the wake of the Cup exit, Iain Munro was signed from Sunderland, too late, of course, to figure in the European Cup semi-final. McLean cited his vast experience and being a talker on the park as the reasons for bringing him to Tannadice. Munro's arrival was timely, with physio Bill Ramsay working overtime as the Tannadice casualty list continued to lengthen.

With five regulars missing, including Hamish McAlpine, which brought a run of 85 consecutive appearances to a halt, John Gardiner took over and, along with Hegarty and Narey, were the Tangerines' heroes in a goalless draw in the glaur of a muddy Tynecastle. With Aberdeen slipping to a rare defeat by Celtic, United's point from Hearts turned out to be one gained, and not lost. But even with a game in hand, United's hopes of retaining their title were becoming increasingly forlorn.

Immediately after the Hearts game, it was Jim McLean and his assistant Walter Smith's turn to spy, taking in Roma's Sunday meeting with Inter Milan, which United's opponents won 1-0. The duo returned home to prepare for a Dens Park date just 24 hours later. A dramatic derby saw United again triumph at Dens, winning 5-2, as Aberdeen's lead was cut to five points.

It has to be said however that, for once, United fans had more than just a derby victory on their mind. The following morning tickets went on sale for what promised to be the greatest night in the club's history. The queues stretched down Tannadice Street and all the way up Arklay

Street. Prices were £10 for the stand and £5 for the terraces, and with no concessions for juveniles and OAPs, that appeared steep. However, the young and old were actually getting three games for the price of their ticket. Entry to two of the remaining home fixtures – against St Johnstone and St Mirren – would be free. Meanwhile, those paying adult prices would gain free admission to the terracings for the visit of St Johnstone, although it would cost them £2 for a seat in the stand. So, once again, the club was looking after its regulars, and none more so than season ticket holders, whose tickets, as already mentioned, were valid for the big occasion.

And the message from Jim McLean, after seeing their semi-final adversaries in action, was: 'We can beat Roma. Roma are good, very good. Their technique and control are fantastic and I have a suspicion that they can play better than the game I saw. But we should not be overawed by their reputation, nor the individual skills of players like Falcao.'

For the moment, the Tannadice boss had difficult decisions to make for the trip to Easter Road. Part-timer Maurice Malpas would be in his usual place and Hamish McAlpine returned in goal, even though John Gardiner had done well enough in the derby – the two goals he conceded were both from the penalty spot.

Unfortunately, it was a boob by the veteran keeper which let Hibs grab the lead and take the points. On the plus side, McLean was happy enough with the performance, but the swollen knee with which Dave Narey left Easter Road rendered him doubtful for the Roma game. For a while his chances of making it were rated only 50-50, but time was on his side. If Narey looked set to play, one of Roma's top players appeared set to miss out. Brazilian international Falcao, although suffering from a knee injury, was however with the Roma party that arrived in Scotland.

European Cup fever approached epidemic proportions. Dundee had joined the elite of football cities – including Belgrade, Glasgow, Madrid and Milan – to have supplied two teams that have contested the semi-final of the premier European competition As the last of the 22,000 tickets was snapped up for the biggest local occasion since Dundee's tie with AC Milan 21 years earlier, the city braced itself for the invasion of around 1,000 Roma fans. Six planes carried 700 fans, whilst a further 300 or so made their own way. Their numbers were swelled by members of the not inconsiderable local Italian community.

The sale of anything in tangerine and black in local sports shops was brisk, as the invading Italians snapped up United souvenirs, further spreading the Tannadice gospel. Norman Cunningham, then manager of Astral Sports, which was located in the recently closed Arnott's store in the High Street, told the *Courier*: 'It's been an amazing week. All we have left are a few scarves. Everything else from flags to mugs has been snapped up and Tannadice should be a sea of tangerine.'

Jim McLean said that this marked the pinnacle of his career, which could only be topped if United reached the final in Rome on 30 May. However, he was in no doubt as to the enormity of the task in hand, given that in previous rounds United had somehow ousted sides with more skilful and technically better players: 'We beat them by playing harder and by being more positive than them.'

Confident that the crowd and the atmosphere generated would inspire his players, McLean continued: 'We have a very hard task ahead. They are a very good side, generally regarded in Italy as different from other sides in their country, and more English in their style of play. But it would be fatal for us to dwell on their strengths, we have got to play to our strengths.'

And didn't they just, with the entire city in a frenzy – including, dare it be said, some Dundee FC supporters – when hearing of the Tangerines' 2-0 win over AS Roma. The local morning paper, the *Courier*, even had a call from Melbourne, Australia, enquiring about the result. As the 20,000-plus trooped elatedly out of Tannadice, 26-year-old Alan Black from St Mary's managed to gasp hoarsely, 'It's the best game I have seen in years. My wife and I were going to go to Spain on holiday this year. When I eventually get home, I'll have to tell her it is Italy instead. Pubs throughout the city were full to overflowing as supporters prepared to celebrate the team's triumph long into the night.

Of course, it was the team's success on the park that gave everyone cause to celebrate and, as had been predicted by their manager, victory was not achieved easily. Despite having Falcao running up and down the corridor outside the dressing room an hour or so before the game, the Brazilian's name was missing from the official teamsheet. It included, however, one of Italy's 1982 World Cup heroes, Bruno Conti, and fellow internationalist Francesco Graziani, plus another Brazilian starter, Toninho Cerezo.

Whilst there were fleeting glimpses of United's potential in the first half, after the break there was frankly only one team in it. As Tommy Gallacher wrote in the *Courier*: 'Unfancied Scottish League champions Dundee United proved themselves once again to be the big-occasion team when they beat Italian champions Roma and put themselves in with a very good chance of a place in the European Cup final.'

All of which must have come as a surprise to the Italian side, who were totally exposed in the second half. Davie Dodds was on hand to knock the ball home from six yards. Spurred on by the crowd, United had Roma pinned back in their own penalty box and it was no surprise when Derek Stark scored a sensational second, sweeping in a swerving low drive from 25 yards – the ball's low trajectory deceiving goalkeeper Franco Tancredi. It seemed only a question of whether United could add to their lead. Some of the visitors' tackling was on the wild side, and more often than not ignored by the referee. Tommy Coyne, a late substitute for the tiring Sturrock, almost made it three, and Tancredi made a sharp save from Billy Kirkwood to keep Italian hopes alive.

A delighted Jim McLean attributed the victory to the players' response to his half-time orders: 'I told the players at half-time that they were out of the competition the way things stood and that they might as well relax in the second half. They did just that and I was really proud of them in the second half. We scored two good goals but deserved more and now are just 90 minutes away from absolute glory.'

Roma's Swedish manager Nils Liedholm looked shattered by the result, acknowledging: 'We missed Roberto Falcao, but I thought my players were beginning to put things together – until United hit with those goals.' And then as an afterthought he added: 'However, Falcao should be able to play in the second leg and he will make a big difference.'

As was the case in the previous round, United's goalscoring heroes were Davie Dodds and Derek Stark. Whilst Doddsie regularly found the net, Stark was one of the midfield Trojans at Tannadice, but this was his third strike of the European campaign and one that he will never forget, even if he at first didn't think it would go in. He recalls: 'Although my shot was swerving, it was too near the middle of the goal and I thought their keeper was bound to save it, but instead of getting his body behind it, he did a kind of Highland fling and was beaten.'

That was Stark's sixth goal of the season and undoubtedly the highlight of his career which, due to injury, went only one way thereafter – downhill. A product of Fife minor football, Derek was of only average build, but was a terrific tackler. His trademark was his seemingly telescopic legs, which so often foiled opposing forwards when they thought they had shrugged off his clutches. Above all, he hated to lose and the magnificent job that he did over a decade was never quite appreciated by everyone other than his team-mates and his manager.

Initially a part-timer, Stark initially made his breakthrough into the side at full-back, forming a useful partnership with Raymond Stewart in 1978-79. The transition to full-time football saw his career blossom and he became a colossus in midfield, though he was equally effective in any of the seven defensive positions in which he was utilised. Sadly, the glitz of that goal against Roma was very quickly tarnished, with Derek's future footballing career soon hanging by a thread.

Sour grapes would probably be the best way of describing Roma's reaction to their shock humiliation. Sneers at the Tannadice facilities, coupled with insinuations by the Roma president that drugs played a part in United's famous victory, were unworthy of such a famous club. Nearer the mark was the fear that the Italians were going to miss out on playing in the European Cup final in their back garden – the final was scheduled for their own Olympic Stadium – instigating a war of words which would manifest itself in some extraordinary scenes before the second leg took place.

Dope smears were simply laughed off in the Tannadice camp. Light-heartedly, Jim McLean commented, 'If I find out what the players were on, I will make sure they get it before every game!' Refusing to become embroiled in further controversy, he astutely acknowledged, 'This is only the start of their campaign. It just shows you what bad losers they are, and I am sorry to say it will get worse before the second leg. Actually, it is only a cover up for their own performance against us, and, as far as I am concerned, it suggests the Italians are running scared. That suits us. It's all done to whip up the emotions of the Roma fans for our visit to the Olympic Stadium.' On that score, the United boss couldn't have realised just how successful this smear campaign would be, and against him personally.

For the moment, more urgent matters rested with the visit of St Johnstone. With free admission for most, a crowd of over 11,000 saw a less emotive encounter, clinched 3-0 by United with the help of two late goals. Even although Aberdeen were otherwise engaged in reaching the Scottish Cup final, beating Dundee 2-0 at Tynecastle, Alex Ferguson's side were still firm title favourites.

Despite it being mid-April, and only a month of the season left, both United and Aberdeen still had a quarter of their league games to play, including two outstanding fixtures between the New Firm. By the time United flew out to Rome, Aberdeen's lead over United extended to ten points, and with only seven games left, that was surely unbridgable.

The end of the league road was, pragmatically, if not theoretically, reached on a miserable Wednesday evening at Pittodrie where Aberdeen strolled to a 5-1 win over a United side who uncharacteristically showed little relish for the fight.

Clearly, McLean regarded hopes of retaining the title as dead, indicating that he would, if the rules permitted, field a reserve side to take on Dundee at Tannadice to protect his players for Roma four days later.

As it was, Maurice Malpas, Richard Gough and Tommy Coyne all missed a derby which was a tale of two halves. United created nearly all the chances in the opening period, but their only reward was a John Clark strike on the stroke of half-time. However, with Dundee desperately battling against relegation, as the *Sunday Post* put it, 'Any thoughts of United receiving a fond farewell before flying out to Rome were well and truly thrown out of Tannadice from the kick-off.' Sheer endeavour won Archie Knox's side a priceless point but, from a Tannadice stance, the good thing was that there were no fresh injuries to worry about.

Wary of the reputation of Italian clubs in Europe, especially with the hullabaloo after the first leg, United took the precaution of enlisting Scotland's top administrators in their quest to reach the final. Accompanying the official party to Rome were Scotland manager Jock Stein, SFA president David Will and secretary Ernie Walker, Scottish League president David Letham and secretary Jim Farry. For his part, Roma president Guiseppe Viola retracted his drug accusations in a telexed apology to the SFA. However, that was nothing compared to the hot water that Viola was to land himself in long after the dust had settled on the second leg.

United flew into a pressure cooker atmosphere from the moment their charter flight landed at Rome's Ciampino Airport on a sweltering Easter Monday. The United party was besieged by Italian reporters and television crews. In addition to those supporters travelling with the official party, around 500 United fans made the journey to Rome to see if their heroes could become only the second Scottish club to reach the European Cup final.

Jim McLean elected to rely on the eleven who had achieved half the job, naming his side after a light training session 24 hours ahead of the biggest game in the club's 75-year history.

The torrid Olympic Stadium was turned into a torture chamber as Tannadice dreams melted in the afternoon heat. Perhaps the most disappointing aspect was how easily Roma scored the three goals they needed to prevent United from becoming the first Scottish club since Celtic in 1970 from reaching the final.

Yet, it all might have turned out so differently had Ralph Milne not fired over after Bannon's cut-back had been cleared into the winger's path. That was the best of the few chances United created, and a goal then would surely have taken the sting out of the Italians, for they would then have needed to score four times to progress. Instead, two first-half goals from Roberto Pruzzo turned the tie in the Italian club's favour, and it was no surprise when they went ahead on the hour after Di Bartolemi converted from the spot after keeper Hamish McAlpine was forced into bringing down Pruzzo.

United, playing in their all-white change strip, were a pale imitation of the side that had subdued the Italians at Tannadice. Only after going behind was there any kind of fluency in their play, but even then they were far from their best. The withdrawal of ballboys by the Italians was only an academic exercise, so little threat was there of the Scots scoring. As if victory wasn't enough for Roma, there followed some extraordinary scenes at the end of the match as the United manager walked from the dug-out to the tunnel.

Roma players surrounded McLean, making threatening gestures as a result of a hate campaign in the Italian press after the first leg. One might only speculate what might have happened had the Romans not booked their place in the final against Liverpool.

McLean offered no excuses for his side's anticlimactic demise when history was there to be made. 'Falcao's presence was really important to Roma and he made all the difference. We had too many players who just did not play as they can,' he commented dejectedly.

Ironically, the one player who could claim exemption from that statement was the youngest in the United side, because he was the one player to play to his potential. Maurice Malpas had made his first-team debut less than three years earlier, and to say that he grabbed the opportunity with both hands is something of an understatement. A series of mature performances at left-back earned him a near permanent place in the back four, yet not only was he still only 21, he was still a part-timer and a genuine part-time player at that.

As Malpas was a student, you might think that that gave him plenty of time off, but his electrical and electronic engineering studies entailed 26 weeks course work and the other 26 in a working environment, so training had to be fitted in when it could. Maurice recalls, 'Normally, I trained on Monday, Tuesday and Thursday evenings either with Graham Low or Wattie Smith and literally only saw my team-mates on matchdays. Not having been in the dressing room on a daily basis perhaps helped for this big occasion because I perhaps didn't feel the pressure as much. Besides, since I had come into the team, we had won the league and now reached the semi-final of the European Cup and naively thought that success on that scale would just carry on and on.'

For Malpas, that game in Rome was the launchpad to an international career which would eventually lead to the talented defender playing in two World Cup finals, earn over 50 caps, enter Scotland's Hall of Fame, and to this day be Dundee United's most capped player. Maurice reveals:

'After the game Jock Stein came over to me and said that I had a good game and before the end of the season I was capped for the first time.'

That first cap, in Marseille against France in June 1984, was the last occasion a part-time player was capped by Scotland and, having obtained his degree, it was also Malpas's last before joining the full-time ranks. However, in keeping with his hectic life-style, 'Mo' touched down in Scotland after that first full cap with just enough time to get changed for his wedding to Maria later that day.

Maurice might have been the apprentice of an outstanding Tannadice back four, which would be the envy of many a top club these days, but that isn't to say that he contributed any less, as the long and distinguished career that followed proves.

Defeat in Rome was bad enough for the contingent of United fans who had travelled to the Italian capital because, like their manager, they too had to contend with a torrent of abuse. It was a dejected 500-strong band of supporters that sped away from the Olympic Stadium after the whistle, protected by a ring of police steel. From the moment they had entered their supposedly segregated area inside the ground, there had been problems. The first group were driven away by hostile home fans who then pelted them with bottles and fruit. Some local 'supporters' ran up to United fans and tore their tangerine and black scarves from their necks. George Aimer, secretary of the United Away Club recalled, 'I have never seen anything like it. We were all really frightened. We were minding our own business, making our way to our seats, when all hell broke loose. Seeing their plight, police and stadium officials led them to a 'safe section' at the top of the south tier of the terracing.

There they were eventually joined by hundreds more United fans and the gathering were forced to stand and watch the match until being escorted away six hours later, which only added to the misery of an afternoon which turned so sour.

After all that, you couldn't imagine that it could get much worse, but it did for the official party and accompanying press corps and supporters. A fault in the oxygen system of the Dan Air chartered aircraft meant a six-hour delay. A tired and dejected party arrived back at Glasgow Airport in the wee small hours.

For fans back home, United's date with European Cup destiny in Rome was televised live but, unfortunately for exiled Arabs, it was only transmitted on BBC2 in Scotland. For Gerry Brady, this didn't seem to pose too many problems as he was based in Newcastle, and the border is only just over an hour's drive away. As the long-standing United and Scotland fan explained, that was the easy bit: 'My mates and I found a pub in Cornhill, a village, a stone's throw from the Tweed. It was about half an hour before the kick-off and the bar, apart from the landlord who was watching Steve Davis playing in the Embassy Snooker World Championships, was empty. Having asked for a drink and a bite to eat, we then asked if he could turn over to BBC2 so that we could watch the game and were horrified when he refused because he wanted to watch the snooker. He at least had the courtesy to tell us that if we wanted to watch the match, we'd have to go up to Coldstream, which was only just across the river. As it turned out, he did us a favour, because the first pub that we went into was full of Arabs from Carlisle and Manchester waiting for the game. So even if we didn't enjoy the game, we all had a right good time, so much so that we ended up stopping over.'

The cost to United of losing out on a return trip to Rome for the final at the end of May was too massive to contemplate, but coming so close was a monumental achievement and was marked by a second civic reception twelve months after the first.

On the field, with seven league games to be crammed in, and with the two teams above them contesting the Scottish Cup final, United's participation in next season's UEFA Cup had long been assured. No matter how much McLean tried to motivate them, for the players it was a case of limply playing out the rest of a season which nevertheless harboured a host of golden memories. Mathematically, United still harboured faint hopes of hanging on to their crown until 2 May, when United's 2-2 draw at Ibrox, coupled with Aberdeen's victory at Hearts, put the Tangerines out of contention:

|          | P  | W  | D | L | F  | A  | Pts |
|----------|----|----|---|---|----|----|-----|
| Aberdeen | 32 | 25 | 4 | 3 | 74 | 16 | 54  |
| Celtic   | 34 | 21 | 6 | 7 | 78 | 39 | 48  |
| Dundee U | 32 | 18 | 8 | 6 | 63 | 34 | 44  |

The Dons went on to claim the championship, thumbing their noses at United in the process by claiming one more point, 57, to United's 56 a year earlier.

Chapter 8

# ~ How the Mighty Fell ~

## (1984 – 1995)

United's fall from grace and the eventual ignominy of relegation in 1995 was a gradual process, but that is hardly surprising given that the men instrumental in taking the club to such unprecedented heights stayed in situ a long time. Indeed, three years after claiming the championship, what was effectively the same side came closer than most people realise to taking the title again. Everyone recalls the climax to the 1985-86 campaign as the one where Hearts blew it at Dens Park when they lost 0-2 to Dundee, letting Celtic – who won 5-0 against St Mirren – in by the back door to steal the crown on goal difference. Yet few remember that had United won their less than demanding final three games, the league flag would have been Tannadice bound.

Great as the achievement in reaching the semi-final of the European Cup had been, apart from embellishing the club's name across the continent, the only tangible reward from 1983-84 was that a third-place finish earned a place in Europe for the eighth consecutive season. Nevertheless, with the signings of goalkeeper Billy Thomson from St Mirren and midfielder Stuart Beedie from St Johnstone, McLean was at last able to make acquisitions who were to put pressure on the championship squad, which over a year after taking the title remained fully intact.

The ink was hardly dry on those signings when the club suffered a great loss with the passing of Johnston Grant, one of the men instrumental in dragging United up by its boot straps from the dim and dark days of the mid-1950s to unprecedented heights. In truth, Grant hadn't enjoyed the best of health during the club's run to the semi-final and he passed away during the club's pre-season tour of Germany in July 1984. For his successor, George Fox, it was a double blow. Paying tribute to his colleague in the programme for Jim McLean's testimonial match against Nottingham Forest, he stated: 'Johnston and I joined the board almost 30 years ago. Apart from being colleagues on the board, we were very good friends and his death is a great personal loss.' As indeed it was for Dundee United, though, at least Grant had lived to see United win the championship and become only the fifth Scottish club to reach the last four of the European Cup.

Of the players, one of the twelve that Jim McLean always gave credit to for the title win had already played his last game in a tangerine jersey. Derek Stark, scorer of three goals in the European Cup, had been a
regular member of the side. But he was to spend 1984-85 battling against
a cartilage injury which eventually was to bring a premature end to a
career before it had even peaked. He was only 26. Derek finally had to
admit defeat in August 1985, after a specialist advised him that his knee
would no longer stand up to the rigours of top-level football. Ironically,
Dens Park, the scene of his finest hours, was also his departure point. He
figured there for what was to be his last game in tangerine. The occasion
was a reserve fixture some sixteen months following his final first-team
outing against St Mirren in April 1984. So, from policing the midfield,
Starkie switched to being a bobby on the beat, something that he had
threatened to do voluntarily earlier during his career. This time, sadly, it
was enforced upon him. Eighteen years on, he remains a member of the
Fife Constabulary.

The thinking behind bringing goalkeeper Billy Thomson to Tannadice
had been two-fold. Firstly, it was a case of looking to the future. Hamish
McAlpine, the oldest member of the league title winning combine, was
now 36. Additionally, since Sandy Davie's departure a decade earlier,
Hamish's place between the sticks had never been under any real threat
from his understudies. That was evident by the fact that in the following
ten years Hamish missed only eleven league games. Apart from the start
of season 1979-80 – when Peter Bonetti briefly took over following
Hamish's row with McLean over the keeper's positioning at corner-kicks
in a close-season tournament in Japan – only the occasional injury had
kept him out of the side.

Just as he had seen off Bonetti, McAlpine would do likewise with Billy
Thomson, who started the 1984-85 campaign as first-choice goalkeeper.
Within weeks, however, the newcomer had been usurped and Hamish
would carry on for another year before a serious injury sidelined him,
eventually leading to him being freed in May 1986.

Beforehand, the European spotlight would fall on him again. Not
only did Hamish help United post a positive result on their European
travels, but he made Saint and Greavsie – so often the scourge of Scottish
goalkeepers on their Saturday lunchtime show – eat humble pie. Hamish
gave a magnificent performance at Old Trafford where United, having
eliminated AIK Stockholm and Lask from Austria, faced Manchester
United in the third round of the UEFA Cup in November 1984. Under
the cosh from Ron Atkinson's side, McLean's men were grateful to
Hamish for keeping the tie alive, providing the platform from which the

Tangerines salvaged a 2-2 draw. Unfortunately, there was to be no lasting glory: a deflected Arnold Muhren shot gave the Manchester giants a 3-2 second-leg win and passage to the quarter-finals.

McAlpine has made more appearances than any other Tannadice keeper (698 in all competitions). With his three penalty conversions, he is the only keeper ever to score for the club. Certainly, he is the only United player to be immortalised in song, witness Michael Marra's record entitled 'Hamish the Goalie'. Leaving Tannadice wasn't quite the end of his footballing career, because Hamish spent two seasons with Raith Rovers and a few months with Arbroath. In addition, he enjoyed a couple of cameo roles for Celtic when they were stuck for a goalkeeper. Over the years, he has periodically helped behind the scenes at Tannadice, but now he sells fitted kitchens, and is equally as recognisable today as he was during his playing days.

Before McAlpine's departure, United went close to winning a fourth trophy by reaching the final of the Skol Cup in October 1984. Having eliminated Celtic to reach the semi-final, Hearts were beaten home and away as United cruised into their fourth League Cup final in six years. There they faced bogey-team Rangers, who were still playing fourth fiddle behind Aberdeen, Celtic and United. Surely, given that scenario, United would finally vanquish not only their Hampden Hoodoo but also their stage fright against Rangers in the cups. It was not to be, as a lacklustre final saw Rangers win their only trophy of Jock Wallace's second spell at Ibrox. Ironically, Iain Ferguson, as Ian Redford had done three years earlier in the same competition, scored the winner to deny future team-mates.

After an indifferent start to the 1984-85 season, which included a home defeat by Dundee in a seven-goal thriller, defeats by Rangers and Manchester United were all that marred a healthy sequence of results, which included wins at Pittodrie, Parkhead and at home to Aberdeen in successive matches to thrust Jim McLean's men back into the title race. However, in the event, United finished five points adrift of Celtic, who were themselves runners-up to Aberdeen. The Dons retained their crown to deprive the Old Firm for three consecutive seasons, the first and last time that has happened.

United, however, still had an opportunity to collect silverware. The prize for finally getting the better of Aberdeen was a third Scottish Cup final. In was also to be the second time United had reached the finals of both cup competitions, emulating the 1980-81 achievement. Leading through Stuart Beedie against Celtic in the final, it looked as though the Tangerines would complete a set of domestic honours, but a Provan free-kick and a Frank McGarvey header saw Celtic come from behind to steal the trophy. Of the team that started the final, Beedie in place of Stark was the only change to the championship winning side of two years earlier.

The following season, 1985-86, would be the last campaign to feature the title-winning heroes as a unit. Barely had that campaign got under way than another member of the championship side departed. Centre-forward John Reilly was transferred to Motherwell in August 1985 for a fee of around £50,000, but an Achilles tendon injury was thought to have brought his career to a premature halt, aged only 24. However, innovative surgery enabled him to make a comeback and he resumed his career at Motherwell before going on to play for Dunfermline and East Fife. Later he briefly managed Cowdenbeath and had a spell as community officer back at Tannadice.

The consensus was that after Hearts defeated a United side containing eight title holders 3-0 at Tannadice in April – opening up a five-point lead with just four games remaining – that United's chances were scuppered. But by beating Aberdeen at Pittodrie the following week, United were still very much in contention. All that remained was to win their last three games, at Clydebank, at home to St Mirren, and at Hibs. Had they done so, the title would again have been Tannadice bound.

That they failed to do what was required, with a side far from past its peak, is a source of puzzlement. As Mike Watson suggested in *Rags to Riches*, the official history of the club (in the 1992 updated edition): 'United fans analysing that outcome reflected ruefully that they had taken seven points out of eight from Celtic over the season.'

Testimony to the talent within the Tannadice ranks came from Aberdeen boss Alex Ferguson, who was in charge of Scotland for the 1986 World Cup in Mexico following the tragic death of Jock Stein during a vital tie against Wales in Cardiff. Ferguson selected no fewer than five Dundee United players in his squad, thereby equalling the record set by Leeds United for the 1974 finals in West Germany. Richard Gough, Maurice Malpas, David Narey, Eamonn Bannon and Paul Sturrock were all included, and none was just making up the numbers. All five figured in the 'Group of Death', which comprised Denmark, West Germany and Uruguay.

Assistant manager Walter Smith was made a director of Dundee United in February 1986, in the hope of cementing his long-term future, but it proved to be a fruitless exercise. Less than two months later, Smith, who would have gone to Ibrox as assistant had McLean taken the job two years earlier, joined the club he supported as a boy by becoming right-hand man to Graeme Souness. Between them, Souness and Smith were to revolutionise the Ibrox club, which would almost totally dominate Scottish football for the next decade.

The end of 1985-86 saw the departure of two of the title-winning team, but for different reasons. As already mentioned, Hamish McAlpine took his bow, leaving Billy Thomson as first-choice keeper. The other departure seemed at first to leave a bigger void. Top scorer Davie Dodds announced that he was joining Neuchatel Xamax of Switzerland – the club which had ended United's UEFA Cup run six months earlier. Dodds cost the Swiss club £175,000, but it turned out to be a transfer of convenience, as the lanky striker returned to Scotland to play for Aberdeen within months.

As Jim McLean started to re-shape his side, Billy Kirkwood and Stuart Beedie joined Hibs. Beedie had been at Tannadice for two seasons, while Kirkwood enjoyed a six-month sabbatical before returning to Tannadice. Not for seven years, however, since Raymond Stewart, had United parted with one of its crown jewels, but Richard Gough was determined to better himself. He demanded a transfer which eventually earned a £750,000 fee from Tottenham. Like Dodds, Gough's leaving left a sour taste. Within a year, the defender was back in Scotland, playing for Rangers, the side which had rejected him six years previously when they could have signed him for nothing.

Not that the loss of four of the championship squad in the space of two months had any immediate detrimental effect. On the contrary, because 1986-87 was to be a monumental one in the club's history as the side actually reached the final of a European competition. It was a remarkable campaign, not least for seeing the class of '83 finally split up. Yet Maurice Malpas, David Narey, Paul Hegarty, Ralph Milne, John Holt, Eamonn Bannon and Paul Sturrock remained. Billy Kirkwood began the season at Easter Road but was brought back to Tannadice on Hogmanay to play his part as United became the first Scottish side to reach the final of the UEFA Cup.

Tommy Coyne was first to go. He had never quite established himself, even in the wake of Dodds' departure, and six months later he moved across the road to Dens Park. His fee was £75,000, and he finally stepped out of the shadows. His play developed to the extent that he ended up on Celtic's books and represented the Republic of Ireland in the 1994 World Cup.

If Coyne's career flourished on leaving Tannadice, the same cannot be said about Ralph Milne. From being instrumental in winning the title and a match-winner in Europe, the winger's form slumped, culminating with his transfer to Charlton Athletic in January 1987 for a £125,000 fee. After moving on to Bristol City, Alex Ferguson attempted to resurrect the player's career by signing him for Manchester United. Milne failed to rise to the challenge, and ended a career which ought to have achieved so much more than in the backwaters at Bury. These days he runs a pub in Nailsea, near Bristol.

It wasn't long before the magnificent Narey-Hegarty partnership was fractured. Initially it was an injury sustained by the United skipper which showed the cracks, but the writing was already on the wall. The man who stepped into Hegarty's shoes was, ironically, John Clark. Like Hegarty, 'Clarkie' came to the club as a striker, but took a step back into defence in order that his career might move forward. The trail to the UEFA Cup final was to provide Clark with his finest hour, for he scored six goals in that memorable run. Although he scored in the final against Gothenburg at Tannadice, the goal for which he will always be remembered came in the palatial setting of Barcelona, when he bulleted home an equalising header five minutes from the end of the second leg. United even scored again to set an incredible record of having played the Catalan giants four times and beaten them four times.

Sandwiched between the two-legged final against Gothenburg, United also contested the Scottish Cup final. With Rangers and Celtic having failed to even reach the semi-finals, United were clear favourites to win what was their fourth final in thirteen years. Instead they lost 0-1 to St Mirren.

That season United played in every game it was possible to play except the League Cup final. John Holt finally severed his fourteen-year Tannadice ties by signing for Dunfermline in September 1987, where he joined Billy Kirkwood, who had signed a matter of weeks earlier. Both were later to resume their careers at Tannadice on the coaching side, but neither with anything like the success they enjoyed as players.

The 1987-88 season saw United reach the final of the Scottish Cup for a fifth time. Celtic's Frank McAvennie scored both Celtic's late goals to complete a league and cup double, which at least gave United the 'consolation' of a place in the European Cup-Winners' Cup. They might have earned that place on merit had a header from Bannon not careered up off the baked hard ground and up and over the bar when United led 1-0.

That losing final was the last contribution by Bannon to United's cause. With his contract up, he ended his nine-year Tannadice connection and joined Hearts at the start of the following season. It had been Bannon's arrival at Tannadice which had been the catalyst to silverware, and it was a pity that he didn't bow out with more than a fourth Scottish Cup loser's medal. Although 30 when he left, there was still some mileage in his career. He spent five seasons back at Tynecastle before taking up a coaching post with Hibs. He won one more medal, famously being a member of the Stenhousemuir side which defeated United in the final of the League Challenge Cup in 1995.

The 1988 Scottish Cup final was also the beginning of the end of Paul Sturrock's illustrious career. Battling, as ever, against injury he was named as a sub at Hampden, and stayed on the bench, something that would have been unthinkable in the past. Twelve months later, with only ten appearances during 1988-89, Luggy made his final competitive appearance in a tangerine jersey against Hamilton in the final game of the season. The last time he pulled on the tangerine was against Real Sociedad in his testimonial at the start of the following season.

Far from severing his Tannadice connection, Sturrock's long-term ambition was realised when he was appointed to the Tannadice coaching staff, along with Steve Murray, Jim McLean's new assistant for the 1988-89 term. League-wise United improved by one place to finish fourth. That meant that they had never finished below the top half of the Premier Division since that inaugural season, when they had diced with relegation.

1988-89 was also the last campaign in which the Narey-Hegarty partnership ruled the defence. Ironically, given that Paul had played 68 times in Europe, a 0-4 defeat at Antwerp in the UEFA Cup marked the last of his 706 appearances for the club. Like Sturrock, Heggie's farewell appearance was in a testimonial, in his case against Gothenburg a month after Luggy's. In January 1989 Hegarty joined St Johnstone, helping them to win the First Division title and return to the Premier Division. He then became player-manager at Forfar for eighteen months and after a spell out of the game returned to Tannadice in a coaching capacity. He moved on to Hearts in 1995, but that was far from the end of his United connection. Brought back as a coach in September 2000, he was appointed manager on a caretaker basis. Inheriting a struggling squad, Hegarty was given only eighteen games in charge before being sacked in January 2003.

By 1991, only Dave Narey and Maurice Malpas of the championship heroes remained at Tannadice, alongside Jim McLean as manager. Although United finished fourth in 1991 and reached the Scottish Cup final, they missed out on Europe for the first time since 1976-77. That was confirmed by a defeat by Motherwell in United's sixth Scottish Cup final. It had been dubbed the 'Family Final' as the winning manager was Jim McLean's wee brother Tommy. Of the title-winning survivors, only Maurice Malpas picked up a loser's medal, because a back injury had sidelined Dave Narey for almost the entire season.

Jim McLean's United were nothing if not consistent, finishing fourth for the fourth consecutive year in 1991-92. They were fourth yet again the following season, and this time it earned entry to the UEFA Cup. But that would be conducted without Jim McLean at the helm. He announced his retirement and brought his 21 and a half years in charge to an end when the curtain came down on the 1992-93 campaign. Almost at once, the club's fortunes started to dip.

Stepping into McLean's shoes was the flamboyant Ivan Golac, who had formerly managed Partizan Belgrade, but the Yugoslav was better known in Britain for his colourful playing career with Southampton. The comparison with his predecessor could scarcely have been greater. 'From Belsen to Butlins,' was how one player described the change of regime. On the face of it, a sixth-place finish out of twelve looked okay, but it didn't tell the whole story. The dreaded prospect of relegation was only banished with four games remaining.

But whatever Ivan Golac's failings, he finally guided the club to the Holy Grail of the Scottish Cup in 1994. Maurice Malpas, who was only a raw youngster at the time of United's two League Cup triumphs, finally got his hands on a cup when collecting the trophy as captain after a 1-0 win over Rangers at Hampden. It was United's first ever cup win of any description over the Ibrox men.

Unfortunately, David Narey wasn't in that Hampden side. The last of his record 866 competitive appearances for United came against Celtic at the beginning of April. He was released a month later. The following season was his last of an illustrious 22-year playing career. Narey added to his medal haul by picking up a First Division championship and a third League Cup winners medal in his single season with Raith Rovers. He retired in 1995.

While Narey was winning more medals with Raith, Dundee United were being relegated for the first time in 35 years. Ivan Golac was sacked – though it was publicly announced as a parting by mutual agreement – after United's quarter-final Scottish Cup exit at Hearts. Billy Kirkwood was appointed manager with just seven games remaining and, with the transfer deadline passed, could do little to prevent the club slipping out of the top division after 35 years. Maurice Malpas was the sole playing survivor, but he was also on the coaching staff, and indeed, was appointed assistant manager under Billy Kirkwood, who also had Paul Hegarty plus former coach Gordon Wallace as part of his backroom team.

In the years since, Paul Sturrock had a shot as manager before heading off to Plymouth Argyle. Maurice Malpas, then 37, was still combining playing with coaching, but called it a day in the summer of 2000.

Jim McLean was forced to resign as chairman after an incident with BBC reporter John Barnes during a post-match interview after a 0-4 home thrashing by Hearts in October 2000. An exceptional career appeared to have come to an unworthy end. In January 2002, a consortium in which Jim McLean was the major shareholder, ousted the board, but nine months later Eddie Thompson bought a controlling interest to finally terminate Jim McLean's 31-year association with the club.

Within weeks Paul Hegarty was placed temporarily in charge but in January 2003 he too was shown the door, along with title-winning teammates Maurice Malpas and John Holt, both coaches. It was an inglorious finale to what had been a glorious era in the history of Dundee United.

# GUIDE TO SEASONAL SUMMARIES

Col 1: Match number (for league fixtures); Round (for cup-ties).
e.g. 4R means 'Fourth round replay.'

Col 2: Date of the fixture and whether Home (H), Away (A), or Neutral (N).

Col 3: Opposition.

Col 4: Attendances. Home gates appear in roman; Away gates in *italics*.
Figures in **bold** indicate the largest and smallest gates, at home and away.
Average home and away attendances appear after the final league match.

Col 5: Respective league positions of Dundee U and opponents after the game.
Dundee U's position appears on the top line in roman.
Their opponents' position appears on the second line in *italics*.
For cup-ties, the division and position of opponents is provided.
e.g. 2:12 means the opposition are twelfth in Division 2.

Col 6: The top line shows the result: W(in), D(raw), or L(ose).
The second line shows Dundee U's cumulative points total.

Col 7: The match score, Dundee U's given first.
Scores in **bold** show Dundee U's biggest league win and heaviest defeat.

Col 8: The half-time score, Dundee U's given first.

Col 9: The top line shows Dundee U's scorers and times of goals in roman.
The second line shows opponents' scorers and times of goals in *italics*.
A 'p' after the time of a goal denotes a penalty; 'og' an own-goal.
The third line gives the name of the match referee.

Team line-ups: Dundee U line-ups appear on top line, irrespective of whether
they are home or away. Opposition teams are on the second line in *italics*.
Players of either side who are sent off are marked !
Dundee U players making their league debuts are displayed in **bold**.

Substitutes: Names of substitutes appear only if they actually took the field.
A player substituted is marked *

N.B. For clarity, all information appearing in *italics* relates to opposing teams.

# SCOTTISH PREMIER DIVISION

**Manager: Jim McLean**   **SEASON 1982-83**

| No | Date | Att | Pos | Pt | F-A | H-T | Scorers, Times, and Referees | 1 | 2 | 3 | 4 | 5 | 6 | 7 | 8 | 9 | 10 | 11 | subs used |
|---|---|---|---|---|---|---|---|---|---|---|---|---|---|---|---|---|---|---|---|
| 1 | H ABERDEEN 4/9 | 11,683 | 2 | W 2 | 2-0 | 2-0 | Malpas 18, Dodds 40; Ref: A Ferguson | **McAlpine** | **Malpas** | **Stark*** | **Gough** | **Hegarty** | **Narey** | **Britton** | **Milne** | **Kirkwood** | **Sturrock** | **Dodds** | **Bannon** |
|  |  |  |  |  |  |  |  | *Leighton* | *Kennedy* | *McMaster* | *Cooper* | *McLeish* | *Miller* | *Strachan* | *Simpson* | *McGhee* | *Bell** | *Black^* | *Weir/Hewitt* |
| 2 | A RANGERS 11/9 | 22,200 | 5 | D 3 | 0-0 | 0-0 | Ref: D Ramsay | **McAlpine** | **Kirkwood** | **Malpas** | **Gough** | **Hegarty** | **Narey** | **Britton** | **Bannon** | **Payne*** | **Sturrock** | **Dodds** | **Milne** |
|  |  |  |  |  |  |  |  | *Stewart* | *McKinnon* | *Dawson* | *McClelland* | *Paterson* | *Bett* | *Cooper** | *Prytz* | *Johnston* | *Redford* | *MacDonald* | *Russell* |
| 3 | A HIBERNIAN 18/9 | 5,562 | 6 | D 4 | 0-0 | 0-0 | Ref: H Young | **McAlpine** | **Malpas** | **Stark** | **Gough** | **Hegarty** | **Narey** | **Britton*** | **Bannon** | **Payne*** | **Sturrock** | **Dodds** | **Milne/Kirkwood** |
|  |  |  |  |  |  |  |  | *McArthur* | *Sneddon* | *Schaedler* | *McNamara* | *Rae* | *Brazil^* | *Callachan* | *Welsh* | *Jamieson** | *Thomson* | *Murray* | *Duncan/Flavell* |
| 4 | H ST MIRREN 25/9 | 6,832 | 9 | W 6 | 3-0 | 1-0 | Milne 16, Sturrock 76, 88; Ref: J Duncan | **McAlpine** | **Phillip*** | **Stark** | **Gough** | **Hegarty** | **Narey** | **Bannon** | **Milne^** | **Kirkwood** | **Sturrock** | **Dodds** | **Britton/Malpas** |
|  |  |  |  |  |  |  |  | *Thomson* | *Wilson* | *McCormack* | *Fitzpatrick* | *McAveety* | *Copland* | *Stark* | *Richardson* | *McAvennie* | *Abercromby* | *Scanlon^* | *McDougall* |
| 5 | H CELTIC 2/10 | 20,009 | 7 | D 7 | 2-2 | 0-1 | Dodds 76, Milne 85 / McStay 20, Aitken 46; Ref: D Syme | **McAlpine** | **Holt** | **Stark** | **Gough** | **Hegarty** | **Narey** | **Bannon^** | **Milne** | **Kirkwood** | **Sturrock** | **Dodds** | **Britton** |
|  |  |  |  |  |  |  |  | *Bonner* | *McGrain* | *Reid* | *Aitken* | *McAdam* | *Sinclair* | *Provan* | *McStay* | *McGarvey** | *MacLeod* | *Nicholas* | *McCluskey* |
| 6 | A KILMARNOCK 9/10 | 2,446 | 8 | D 8 | 1-1 | 0-1 | Milne 74p / Gallacher 26; Ref: B Robertson | **McAlpine** | **Malpas** | **Stark** | **Gough** | **Hegarty** | **Narey** | **Britton*** | **Milne** | **Kirkwood** | **Sturrock** | **Dodds** | **Holt** |
|  |  |  |  |  |  |  |  | *McCulloch* | *McDicken* | *MacLeod* | *J Clark* | *Armstrong* | *Clarke* | *McGivern* | *McLean^* | *Gallacher* | *McClurg* | *R Clark* | *Bryson/Bourke* |
| 7 | H MORTON 16/10 | 5,986 | 6 | W 10 | 6-0 | 5-0 | Narey 15, 19, Dodds 17, 42, 86, Kirkwood 21; Ref: L Thow | **McAlpine** | **Holt** | **Stark** | **Gough** | **Hegarty** | **Narey** | **Bannon*** | **Milne** | **Kirkwood^** | **Sturrock** | **Dodds** | **Malpas/Payne** |
|  |  |  |  |  |  |  |  | *Baines* | *Houston* | *Holmes* | *Duffy* | *McLaughlin* | *Jackson* | *McNab* | *Docherty** | *Hutchison* | *Rooney* | *Ritchie* | *Cochrane* |
| 8 | A MOTHERWELL 23/10 | 4,555 | 10 | W 12 | 2-0 | 0-0 | Narey 88, Kirkwood 89; Ref: A Ferguson | **McAlpine** | **Holt** | **Stark** | **Gough** | **Hegarty** | **Narey** | **Malpas** | **Milne** | **Kirkwood** | **Britton*** | **Dodds** | **Reilly** |
|  |  |  |  |  |  |  |  | *Sproat* | *MacLeod* | *Forsyth* | *Carson* | *Edvaldsson* | *Mauchan* | *Burns** | *Flavell* | *McLelland* | *McLaughlin* | *O'Hara* | *Gahagan/Rafferty* |
| 9 | H DUNDEE 30/10 | 14,959 | 5 | W 14 | 1-0 | 0-0 | Dodds 86; Ref: D Downie | **McAlpine** | **Phillip** | **Stark** | **Gough** | **Hegarty** | **Narey** | **Taylor*** | **Milne** | **Kirkwood*** | **Holt** | **Dodds*** | **Reilly** |
|  |  |  |  |  |  |  |  | *Kelly* | *Glennie* | *McKimmie* | *Fraser* | *Smith* | *MacDonald* | *Ferguson* | *Scrimgeour** | *Davidson* | *Mackie* | *Stephen^* | *Bell/Kidd* |
| 10 | A ABERDEEN 6/11 | 13,968 | 2 | L 14 | 1-5 | 1-3 | Gough 20 / Cooper 23, Rougvie 29, 41, Black 72 (Strachan 85); Ref: G Smith | **McAlpine** | **Malpas** | **Stark** | **Gough** | **Hegarty** | **Narey** | **Bannon** | **Milne** | **Kirkwood** | **Holt** | **Dodds*** | **Reilly** |
|  |  |  |  |  |  |  |  | *Leighton* | *Kennedy* | *Rougvie* | *Cooper* | *McLeish* | *Miller* | *Strachan* | *Simpson* | *McGhee* | *Black* | *Weir* |  |
| 11 | H RANGERS 13/11 | 16,470 | 4 | W 16 | 4-2 | 1-1 | Milne 31, 87, Dodds 71, Gough 86 / Cooper 33, Johnstone 65; Ref: J McGilvary | **McAlpine** | **Stark** | **Malpas** | **Gough** | **Hegarty** | **Narey** | **Bannon** | **Milne** | **Kirkwood** | **Sturrock** | **McDonald*** | **Dodds** |
|  |  |  |  |  |  |  |  | *Stewart* | *McKinnon* | *Dawson* | *McClelland* | *Stevens* | *Bett* | *Cooper* | *McPherson* | *Johnstone* | *Redford* | *MacDonald** | *Dalziel* |

**Match reports**

1. Alex Ferguson's side suffer only their second defeat in 32 outings as Jim McLean's side get the league campaign off to a flying start. First-half domination sees Malpas fire home from 20 yards, whilst Dodds rises high to head home the second from a Gough cross for an important win...

2. Ian Britton bangs one against the post but that was the closest either side came to scoring. Kirkwood is booked for dissent. Disappointment for failing to make it eight straight wins is tempered by taking a point from Ibrox, scene of just two victories in the last 14 Premier Division visits.

3. To say Jim McLean's men have played better would be understating this undistinguished sterile stalemate. Young doesn't help United's cause. Refereeing his first top ten game, he at last books Gordon Rae for fouling Sturrock after several cynical tackles by Hibs men went unpunished.

4. Two late goals finally subdue Saints. Milne, on the end of a Bannon cross, stylishly angles in a fierce volley. Sturrock seals a very comfortable win from two further Bannon assists. Sent clear, he slips the ball under the keeper and easily tucks away his second after being left unmarked.

5. Having given Billy McNeill's side two goals of a start, United stage a classic comeback. Paul McStay blasts Celtic ahead and it looks all over when Roy Aitken adds a second. Davie Dodds poaches one back and Ralph Milne sweeps in an equaliser to dent Celtic's 100% record.

6. Eccentric refereeing contributes to both goals. Brian Gallacher slips the home side ahead, though clearly offside. Derek McDicken looks more than transgressor as Paul Sturrock went down, but Ralph Milne scores from the spot. McDicken, McGivern and Holt are booked.

7. A Rolls-Royce performance mows down Benny Rooney's side. Dave Narey ghosts in to nod the first and a glancing header from Davie Dodds brings a delightful second. Dave Narey hammers in the third and Billy Kirkwood the fourth. Davie Dodds goes on to complete his hat-trick.

8. Staging a late, late, show. United snatch victory against the league's bottom-markers. Just two minutes are left when Dave Narey lashes home a low drive for the opener. Billy Kirkwood side-foots the second from a Ralph Milne cut-back that leaves Jock Wallace's troops reeling.

9. It took another late strike to bag two points as Dundee fight tooth and nail as bookings for Gerry Davidson, Bobby Glennie and Brian Scrimgeour indicates. Alex Taylor fires in a low drive which keeper Colin Kelly spills and Davie Dodds drills the rebound high into the net.

10. Richard Gough's header from a Ralph Milne cross gives United the lead, but United stumble to their first league defeat. Neale Cooper's 18-yarder draws the Dons level and two Doug Rougvie goals put them ahead. Eric Black and Gordon Strachan's goals make final score flattering.

11. Milne heads in a Paul Sturrock cross as United forge ahead, but Davie Cooper hooks John Grieg's side level and Derek Johnstone gives Gers the lead. Davie Dodds soon levels and in a frenetic finale, goals from Richard Gough and Ralph Milne give United a fully deserved victory.

Dundee United season record (matches 12–23)

---

**12. H HIBERNIAN — 20/11**
Result: W 3-0 (HT 1-0) · Meeting 2 · Att 7,347 · Pos 9 · Pts 18
Scorers: Bannon 34, Reilly 77, Dodds 79
Ref: B McGinlay

United: McAlpine, Stark, Malpas, Gough, Hegarty, Narey, Bannon, Milne*, Kirkwood^, Sturrock^, Dodds
Hibernian: McArthur, Sneddon, Duncan, Conroy, Rae, Turnbull, Callachan, Smith, Irvine*, Thomson, Murray
Subs: Reilly/Taylor — Jamieson

Eamonn Bannon taps in the first-half opener, but it is substitute Reilly's second as he steers in Gough's through ball which is the goal of the game. Dodds sticks away a Paul Sturrock cross from close range for the third, leaving Pat Stanton's unimpressive visitors well beaten.

---

**13. A ST MIRREN — 27/11**
Result: W 2-0 (HT 0-0) · Meeting 2 · Att 3,823 · Pos 7 · Pts 20
Scorers: Bannon 70, Dodds 83
Ref: H Alexander

United: McAlpine, Holt, Malpas, Gough, Hegarty, Narey, Bannon, Milne, Kirkwood, Sturrock*, Dodds
St Mirren: Thomson, Wilson, Clark, Richardson, Fulton, Copland, Stark, McDougall, Somner, McAvennie*, Abercromby
Subs: Reilly — Scanlon

The only surprise was that Rikki McFarlane's men held out so long. Bannon, who was booked along with Saints' Lex Richardson, eventually rectifies that with a fierce first-time grounder. Dodds makes sure the disjointed Saints are beaten, tapping in a Bannon cut-back from close in.

---

**14. H KILMARNOCK — 11/12**
Result: W 7-0 (HT 1-0) · Meeting 2 · Att 7,259 · Pos 10 · Pts 22
Scorers: Reilly 38, 68, Bannon 48, Narey 73, [Milne 78, Dodds 87, 90]
Ref: J Renton

United: McAlpine, Stark, Malpas, Gough, Hegarty, Narey, Bannon, Milne*, Kirkwood^, Sturrock*, Reilly^
Kilmarnock: McCulloch, Robertson, Cockburn, J Clark, McDicken, Clarke, McGivern, McLean*, Bourke, MacLeod, Gallacher
Subs: Dodds/Holt — Bryson

Jim Clunie's side are routed. John Reilly raps in the only goal of the first half after a Paul Sturrock shot breaks to him. Bannon slams in the second. Reilly scores a third and Narey crashes in a fourth. Milne hits a fabulous fifth and two goals by Dodds to make it seventh heaven.

---

**15. A MORTON — 18/12**
Result: W 2-1 (HT 1-1) · Meeting 2 · Att 1,887 · Pos 8 · Pts 24
Scorers: Reilly 31, Sturrock 67 · McNab 12
Ref: E Pringle

United: McAlpine, Stark, Malpas, Gough, Hegarty, Narey, Bannon, Milne, Kirkwood*, Sturrock, Reilly*
Morton: Baines, Hayes, Holmes, Rooney, McLaughlin, Duffy, McNeil^, Docherty, Cochrane, Houston*, McNab
Subs: Holt — Doak/Ritchie

No slip up in icy conditions, despite trailing to Eddie McNab's stylish opener. Reilly hooked home the equaliser and Sturrock flicks a Bannon cross past Baines for the winner. Conditions contributed to the four bookings – United's Reilly, Holt and Gough plus Morton's McNab.

---

**16. H MOTHERWELL — 27/12**
Result: W 5-0 (HT 2-0) · Meeting 2 · Att 7,682 · Pos 9 · Pts 26
Scorers: Milne 33, Bannon 37p, Reilly 59, [Hegarty 63, Sturrock 82]
Ref: H Williamson

United: McAlpine, Stark, Malpas, Gough, Hegarty, Narey, Bannon, Milne, Kirkwood*, Sturrock, Reilly*
Motherwell: Sproat, MacLeod, Forsyth, Forbes, Edvaldsson, Mauchlan, Gahagan^, Flavell, McLaughlin*, McClair, O'Hara
Subs: Kirkwood — McClelland/Clinging

A scoring spree brings a sixth consecutive victory. Milne polishes off a fine move to make the breakthrough and Bannon makes it two from the spot after a foul on Sturrock. Reilly prods in after Sturrock strikes the bar and headers from Hegarty and Sturrock cap the second-half rout.

---

**17. A DUNDEE — 1/1**
Result: W 2-0 (HT 1-0) · Meeting 2 · Att 18,109 · Pos 5 · Pts 28
Scorers: Milne 24, 83
Ref: H Alexander

United: McAlpine, Stark, Malpas, Gough, Hegarty, Narey, Bannon, Milne*, Kirkwood, Sturrock, Reilly
Dundee: Kelly, Glennie*, McKimmie, Bell^, Smith, MacDonald, Ferguson, McGeachie, Stephen, Mackie, Murphy
Subs: Kirkwood — Scrimgeour/Sinclair

United are streets ahead of Donald Mackay's side and, volleying the second, Milne is the local boy made good, deftly nodding the opener from Bannon's cross and volleying the second. Dundee's skipper Glennie is booked as are Ferguson and United's Malpas.

---

**18. H ABERDEEN — 3/1**
Result: L 0-3 (HT 0-2) · Meeting 3 · Att 17,852 · Pos 2 · Pts 28
Scorers: Simpson 27, Weir 43, McGhee 88
Ref: B McGinlay

United: McAlpine, Stark, Malpas*, Gough, Hegarty, Narey, Bannon, Milne, Kirkwood, Sturrock, Reilly
Aberdeen: Leighton, Kennedy, Rougvie, Cooper, McLeish, Miller, Strachan*, Simpson^, McGhee, Weir, Bell
Subs: Holt/Reilly — Black/McMaster

Simpson slams Dons opener and Weir first-times the second from McGhee's low cross. Plenty of United possession produces little of note in front of goal. McGhee disposses Narey to score a late third and wreck United's unbeaten home record. Weir, McGhee and Rougvie are booked.

---

**19. A RANGERS — 8/1**
Result: L 1-2 (HT 1-1) · Meeting 3 · Att 15,200 · Pos 4 · Pts 28
Scorers: Reilly 12 · Prytz 41, Kennedy 62
Ref: G Smith

United: McAlpine, Stark*, Malpas, Gough, Hegarty, Narey, Bannon, Milne^, Kirkwood, Sturrock, Reilly*
Rangers: McCloy, McKinnon, Redford, Stevens, McClelland, Bett, Prytz, Russell*, Kennedy, Black, Johnstone
Subs: Holt/McNeil — Cooper

Reilly's fastest goal of the day from close range fails to spark United. Kennedy silences the 'Greig must go chants', setting up Prytz's headed equaliser, before volleying the winner from close range. Black of Rangers, plus Malpas and Bannon, are yellow-carded as Saints lose again.

---

**20. A HIBERNIAN — 15/1**
Result: D 0-0 (HT 0-0) · Meeting 3 · Att 5,500 · Pos 6 · Pts 29
Ref: A Ferguson

United: McAlpine, Holt, Malpas, Gough, Hegarty, Narey, Bannon, Britton^, Kirkwood, Sturrock, Reilly*
Hibernian: Rough, Sneddon, Turnbull, Welsh, Rae, McNamara, Conroy, Rice, Duncan, Thomson*, Murray
Subs: Milne/Stark — Irvine

Hamish McAlpine is the hero, saving Rae's penalty after Bannon is harshly judged to arm away the ball. Earlier, Murray does net but the goal is disallowed despite Narey being booked for a foul on the home striker. A strange decision. but one that allows lucky United to take a point.

---

**21. H ST MIRREN — 22/1**
Result: W 3-2 (HT 3-1) · Meeting 3 · Att 6,714 · Pos 8 · Pts 31
Scorers: Kirkwood 10, Dodds 17, 19 · McDougall 45, Somner 87
Ref: D Syme

United: McAlpine, Stark, Malpas, Gough, Hegarty, Narey, Bannon, Milne, Kirkwood, Holt, Reilly^
St Mirren: Thomson, Wilson, Clarke, Walker, Fulton, Abercromby, Clark*, Richardson, McDougall, McAvennie, Scanlon*
Subs: Dodds/Reilly — Somner

Kirkwood chips into the top corner from the edge of the box and Dodds side-foots Kirkwood's low cross. A minute later Dodds nets again as Saints suffer. But McDougall scores with a low drive off Malpas. Fortunately as Saints take control they can only muster a late Somner strike.

---

**22. H CELTIC — 5/2**
Result: D 1-1 (HT 1-1) · Meeting 3 · Att 17,289 · Pos 1 · Pts 32
Scorers: Dodds 40 · Nicholas 4
Ref: E Pringle

United: McAlpine, Stark, Malpas, Gough, Hegarty, Narey, Bannon, Holt, Kirkwood, Sturrock, Dodds
Celtic: Bonner, McGrain, Reid, Aitken, McAdam, Sinclair, Provan, Rae, Nicholas, McStay, MacLeod
Subs: — McCluskey

All square at the end of a pulsating contest. Celtic's Nicholas stabs the leaders in front from close range, but Dodds gets on the end of a Stark up and under to toe the ball into the bottom corner. Two minutes later, Sinclair handles in the box, but Bonner at full stretch saves Bannon's kick.

---

**23. A KILMARNOCK — 12/2**
Result: W 5-0 (HT 2-0) · Meeting 3 · Att 1,830 · Pos 10 · Pts 34
Scorers: Holt 10, 17, 54, Bannon 56, Dodds 78
Ref: D Downie

United: McAlpine, Phillip, Malpas, Gough, Hegarty, Narey, Bannon, Holt, Kirkwood^, Sturrock*, Dodds
Kilmarnock: Wilson, McDicken, Clark R, Clark J, Armstrong, Clarke, McGivern, MacLeod, Gallacher, Simpson^, Muir
Subs: Dodds — McClurg/McKenna

John Holt is the unlikely hat-trick hero. His header from a Malpas cross brings the first and he forces home Bannon crosses for his second and third. Bannon thrashes in a fourth and in the gathering fog, Dodds' crisp volley takes the season's tally to thirteen against hapless Kilmarnock.

# SCOTTISH PREMIER DIVISION — Manager: Jim McLean — SEASON 1982-83

| No | Date | Att | Pos | Pt | F-A | H-T | Scorers, Times, and Referees | 1 | 2 | 3 | 4 | 5 | 6 | 7 | 8 | 9 | 10 | 11 | subs used |
|---|---|---|---|---|---|---|---|---|---|---|---|---|---|---|---|---|---|---|---|
| 24 | H MORTON 26/2 | 5,986 | 9 | 35 | 1-1 | 0-0 | Gough 57 / Hutchison 81 / Ref: J Duncan | McAlpine / *Baines* | Stark / *Doak* | Malpas / *Holmes* | Gough / *Rooney* | Hegarty / *McLaughlin* | Narey / *Duffy !* | Bannon * / *Payne* | Milne / *Hutchison* | Holt ^ / *Docherty* | Sturrock / *McNeil* | Dodds / *Houston ^* | Reilly/Kirkwood Gavigan |
|  |  |  |  |  |  |  | *Ten-man Morton pull off daylight robbery by stealing a vital point from careless United. Ten minutes after Duffy was dismissed for yet again clattering Sturrock, Baines makes his one mistake and Gough nods home. Hutchison's low drive via McAlpine gives Ton a shock equaliser.* |  |  |  |  |  |  |  |  |  |  |  |  |
| 25 | A MOTHERWELL 5/3 | 3,589 | 8 | 37 | 4-1 | 2-1 | Gough 16, 30, Dodds 46, Milne 70 / Gahagan 15 / Ref: R Cuthill | McAlpine / *Walker* | Stark / *Dornan* | Murray / *MacLeod* | Gough / *Forbes* | Hegarty / *Edvaldsson* | Narey / *Mauchlan* | Bannon / *Gahagan* | Milne / *Rafferty* | Kirkwood * / *Harrow* | Holt / *McClair* | Dodds / *O'Hara* | Malpas |
|  |  |  |  |  |  |  | *Gahagan slots the home side ahead after McAlpine saves from Harrow. Not for long though as Gough heads home a right-wing corner and then does likewise to one from the left as United go ahead. Dodds strokes a Gough cross and Milne diverts a Bannon cross in for the fourth.* |  |  |  |  |  |  |  |  |  |  |  |  |
| 26 | H DUNDEE 12/3 | 13,443 | 5 | 39 | 5-3 | 1-0 | Gough 30, 51, Reilly 82, Hegarty 85, Ferg 53p, Kidd 69, Fraser 74 [Dodds 87] / Ref: K Hope | McAlpine / *Geddes ** | Stark / *McGeachie* | Malpas / *McKimmie* | Gough / *Fraser* | Hegarty / *Smith* | Narey / *MacDonald* | Bannon / *Ferguson* | Milne * / *Bell ^* | Kirkwood / *Sinclair* | Sturrock / *Scrimgeour* | Dodds ^ / *Kidd* | Reilly/Holt Mackie/McClelland |
|  |  |  |  |  |  |  | *Gough strikes a superb 20-yarder and heads home after a Sturrock flick comes off the bar. Ferguson scored from the spot after Gough impedes Sinclair. Kidd equalises and Fraser blasts Dundee in front. Reilly restores parity and Hegarty and Dodds get late goals that secure victory.* |  |  |  |  |  |  |  |  |  |  |  |  |
| 27 | A ABERDEEN 19/3 | 22,800 | 1 | 41 | 2-1 | 2-0 | Milne 25, 30 / Strachan 65p / Ref: E Pringle | McAlpine / *Leighton* | Stark / *Cooper* | Malpas / *Rougvie* | Gough / *McMaster* | Hegarty / *McLeish* | Narey / *Miller* | Bannon / *Strachan* | Milne ! / *Bell ^* | Kirkwood / *McGhee* | Phillip / *Hewitt* | Dodds / *Weir ^* | Black/Simpson |
|  |  |  |  |  |  |  | *The Dons had just conquered Bayern Munich, but couldn't do likewise to United. Milne is saint and sinner, being sent off for kicking McLeish after scoring both goals. His first is off the bar and he sweeps in a second on the turn. Dodds fouls Miller and Strachan converts the penalty.* |  |  |  |  |  |  |  |  |  |  |  |  |
| 28 | H HIBERNIAN 26/3 | 7,279 | 7 | 42 | 3-3 | 3-1 | Dodds 7, Britton 22, Gough 44 / Rae 3, Irvine 64, Rice 62 / Ref: T Muirhead | McAlpine / *Rough* | Stark / *Sneddon* | Malpas / *Duncan* | Gough / *Turnbull* | Hegarty / *Rae* | Narey / *McNamara* | Bannon * / *Conroy ** | Britton / *Rice* | Kirkwood / *Irvine* | Reilly / *Thomson* | Dodds / *Harvey* | Taylor Callachan |
|  |  |  |  |  |  |  | *Hibs secured their third draw with a battling performance. Rae's blistering 35-yarder deceives McAlpine, but Dodds flicks in a near-post equaliser. Britton fires United in front and Gough squeezes in a third. United's second-half fade is punished by Irvine and Rice as Hibs draw.* |  |  |  |  |  |  |  |  |  |  |  |  |
| 29 | H RANGERS 2/4 | 14,142 | 4 | 44 | 3-1 | 1-0 | Milne 33, Sturrock 77, 89 / Clark 66 / Ref: A Ferguson | McAlpine / *McCloy* | Stark / *Dawson* | Malpas / *Redford* | Gough / *McClelland* | Hegarty / *Paterson* | Narey / *Bett* | Bannon / *Cooper* | Milne / *McKinnon* | Holt / *Clark* | Sturrock / *Prytz ** | Dodds / *McDonald* | Dodds Lyall |
|  |  |  |  |  |  |  | *Only Sturrock's late double downs Rangers. Milne guides a Bannon cross for the opener and is unlucky when he hits the bar just before the break. Clark's equaliser is helped into the net by Dodds, but Sturrock pounces on Paterson's poor clearance and also scores from Stark's pass.* |  |  |  |  |  |  |  |  |  |  |  |  |
| 30 | A CELTIC 6/4 | 34,508 | 1 | 44 | 0-2 | 0-0 | McGarvey 60, Nicholas 79 / Ref: C White | McAlpine / *Bonner* | Stark / *McGrain* | Malpas / *Reid* | Gough / *Aitken* | Hegarty / *McAdam* | Narey * / *MacLeod* | Bannon / *Provan* | Milne / *McStay* | Holt / *Nicholas* | Sturrock / *Burns* | Dodds / *McGarvey* | Reilly |
|  |  |  |  |  |  |  | *Championship dreams fade as United lose ground to the reigning champions. This physical contest is tipped Celtic's way when McGarvey nips in on Hegarty's half-hit pass-back to score. A cheeky Nicholas chip seals a victory that leaves United trailing leaders Celtic by three points.* |  |  |  |  |  |  |  |  |  |  |  |  |
| 31 | A ST MIRREN 9/4 | 4,617 | 4 | 46 | 2-1 | 2-1 | Bannon 31p, Sturrock 35 / Somner 42 / Ref: E Pringle | McAlpine / *Thomson* | Holt / *Wilson* | Malpas / *Clarke* | Gough / *Fitzpatrick* | Hegarty / *Fulton* | Narey / *McCormack* | Bannon / *Logan* | Milne / *Richardson ** | Kirkwood / *Somner* | Sturrock / *McVennie* | Dodds / *Abercromby* | McEachran |
|  |  |  |  |  |  |  | *United complete a whitewash over Rikki McFarlane's side with a fourth win. Eamonn Bannon converts a softish penalty award after Sturrock was fouled by McCormack to break the deadlock. Sturrock heads the second goal before Somner pulls one back just before the break.* |  |  |  |  |  |  |  |  |  |  |  |  |
| 32 | A CELTIC 20/4 | 23,965 | 1 | 48 | 3-2 | 1-1 | Hegarty 14, Bannon 52p, Milne 84 / Nicholas 38p, Burns 73 / Ref: D Syme | McAlpine / *Bonner* | Stark / *Sinclair ** | Malpas / *Reid* | Gough ! / *Aitken* | Hegarty / *McAdam* | Narey / *MacLeod* | Bannon / *Provan* | Milne / *McStay* | Holt * / *Nicholas* | Sturrock / *Burns* | Dodds / *McGarvey* | McCluskey |
|  |  |  |  |  |  |  | *Hegarty's opportunism has United in front but Nicholas sinks a spot-kick after Stark impedes Burns. MacLeod then does likewise on Dodds for Bannon to bang home a penalty. Gough is then sent off and Burns sweeps home the equaliser, but Milne grabs a dramatic and crucial winner.* |  |  |  |  |  |  |  |  |  |  |  |  |
| 33 | H KILMARNOCK 23/4 | 7,516 | 10 | 50 | 4-0 | 4-0 | Stark 13, 34, Holt 21, Sturrock 40 / Ref: A Huett | McAlpine / *McCulloch* | Stark / *McLean* | Malpas / *R Clark* | Kirkwood / *J Clark* | Hegarty / *Armstrong ^* | Narey / *Clarke* | Bannon / *McGivern* | Milne / *MacLeod* | Holt * / *Burke* | Sturrock / *Simpson* | Dodds / *Muir ^* | Britton Gallacher/McDicken |
|  |  |  |  |  |  |  | *Emphatic as the scoreline appears, this is not one of the better displays, but a tremendous 20-minute spell brings four goals to floor the visitors. Stark heads home the first and Holt angles in a second. Stark scores the third and Sturrock rifles in a fourth. Clark and Simpson are booked.* |  |  |  |  |  |  |  |  |  |  |  |  |
| 34 | A MORTON 30/4 | 6,820 | 9 | 52 | 4-0 | 1-0 | Dodds 31, 68, Narey 52, Milne 63 / Ref: M Delaney | McAlpine * / *Baines* | Stark / *Hayes* | Malpas / *Holmes* | Gough / *Rooney ^* | Hegarty / *McLaughlin* | Narey / *Duffy* | Bannon / *Payne* | Milne / *Slaven ** | Holt / *Hutchison* | Sturrock / *Cochrane* | Dodds / *Houston* | Kirkwood Ritchie/Gavigan |
|  |  |  |  |  |  |  | *Another four-goal romp, as Benny Rooney's men are swept aside. Bannon's swerving free-kick comes back off the post for Dodds to trundle in. Narey stylishly slots in a second after taking a Dodds flick in his stride. Milne outstrips the defence to add a third and Dodds makes if four.* |  |  |  |  |  |  |  |  |  |  |  |  |

## 35 — H MOTHERWELL, 7/5 — 11,933 (8, 54) — 1-0 / 4-0 W

Scorers: Bannon 27, 53p, Dodds 72, 82
Ref: D Syme

| Dundee United | Motherwell |
|---|---|
| McAlpine | Walker |
| Stark | Dornan |
| Malpas | MacLeod |
| Kirkwood | Forbes |
| Hegarty | Carson |
| Narey | Flavell |
| Bannon | Gahagan |
| Milne | Rafferty^ |
| Holt | Edvaldsson |
| Sturrock | McClair |
| Dodds | Mauchlan * |
| | O'Hara/McAllister |

Bannon's dead-ball skills win this game. Early jitters are soothed as his Brazilian style free-kick from 30 yards finds the net and ... penalty after Forbes decked Sturrock. Milne squares for Dodds to make it three and a brilliant move sees Dodds 26th goal take the tally to four.

## 36 — A DUNDEE, 14/5 — 29,106 (6, 56) — 2-1 W

Scorers: Milne 4, Bannon 11
Ferguson 28
Ref: G Smith

| Dundee United | Dundee |
|---|---|
| McAlpine | Kelly |
| Stark | Glennie * |
| Malpas | McKimmie |
| Kirkwood | Fraser |
| Hegarty | Smith |
| Narey | MacDonald Ferguson |
| Bannon | McGeachie |
| Milne | Kirkwood |
| Holt | Sinclair |
| Sturrock | Stephen Kidd |
| Dodds | Mackie |

Milne chips home from 35 yards and, in a rampaging start, Narey is brought down in the box by MacDonald. Kelly saves Bannon's kick, but is helpless to prevent him netting the rebound. Dodds hits the bar, but Ferguson volleys one back from 20 yards to set an hour of nail-biting.

Home 11,133  Away 12,249
Average

---

## League Cup - Section 4

### 1 — H ST JOHNSTONE, 14/8 — 7,001 — W 3-0

Scorers: Kirkwood 20, Dodds 22, Sturrock 36
Ref: R Cuthill

| Dundee United | St Johnstone |
|---|---|
| McAlpine | Tulloch |
| Phillip | Mackay * |
| Stark | McNeil |
| Gough | Beedie |
| Hegarty * | Kennedy |
| Narey | Caldwell |
| Britton | Addison |
| Malpas | Brogan |
| Payne ^ | Pelosi |
| Sturrock | Morton |
| Dodds | Bramigan ^ |
| | Rutherford/Fleming, Kirkwood/Taylor |

Scintillating stuff to start as Kirkwood scores with his first touch from Payne's lay-off and from the re-start Dodds nets a rebound after Tulloch saved Narey's long-ranger. Magic from Sturrock sees him best four defenders to score. By comparison, the second half seems very flat indeed.

### 2 — A FALKIRK, 18/8 — 2,500 — W 4-0

Scorers: Narey 21, Sturrock 22, Malpas 47, [Milne 49]
Ref: D Downie

| Dundee United | Falkirk |
|---|---|
| McAlpine | Watson |
| Phillip | Hoggan |
| Stark | Nicol |
| Gough | Brown |
| Hegarty ^ | M Oliver |
| Narey | Wilson |
| Britton | A Oliver * |
| Malpas | Herd |
| Payne | Ford |
| Sturrock * | Smith |
| Dodds | Perry |
| | Milne/Kirkwood, Fowler |

Free-flowing United coast to victory. Narey's strong header from Sturrock's cross is quickly followed by the latter firing through a bewildered home defence. Malpas hits a fine 30-yarder – his first for the club. The fourth is a simple tap in by Milne. Gough's booking is the only flaw.

### 3 — H RAITH ROVERS, 21/8 — 5,039 — W 5-1

Scorers: Narey 9, 77, Payne 12, Britton 52, Harris 43 [Milne 65]
Ref: K Hope

| Dundee United | Raith Rovers |
|---|---|
| McAlpine | Walker |
| Phillip | Houston |
| Stark | Candlish |
| Gough | Robertson |
| Hegarty | Forsyth |
| Narey | More |
| Britton ^ | Steen |
| Malpas * | Thomson |
| Payne | Ballantyne |
| Sturrock | Gibson * |
| Dodds | Harris |
| Milne/Kirkwood | Russell |

A stroll in the rain as Raith are run ragged. Walker lets a Narey 30-yarder through his hands and Payne blasts in a second from Sturrock's pass. Raith retort through Harris following a McAlpine slip, but Britton hammers home from close range and Milne and Narey take the tally to five.

### 4 — H FALKIRK, 25/8 — 4,391 — W 4-0

Scorers: Dodds 5, 17, Sturrock 73, Payne 80
Ref: D Galloway

| Dundee United | Falkirk |
|---|---|
| Gardiner | Watson |
| Phillip * | Hoggan |
| Stark | Nicol |
| Gough | Brown |
| Hegarty | Fowler |
| Narey | Wilson |
| Britton | A Oliver * |
| Malpas ^ | Herd |
| Payne | Smith |
| Sturrock | Ward |
| Dodds | Thompson |
| Bannon/Holt | Hendrie |

Pounded for 90 minutes, Falkirk are lucky only to lose by four. Dodds heads a Sturrock cross high into the net and bullets in a low Gough cross for his second. Sturrock cracks in a third from 15 yards, whilst Payne pounces to make it four from eight yards after a Dodds shot was blocked.

### 5 — A ST JOHNSTONE, 28/8 — 4,092 — W 3-0

Scorers: Dodds 40, Bannon 69, Kirkwood 74
Ref: W Knowles

| Dundee United | St Johnstone |
|---|---|
| McAlpine | Tulloch |
| Holt * | Mackay |
| Stark | McNeil |
| Gough | Beedie |
| Hegarty | Caldwell |
| Narey | Rutherford |
| Britton | Addison |
| Malpas | Brogan |
| Bannon | Pelosi |
| Sturrock | Morton |
| Dodds | Fleming |
| Kirkwood | |

United clinch the section, turning on the style in the second period after Dodds' glancing header from Britton's cross gives them an interval lead. Bannon screws the ball in from an acute angle increases the lead, and Kirkwood rams a Sturrock flick high into the net for a third goal.

### 6 — A RAITH ROVERS, 1/9 — 1,764 — W 3-1

Scorers: Bannon 45p, Dodds 70, Sturrock 74
Harris 47 [Milne 74]
Ref: E Pringle

| Dundee United | Raith Rovers |
|---|---|
| McAlpine | Walker |
| Holt * | Robertson |
| Stark | Candlish |
| Gough | Thomson |
| Hegarty | Forsyth |
| Narey | More |
| Britton | Robinson |
| Malpas | Gibson ^ |
| Bannon | Harris |
| Sturrock | McCulloch * Mitchell |
| Dodds * | Urquhart/Spence |
| Kirkwood | |

Closest game of section, but 100% record is maintained. Walker impedes Dodds and Bannon scores from the resultant spot-kick. Harris shocks United with a fierce equaliser from an acute angle, but Dodds hooks in a Bannon cross to regain the lead and a silky Sturrock finish seals it.

### Qual

| | | | | | | | |
|---|---|---|---|---|---|---|---|
| DUNDEE UNITED | 6 | 6 | 0 | 0 | 22 | 2 | 12 |
| St Johnstone | 6 | 3 | 1 | 2 | 15 | 10 | 7 |
| Falkirk | 6 | 1 | 1 | 4 | 3 | 15 | 3 |
| Raith | 6 | 0 | 2 | 4 | 5 | 18 | 2 |

### QF 1 — A ABERDEEN, 22/9 — 14,292 — W 3-1

Scorers: Gough 25, Bannon 35, Kirkwood 80
McGhee 15
Ref: H Alexander

| Dundee United | Aberdeen |
|---|---|
| McAlpine | Leighton |
| Phillip * | Rougvie |
| Stark | McMaster |
| Gough | Cooper |
| Hegarty | McLeish |
| Narey | Miller |
| Bannon | Strachan |
| Malpas | Watson ^ |
| Kirkwood | McGhee |
| Sturrock | Hewitt |
| Dodds | Weir |
| | Kennedy/Black |

McGhee fastens on to a long ball from Rougvie to stroke Dons ahead. Gough's low diving header from Milne levels. Bannon's swerving fully 25 yards into the top corner is a joy to behold. Kirkwood with a free header scores a vital third. He and Aberdeen's Neale Cooper are booked.

### QF 2 — H ABERDEEN, 6/10 — 11,753 — W 1-0

Scorers: Sturrock 73p
Ref: G Smith
(United win 4-1 on aggregate)

| Dundee United | Aberdeen |
|---|---|
| McAlpine | Leighton |
| Phillip | Cooper |
| Stark | Rougvie |
| Gough | McMaster |
| Hegarty | McLeish |
| Narey | Miller |
| Bannon | Strachan |
| Malpas | Simpson |
| Kirkwood | McGhee * |
| Sturrock | Hewitt |
| Dodds | Weir |
| | Black |

Dons exit from this competition at the hands of a Dundee team for the fourth year in a row. Strachan smashes a header off the post before the tie is sealed by a Paul Sturrock penalty after Rougvie handled a Hegarty header. Weir joins Gough and Phillip in the ref's book for protesting.

# SCOTTISH PREMIER (CUP-TIES)     Manager: Jim McLean

## League Cup (continued)

| | | | | F-A | H-T | Scorers, Times, and Referees | 1 | 2 | 3 | 4 | 5 | 6 | 7 | 8 | 9 | 10 | 11 | subs used |
|---|---|---|---|---|---|---|---|---|---|---|---|---|---|---|---|---|---|---|
| SF | A | CELTIC | 19,149 | 0-2 | 0-2 | Nicholas 39p, McGarvey 44 | McAlpine | Phillip | Stark | Gough | Hegarty | Narey | Holt | Milne | Kirkwood | Payne * | Dodds | Reilly |
| 1 | 27/10 | | L | | | Ref: K Hope | Bonner | McGrain | Reid | Aitken | McAdam | Sinclair | Provan | McStay | McGarvey * | MacLeod | Nicholas | Crainie |

Dodds hits a post in the early stages, but two goals just before the interval give United an uphill task. Nicholas slots away a hotly disputed penalty after Stark allegedly fouled Provan. Nicholas flicks a Provan cross on and McGarvey hooks home from close range right on half-time.

| | | | | F-A | H-T | Scorers, Times, and Referees | 1 | 2 | 3 | 4 | 5 | 6 | 7 | 8 | 9 | 10 | 11 | subs used |
|---|---|---|---|---|---|---|---|---|---|---|---|---|---|---|---|---|---|---|
| SF | H | CELTIC | 15,426 | 2-1 | 0-0 | Sturrock 51, 65 | McAlpine | Holt ! | Malpas | Gough | Hegarty | Narey | Bannon | Milne | Kirkwood | Sturrock | Dodds | |
| 2 | 10/11 | | W | | | Nicholas 90 | Bonner | McGrain | Sinclair | Aitken | McAdam | Burns * | Provan * | McStay | McGarvey | MacLeod | Nicholas | McCluskey |
| | | | | | | Ref: B McGinlay | | | | | | | | | | | | |
| | | | | | | (United lose 2-3 on aggregate) | | | | | | | | | | | | |

Aitken gets the last touch, but Sturrock gets the credit for the opener. Sturrock then levels tie, chasing a Narey free-kick to squeeze it past Bonner. Holt is dismissed after a second caution. Aitken and McStay are booked. Nicholas nicks the winner with a low 18-yard drive from Burns' pass.

## Scottish Cup

| | | | | F-A | H-T | Scorers, Times, and Referees | 1 | 2 | 3 | 4 | 5 | 6 | 7 | 8 | 9 | 10 | 11 | subs used |
|---|---|---|---|---|---|---|---|---|---|---|---|---|---|---|---|---|---|---|
| 1 | A | ST MIRREN | 7,020 | 0-1 | 0-1 | Sommer 28 | McAlpine | Stark | Malpas | Gough | Hegarty | Narey | Holt | Milne | Kirkwood * | Sturrock | Dodds | Clark |
| 29/1 | | | L | | | Ref: D Syme | Thomson | Wilson | Clarke | McCormack | Fulton | Abercromby | Stark | Richardson | McDougall | McAvennie | Sommer | |

Saints cup jinx strikes again, knocking United out for the sixth time in seven meetings over 22 years. Sommer strikes from a narrow angle for the winner. Thomson brilliantly keeps out United's only shot on target from Sturrock. Kirkwood, McCormack and McDougall are all booked.

## UEFA Cup

| | | | | F-A | H-T | Scorers, Times, and Referees | 1 | 2 | 3 | 4 | 5 | 6 | 7 | 8 | 9 | 10 | 11 | subs used |
|---|---|---|---|---|---|---|---|---|---|---|---|---|---|---|---|---|---|---|
| 1:1 | H | PSV EINDHOVEN | 13,223 | 1-1 | 1-0 | Dodds 37 | McAlpine | Malpas * | Stark | Gough | Hegarty | Narey | Britton | Kirkwood * | Bannon | Sturrock | Dodds | Milne/Phillip |
| 15/9 | | | D | | | W van der Kerkhof 68 | Doesburg | Van Aerle | Stevens | Brandts | Wildschut | vd Kerkhof W vd Kerkhof R Poortvliet | | | Koolhof * | Lokhoff | Thorsen | Landsbergen |
| | | (Holland) | | | | Ref: V Roth (West Germany) | | | | | | | | | | | | |

Dodds re-directs Bannon's half-hit shot into the net from six yards with PSV claiming offside, but it counts. Several saves by Doesburg keeps United at bay. Willy van der Kerkhof slips the ball past McAlpine for a vital away goal. Stevens, Lokhoff and Wildschut are all cautioned.

| | | | | F-A | H-T | Scorers, Times, and Referees | 1 | 2 | 3 | 4 | 5 | 6 | 7 | 8 | 9 | 10 | 11 | subs used |
|---|---|---|---|---|---|---|---|---|---|---|---|---|---|---|---|---|---|---|
| 1:2 | A | PSV EINDHOVEN | 12,000 | 2-0 | 2-0 | Kirkwood 5, Hegarty 29 | McAlpine | Phillip * | Stark | Gough | Hegarty | Narey | Bannon | Milne | Kirkwood | Sturrock | Dodds | Malpas |
| 28/9 | | | W | | | Ref: A Zade (Russia) | Doesburg | Van Aerle * | Stevens | Brandts | Wildschut | vd Kerkhof W vd Kerkhof R Poortvliet | | | Koolhof | Lokhoff * | Thorsen | Moo Huh/ Landst gn |
| | | | | | | (United win 3-1 on aggregate) | | | | | | | | | | | | |

A stunning victory as United outclass the Dutch masters, to the extent the two-goal margin flatters the home side. Kirkwood thumps in the first from a Bannon chip and Hegarty sweeps in a low Bannon cross after Milne dummies. Hegarty – deliberate handball – is the only booking.

| | | | | F-A | H-T | Scorers, Times, and Referees | 1 | 2 | 3 | 4 | 5 | 6 | 7 | 8 | 9 | 10 | 11 | subs used |
|---|---|---|---|---|---|---|---|---|---|---|---|---|---|---|---|---|---|---|
| 2:1 | A | VIKING | 8,890 | 3-1 | 0-0 | Milne 73, 80p, Sturrock 88 | McAlpine | Holt | Stark | Gough | Hegarty | Narey | Malpas | Milne | Kirkwood | Sturrock | Dodds | Kvia/Bjørnsen |
| 20/10 | | | W | | | Henrikson 76 | Haugvaldstad Fjetland * | | Henrikson | Svendsen | Saebo | Brekke | Hammer | Goodchild | Bernstein | Refvik * | Andersen | |
| | | (Norway) | | | | Ref: O Orankangas (Finland) | | | | | | | | | | | | |

Never breaking stride, Milne fastens on to Holt's pass to give his side a deserved lead. Henrikson gets the credit for Viking's equaliser after a scramble. Svendsen handles a Sturrock shot, Milne makes sure from the penalty. Sturrock increases the lead, after running on to Gough's pass.

| | | | | F-A | H-T | Scorers, Times, and Referees | 1 | 2 | 3 | 4 | 5 | 6 | 7 | 8 | 9 | 10 | 11 | subs used |
|---|---|---|---|---|---|---|---|---|---|---|---|---|---|---|---|---|---|---|
| 2:2 | H | VIKING | 10,611 | 0-0 | 0-0 | | McAlpine | Phillip * | Stark | Gough | Hegarty | Narey | Reilly | Milne | Kirkwood | Holt | Dodds ^ | Malpas/Clark |
| 3/11 | | | D | | | Ref: O Amundessen (Denmark) | Johannes'n E Fjetland * | | Henrikson | Svendsen | Fretlberg | Brekke | Hammer | Goodchild | Bernstein ! | Refvik * | Andersen | Joh'nes'n T/ Risanger |
| | | | | | | (United win 3-1 on aggregate) | | | | | | | | | | | | |

For once, a Euro evening is low key. The recently crowned Norwegian champions curiously adopt a defensive approach despite trailing by two goals! Nevertheless, Viking skipper Bernstein manages to get himself sent off after tangling with Kirkwood, whilst Anderson is also booked.

| | | | | F-A | H-T | Scorers, Times, and Referees | 1 | 2 | 3 | 4 | 5 | 6 | 7 | 8 | 9 | 10 | 11 | subs used |
|---|---|---|---|---|---|---|---|---|---|---|---|---|---|---|---|---|---|---|
| 3:1 | H | WERDER BREMEN | 11,545 | 2-1 | 1-0 | Milne 15, Narey 82 | McAlpine | Stark * | Malpas | Gough | Hegarty | Narey | Bannon ^ | Milne | Kirkwood | Sturrock | Dodds | Holt/Reilly |
| 24/11 | | | W | | | Meier 65 | Burdenski | Kemp | Otten | Gruber | Fitchel | Mohlmann | Sidka | Siegmann | Voller | Okudera | Meier * | Bracht |
| | | (W Germany) | | | | Ref: H Fahnler (Austria) | | | | | | | | | | | | |

Otto Rehbagel's men are under the cosh for most of the game. Reward comes with Milne flicking a Bannon cross high into the net. Vollers' shot comes off Hegarty and Meier sinks an equaliser, but in a furious finish Narey chips in from 25 yards and Milne smashes one off the post.

| | | | | F-A | H-T | Scorers, Times, and Referees | 1 | 2 | 3 | 4 | 5 | 6 | 7 | 8 | 9 | 10 | 11 | subs used |
|---|---|---|---|---|---|---|---|---|---|---|---|---|---|---|---|---|---|---|
| 3:2 | A | WERDER BREMEN | 37,500 | 1-1 | 1-0 | Hegarty 3 | McAlpine | Stark | Malpas | Gough | Hegarty | Narey | Bannon | Milne | Kirkwood | Sturrock | Dodds * | Holt |
| 8/12 | | | D | | | Voller 48 | Burdenski | Kemp * | Otten | Gruber ^ | Fitchel | Mohlmann | Sidka | Siegmann | Voller | Okudera | Meier | Bohnke/Schaaf |
| | | | | | | Ref: D Krchnak (Czechoslovakia) | | | | | | | | | | | | |
| | | | | | | (United win 3-2 on aggregate) | | | | | | | | | | | | |

Hegarty's downward header from a Milne corner increases the lead early on and Dodds misses a great chance near the break. Rudi Voller equalises with a header from Schaaf's cross. Hegarty amazingly clears a netbound Voller lob off the line as United survive a second-half siege.

## European Cup-Winners' Cup / UEFA Cup — Quarter Final

| | | Opponent | Attendance | Date | HT | Res | FT | Scorer | Referee |
|---|---|---|---|---|---|---|---|---|---|
| QF | A | BOHEMIANS PRAGUE (Czechoslovakia) | 17,000 | 2/3 | 0-1 | L | 0-1 | Chaloupka 10 | Ref: M Van Langenhove (Belg) |

**Dundee United:** McAlpine, Stark *, Malpas, Gough, Hegarty, Narey, Bannon, Milne *, Kirkwood, Sturrock, Dodds, Holt
**Bohemians:** *Hruska Z, Jakubec, Prokes, Zelensky, Levy, Bicovsky, Marcik, Chaloupka, Cermak, Koukal, Prilozny *, Hruska V*

| | | Opponent | Attendance | Date | HT | Res | FT | Referee |
|---|---|---|---|---|---|---|---|---|
| QF | H | BOHEMIANS PRAGUE | 21,336 | 16/3 | 0-0 | D | 0-0 | Ref: A Daina (Switzerland) |

(United lose 0-1 on aggregate)

**Dundee United:** McAlpine, Stark *, Malpas, Gough, Hegarty, Narey, Bannon, Milne, Kirkwood, Sturrock, Dodds, Reilly
**Bohemians:** *Hruska Z, Jakubec, Prokes, Zelensky, Levy, Bicovsky, Marcik, Chaloupka, Cermak ^, Prilozny *, Koukal, Novak/Micinec*

United's defence is caught stuck in the mud as Chaloupka heads Bicovsky's free-kick. Far from being backs to the wall stuff, Stark and Dodds see shots saved by Hruska. After Stark was booked, Marcik and Prokes receive similar punishment as frustration creeps into the Czechs' play.

It is Czech-mate in Europe. McAlpine is a spectator, whilst Hruska at the opposite end is Bohemians' hero. Time after time he came to his side's rescue, but although under the cosh for almost ninety minutes, there is no way past the keeper. Levy and sub Novak are booked.

## Appearances & Goals

| | Appearances | | | | | | | | Goals | | | | |
|---|---|---|---|---|---|---|---|---|---|---|---|---|---|
| | Lge | Sub | LC | Sub | SC | Sub | Eur | Sub | Lge | LC | SC | Eur | Tot |
| Bannon, Eamonn | 31 | 1 | 4 | 1 | 1 | | 6 | | 10 | 3 | | | 13 |
| Britton, Ian | 7 | 3 | 6 | | | 1 | 1 | | 1 | 1 | | | 2 |
| Clark, John | 1 | | | | | | | | | | | | |
| Dodds, Davie | 34 | 2 | 10 | | 1 | | 8 | | 22 | 5 | | 1 | 28 |
| Gardiner, John | | | 1 | | | | | | | | | | |
| Gough, Richard | 34 | | 9 | | 1 | | 8 | | 8 | 1 | | | 9 |
| Hegarty, Paul | 36 | | 10 | | 1 | | 8 | | 3 | | | 2 | 5 |
| Holt, John | 18 | 8 | 4 | 1 | | | 2 | 3 | 4 | | | | 4 |
| Kirkwood, Billy | 26 | 5 | 4 | 5 | 1 | | 8 | | 3 | 3 | | 1 | 7 |
| McAlpine, Hamish | 36 | | 9 | | 1 | | 8 | | | | | | |
| McNeil, John | | 1 | | | | | | | | | | | |
| Malpas, Maurice | 31 | 3 | 7 | 1 | 1 | | 6 | 2 | 1 | 1 | | | 2 |
| Milne, Ralph | 30 | 4 | 4 | 2 | 1 | | 7 | 1 | 16 | 2 | | 3 | 21 |
| Murray, Derek | 1 | | | | | | | | | | | | |
| Narey, Dave | 36 | | 10 | | 1 | | 8 | | 5 | 3 | | 1 | 9 |
| Payne, Graeme | 2 | 1 | 6 | | | | | | | 2 | | | 2 |
| Phillip, Iain | 5 | | 8 | | | | 2 | 1 | | | | | |
| Reilly, John | 8 | 9 | | | | | 1 | 2 | 7 | | | | 7 |
| Stark, Derek | 31 | 1 | 9 | | 1 | | 8 | | 2 | | | | 2 |
| Sturrock, Paul | 28 | | 9 | | 1 | | 7 | | 8 | 7 | | 1 | 16 |
| Taylor, Alex | 1 | 2 | | | | | | | | | | | |
| **21 players used** | **396** | **40** | **110** | **12** | **11** | **1** | **88** | **11** | **90** | **28** | | **9** | **127** |

## League Table

| | P | W | D | L | F | A | W | D | L | F | A | Pts |
|---|---|---|---|---|---|---|---|---|---|---|---|---|
| | | **Home** | | | | | **Away** | | | | | |
| 1 DUNDEE UTD | 36 | 13 | 4 | 1 | 57 | 18 | 11 | 4 | 3 | 33 | 17 | 56 |
| 2 Celtic | 36 | 12 | 3 | 3 | 44 | 18 | 13 | 2 | 3 | 46 | 18 | 55 |
| 3 Aberdeen | 36 | 14 | 4 | 0 | 46 | 12 | 11 | 1 | 6 | 30 | 12 | 55 |
| 4 Rangers | 36 | 9 | 6 | 3 | 32 | 16 | 4 | 6 | 8 | 20 | 25 | 38 |
| 5 St Mirren | 36 | 8 | 5 | 5 | 30 | 18 | 3 | 7 | 8 | 17 | 33 | 34 |
| 6 Dundee | 36 | 8 | 3 | 7 | 29 | 28 | 1 | 8 | 9 | 13 | 25 | 29 |
| 7 Hibernian | 36 | 8 | 3 | 7 | 21 | 17 | 3 | 4 | 11 | 14 | 34 | 29 |
| 8 Motherwell | 36 | 8 | 2 | 8 | 28 | 27 | 3 | 3 | 12 | 11 | 46 | 27 |
| 9 Morton | 36 | 4 | 5 | 9 | 14 | 26 | 2 | 3 | 13 | 16 | 48 | 20 |
| 10 Kilmarnock | 36 | 3 | 7 | 8 | 17 | 31 | 0 | 4 | 14 | 11 | 60 | 17 |
| | 360 | 87 | 42 | 51 | 318 | 211 | 51 | 42 | 87 | 211 | 318 | 360 |

## Record Against Each Club

| | P | W | D | L | F | A | Pts |
|---|---|---|---|---|---|---|---|
| v Motherwell | 4 | 4 | 0 | 0 | 15 | 1 | 8 |
| v St Mirren | 4 | 4 | 0 | 0 | 10 | 3 | 8 |
| v Dundee | 4 | 4 | 0 | 0 | 10 | 4 | 8 |
| v Kilmarnock | 4 | 3 | 1 | 0 | 17 | 1 | 7 |
| v Morton | 4 | 3 | 1 | 0 | 13 | 2 | 7 |
| v Hibernian | 4 | 3 | 1 | 0 | 6 | 3 | 7 |
| v Rangers | 4 | 2 | 1 | 1 | 8 | 5 | 5 |
| v Celtic | 4 | 1 | 2 | 1 | 6 | 7 | 4 |
| v Aberdeen | 4 | 0 | 2 | 2 | 5 | 9 | 2 |

**Cup**

| | W | D | L | F | A | Pts |
|---|---|---|---|---|---|---|
| v St Mirren | 0 | 0 | 1 | 0 | 1 | 0 |
| v Celtic | | | | | | |

## Odds & Ends

Quadruple wins: (3) Motherwell, St Mirren, Dundee.

Quadruple losses: (0).

Win from behind: (5) Aberdeen (a, LC), Rangers (h), Morton (a), Motherwell (a), Dundee (h).

Lost from in front: (2) Aberdeen (a), Rangers (a).

High spots: the late recovery to draw 2-2 with Celtic in October. Defeating the Dons 2-1 away in March to resurrect title hopes. Posting a crucial 3-2 Parkhead win over Celtic with ten men in April. Winning the title across the road after a 2-1 derby victory.

Low spots: A fourth straight League Cup final spot denied by Celtic. Suffering heavy defeats by Aberdeen both home and away. Going out of the Scottish Cup to St Mirren (0-1) at the first hurdle. Bowing out to Bohemians in the UEFA Cup after beating better sides.

With 56 points and 90 goals, United equalled the then best-ever points total and record goals scored in a top ten campaign, held by Celtic.

Hat-tricks: (2) Dodds, Holt.

Ever Presents: (4) Heagrty, McAlpine, Narey, Dodds (34 + 2 subs).

Leading scorer: Dodds (17).

# SCOTTISH PREMIER DIVISION  

**Manager: Jim McLean**   **SEASON 1983-84**

## Match details, scorers and referees

| No | Date | Opponent | Att | Pos | Pt | Res | F-A | H-T | Scorers, Times, and Referees |
|----|------|----------|-----|-----|----|-----|-----|-----|------------------------------|
| 1 | H 20/8 | MOTHERWELL | 9,465 | | 2 | W | 4-0 | 1-0 | Kirkwood 20, 86, Hegarty 49, Taylor 63. Ref: D Downie |
| 2 | A 3/9 | DUNDEE | 13,656 | 9 | 4 | W | 4-1 | 1-1 | Reilly 17, 70, Milne 78, Stark 85; McCall 6. Ref: B McGinlay |
| 3 | H 10/9 | HIBERNIAN | 7,790 | 9 | 6 | W | 5-0 | 2-0 | Dodds 23, 42, Milne 67, 84, Kirkwood 78. Ref: W McLeish |
| 4 | A 17/9 | ST JOHNSTONE | 6,969 | 10 | 8 | W | 2-1 | 0-0 | Dodds 47, Holt 67; Morton 59p. Ref: J Renton |
| 5 | A 24/9 | ABERDEEN | 21,100 | 4 | 10 | W | 2-1 | 1-0 | Bannon 36, Kirkwood 52; Strachan 78p. Ref: H Alexander |
| 6 | H 1/10 | RANGERS | 16,738 | 6 | 10 | L | 0-2 | 0-2 | McCoist 12, Clark 39. Ref: L Thow |
| 7 | H 8/10 | CELTIC | 20,741 | 3 | 12 | W | 2-1 | 1-0 | Kirkwood 28, Gough 62; Melrose 84. Ref: R Cuthill |
| 8 | H 22/10 | HEARTS | 13,157 | 4 | 14 | W | 1-0 | 1-0 | Dodds 36. Ref: D Hope |
| 9 | A 29/10 | MOTHERWELL | 4,398 | 9 | 15 | D | 2-2 | 2-2 | Dodds 8, 44; Gahagan 14, Alexander 28. Ref: A Huett |
| 10 | H 5/11 | DUNDEE | 14,813 | 6 | 15 | L | 0-1 | 0-1 | Mackie 19. Ref: K Hope |
| 11 | H 12/11 | ST JOHNSTONE | 7,937 | 10 | 17 | W | 7-0 | 4-0 | Hegarty 5, Bannon 11p, 80, Dodds 21, 28, [Gough 73, Kirkwood 86]. Ref: A Ferguson |

## Line-ups (United in roman, opponents in italic)

| No | Team | 1 | 2 | 3 | 4 | 5 | 6 | 7 | 8 | 9 | 10 | 11 | subs used |
|----|------|---|---|---|---|---|---|---|---|---|----|----|-----------|
| 1 | Utd | McAlpine | Kirkwood | Malpas | Gough | Hegarty | Narey | Bannon | Milne | Taylor | Holt | Dodds * | Clark * |
| 1 | Opp | *Sprat* | *Dornan* | *MacLeod* | *Carson* | *Edvaldsson* | *Mauchlen* | *Gahagan* | *Rafferty* | *Gillespie ^* | *Harrow* | *Flavell ^* | *Forbes/Burns* |
| 2 | Utd | McAlpine | Kirkwood * | Malpas | Gough | Hegarty | Narey | Bannon | Milne | Reilly | Holt | Dodds | Stark |
| 2 | Opp | *Kelly* | *McKimmie* | *McKinlay* | *Fraser* | *Glennie* | *Ferguson* | *MacDonald* | *McGeachie * McCall* | *Mackie* | *Kidd* | | *Stephen* |
| 3 | Utd | McAlpine | Stark | Malpas ^ | Gough | Hegarty | Narey | Bannon | Milne | Reilly * | Holt | Dodds | Taylor/Kirkwood |
| 3 | Opp | *Rough* | *Sneddon* | *Duncan* | *Brazil* | *Jamieson* | *McNamara* | *Callachan* | *Conroy* | *Irvine* | *McKee ** | *Murray ^* | *Rice/Kane* |
| 4 | Utd | McAlpine | Kirkwood | Stark | Gough | Hegarty | Narey | Bannon | Milne | Reilly * | Holt | Dodds | Taylor |
| 4 | Opp | *McDonald* | *Kilgour* | *McVicar ** | *Addison* | *Caldwell* | *Rutherford* | *Gibson* | *Brogan* | *Blair ^* | *Morton* | *Beedie* | *Wright/Brannigan* |
| 5 | Utd | McAlpine | Kirkwood | Stark | Gough | Hegarty | Narey | Bannon | Milne | Taylor | Bell * | Dodds | |
| 5 | Opp | *Leighton* | *Rougvie* | *McMaster* | *Cooper* | *McLeish* | *Miller* | *Cowan ^* | *Simpson* | *McGhee* | *Redford* | *Weir* | *Strachan/Hewitt* |
| 6 | Utd | McAlpine | Kirkwood | Stark | Gough | Hegarty | Narey | Bannon | Milne | Taylor * | Holt ^ | Dodds | Payne/McGinnis |
| 6 | Opp | *McCloy* | *Dawson* | *McClelland* | *McPherson* | *Paterson* | *MacKinnon* | *Prytz ** | *McCoist* | *Clark* | *Cooper* | | *Russell* |
| 7 | Utd | McAlpine | Kirkwood | Malpas | Gough | Hegarty | Narey | Bannon | Milne | Reilly * | Holt | Dodds | Stark |
| 7 | Opp | *Bonner* | *McGrain* | *Whittaker ** | *Aitken* | *McAdam* | *Sinclair* | *McStay* | *Melrose* | *McGarvey* | *MacLeod* | *Burns* | *McClair* |
| 8 | Utd | McAlpine | Kirkwood | Stark | Gough | Hegarty | Narey | Bannon | Milne * | Reilly * | Holt | Dodds | Malpas/Clark |
| 8 | Opp | *Smith* | *Kidd* | *Cowie* | *Jardine* | *McDonald R* | *Mackay* | *Bowman* | *Park ** | *Bone* | *Robertson* | *MacDonald* | *A Johnston* |
| 9 | Utd | McAlpine | Kirkwood | Stark | Gough * | Hegarty | Narey | Bannon | Malpas | Johnstone * | Holt | Dodds | Milne/Coyne |
| 9 | Opp | *Walker* | *Dornan* | *MacLeod* | *Carson* | *Edvaldsson* | *Mauchlen* | *Burns ** | *Forbes* | *Harrow ^* | *Alexander* | *Gahagan* | *Rafferty/Shaw* |
| 10 | Utd | McAlpine | Kirkwood | Malpas | Gough | Hegarty | Narey ^ | Bannon | Milne | Johnstone * | Holt | Dodds | Reilly/Coyne |
| 10 | Opp | *Geddes* | *McKimmie* | *McKinlay* | *Fraser* | *Smith* | *Glennie* | *Mackie* | *Richardson* | *Ferguson* | *McCall* | | *Stephen* |
| 11 | Utd | McAlpine | Kirkwood | Malpas | Gough | Hegarty | Narey | Bannon | Milne | Coyne | Holt | Dodds * | Johnstone |
| 11 | Opp | *Baines* | *Mackay* | *Kilgour* | *Caldwell* | *Kennedy* | *Rutherford* | *Gibson* | *Brogan* | *Blair* | *Morton* | *Lyons* | |

## Match reports

1. Jock Wallace's men are routed after the league flag is unfurled. Kirkwood stylishly heads Taylor's cross in. Another Taylor assist sees Hegarty head a second. Taylor's merited goal follows a deflection. Kirkwood heads the fourth. Gillespie, Harrow and MacLeod join Dodds in the book.

2. Late romp by United extends Dundee's derby drought to 13 matches. McCall heads Dundee in front from a Fraser corner. Reilly soon curls in the equaliser and crashes United ahead after going past McKimmie. Milne is sent in by Gough to slip home a third. Stark scores an easy fourth.

3. The Tangerine machine motors on against Pat Stanton's side. Dodds flicks in from an acute angle. Unmarked he heads the second. Milne heads in Bannon's cross as United step up a gear and sub Kirkwood's first touch nets a fourth. It's nap as Milne slips the ball past a prostrate Rough.

4. Alex Rennie's newly promoted side are just edged out. Bookings for Saints Caldwell and McVicar plus Milne sums up the first half. Dodds converts a Bannon cross. Morton levels from the spot after Hegarty fouls Rutherford. Sub Taylor carves out move for Holt's headed winner.

5. A New Firm victory makes it 11 successive league wins – a club record. Bannon who blasts in from 20 yards. McMaster fails from the spot, Kirkwood touches in a Milne cross as Dons go two down. Strachan does better from their second penalty.

6. Crash, bang wallop goes the 100% record. McAlpine punches a Redford cross off the back of McCoist's head and Clark stabs in as a Cooper corner causes confusion. McPherson, Clark and Redford of the hungrier visitors are booked in a win that eases the pressure on boss John Greig.

7. Desperate stuff at the end, but United hang on to depose Celtic at the top. Kirkwood's blistering drive takes a deflection to spin past Bonner. Gough rises to head in a Bannon cross. Melrose scores in similar fashion from a ball delivered by Sinclair. Whittaker is the only name noted.

8. After some heart-stopping moments, United stay top after a teethy tussle in which Stark, Dodds and Narey plus Kidd, MacDonald and Jardine are booked. The long legs of Dodds provides the winner. McAlpine's late great double save stops Alex Macdonald's men rescuing a point.

9. First away point is dropped after an intense contest in which Forbes, MacLeod, Narey and Dodds are booked. Dodds strokes in an opener. Gahagan counters with solo effort and provides the ammo for Alexander. Dodds equalises from ten yards. New signing Coyne come on.

10. First home derby defeat for eight years caps a bad week as McLean ponders Ibrox job offer. Mackie pounces to give Donald Mackay his first derby success, though his side had to defend magnificently in the second half. Holt and McKinlay are booked.

11. Seventh heaven as Jim McLean's decision to stay is stylishly celebrated. Hegarty nets from close range. Bannon scores from the spot after a foul on Dodds who steers in Milne's cross and then fires in a Bannon pass. Gough gets a fifth. Bannon goes solo and Kirkwood nets a seventh.

**12 A RANGERS 19/11** — Att 27,800 — Pos 2, D, 8, Pts 18 — HT 0-0, FT 0-0
United: McAlpine, Kirkwood, Malpas, Gough, Hegarty, Narey, Bannon, Milne*, Coyne, Holt, Dodds
Rangers: McCloy, MacKinnon, Dawson, McClelland, Paterson, McPherson, Nicholl*, McCoist, Clark, Redford, Cooper^
Subs: Johnstone; Russell/Mitchell
Blankety-blank in Jock Wallace's first game back as Ibrox boss. Rangers give 100%, United are below their best, so the Ibrox side halt a run of five straight defeats. McAlpine is the hero, making one exceptional save from Russell. Hegarty is the only name to go in the ref's note-book.
Ref: T Muirhead

**13 A ST MIRREN 22/11** — Att 4,186 — Pos 3, L, 5, Pts 18 — HT 0-2, FT **0-4**
Scorers: Scanlon 20p, McAvennie 42, 62, 70
United: McAlpine, Thomson, Stark, Gough, Hegarty, Narey, Bannon, Milne*, Coyne, Holt, Dodds
St Mirren: Thomson, Clark, Hamilton, Fulton, Abercromby, Fitzpatrick, McAvennie, McDougall, Cooper, Scanlon*, Alexander
Subs: Flavell
Alex Miller's Saints hustle and harry United to their heaviest ever Premier loss to Saints. Malpas fouls McDougall and Scanlon sinks the spot-kick. McAvennie's head-flick doubles the lead. He blasts home his second before side-footing in a McDougall pass to complete his hat-trick.
Ref: E Brolls

**14 H ABERDEEN 26/11** — Att 16,972 — Pos 3, L, 1, Pts 18 — HT 0-1, FT 0-2
Scorers: Bell 8, Strachan 70
United: McAlpine, Malpas, Murray^, Hegarty, Narey, Bannon, Milne, McGinnis*, Reilly, Holt, Dodds
Aberdeen: Leighton, Cooper, Rougvie, Simpson, McLeish, Strachan, Miller, McGhee, Bell, Hewitt, Weir
Subs: Sturrock/Coyne
Alex Ferguson's men get it easy against shot-shy United who fail to score for the third time on the trot. Bell's opener deflects over McAlpine. Strachan robs Narey to round the keeper for a points-sealing second. McGhee joins Dodds and Narey, the other names noted by the referee.
Ref: G Smith

**15 A HIBERNIAN 3/12** — Att 7,000 — Pos 3, W, 6, Pts 20 — HT 1-0, FT 2-0
Scorers: Milne 44, Stark 75
United: McAlpine, Rough, Malpas, Murray, Hegarty, Narey, Bannon, Milne*, Reilly, Stark^, Dodds
Hibernian: Sneddon, Schaedler, Brazil, Jamieson^, Blackley, Callachan, Turnbull*, Irvine, Thomson, Duncan
Subs: McGinnis/Clark; Harvey/Rice
Looking more like champions, Milne cuts inside to deliver an unstoppable drive from 12 yards. Stark slots a Milne cross under Rough to knock the stuffing out of the home side and wrap up United's first win in four games. Blackley (foul on Reilly) and Schaedler (dissent) are booked.
Ref: D Hope

**16 A HEARTS 10/12** — Att 9,288 — Pos 3, D, 5, Pts 21 — HT 0-0, FT 0-0
United: McAlpine, Smith, Malpas, Stark, Hegarty, Narey, Bannon, Milne*, Reilly, Holt, Dodds
Hearts: Smith, Kidd, Cowie, Jardine, MacDonald R Levein, Bowman, Mackay, Bone, Robertson, Park
Subs: Holt
Dull with few thrills is the epitaph of this second successive Saturday in the capital. Both defences dominate, though Narey and Hegarty are booked, as is Hearts' Park. Territorially on top, Milne is missed after he limps off. Two best chances fall to sub Holt but the keeper isn't tested.
Ref: T Muirhead

**17 A CELTIC 27/12** — Att 25,982 — Pos 3, D, 2, Pts 22 — HT 0-1, FT 1-1
Scorers: Bannon 68p, McClair 45
United: McAlpine, Kirkwood, Malpas, Gough, Hegarty, Narey, Bannon, Holt, Sturrock, Coyne, Dodds
Celtic: Bonner, McGrain, Reid, Aitken, McAdam*, Sinclair, Colquhoun^, McStay P, McGarvey, MacLeod, McClair
Subs: Dobbin/McStay W
In driving wind and rain Davie Hay's side boss the first half but United come back in the second. McClair sweeps in a Colquhoun cross. Aitken impedes Coyne and Bannon converts the soft penalty award. McClair, McAdam, Sinclair and Bannon are all booked in a robust encounter.
Ref: D Syme

**18 H MOTHERWELL 31/12** — Att 6,976 — Pos 3, W, 10, Pts 24 — HT 1-0, FT 2-1
Scorers: Stark 37, Hegarty 82, Edvaldsson 75
United: McAlpine, Sproat, Malpas, Stark, Hegarty, Narey, Bannon, Reilly, Sturrock, Coyne, Dodds
Motherwell: Sproat, Dornan, Black, Edvaldsson, Forbes, Mauchlen, Alexander*, McAllister^, Rafferty, Lyall, Gahagan
Subs: Gillespie/MacLeod
Backed by a howling gale, a Stark strike from 20 yards is all United have to show for their first half efforts against Bobby Watson's men. From Gahagan's corner Edvaldsson equalises with a header, but Hegarty saves any blushes. His header bounces in after Sturrock swings and misses.
Ref: B McGinlay

**19 A ST JOHNSTONE 7/1** — Att 5,126 — Pos 3, W, 9, Pts 26 — HT 2-0, FT 2-1
Scorers: Dodds 31, 41, Scott 82
United: McAlpine, Baines, Malpas, Stark, Hegarty, Narey, Bannon, Beaumont, Milne, Holt, Dodds
St Johnstone: Baines, Kilgour*, McVicar, Lyons, Caldwell, Rutherford, Gibson, Blair, Scott, Morton, Beedie
Subs: Branigan
United stay in touch with the top of the table, but only just, as McAlpine saves a Morton penalty. Dodds was the hero, heading in a Beaumont cross at the far post and then diving to head in, when supplied by Sturrock. Scott converts a Blair cross for home consolation. Beedie is booked.
Ref: G Smith

**20 H HIBERNIAN 11/2** — Att 7,675 — Pos 3, W, 7, Pts 28 — HT 1-0, FT 2-0
Scorers: Hegarty 42, Malpas 49
United: McAlpine, Rae R, Malpas, Stark, Hegarty, Narey, Bannon, Holt, Milne, Sturrock*, Dodds
Hibernian: Rae R, Sneddon, Schaedler, Brazil!, Jamieson, Blackley, Callachan, Kane^, Irvine, Thomson, Duncan
Subs: Beaumont; Rae G
Spying Rapid boss Baric learns little as United are still ring-rusty but too hot for Pat Stanton's side. Dodds heads Milne's cross against the post and Hegarty nets. Malpas whistles home a second from 12 yards. Brazil, already booked like Sneddon and Blackley, fouls Sturrock and is off.
Ref: W McLeish

**21 A ST MIRREN 25/2** — Att 4,007 — Pos 3, D, 5, Pts 29 — HT 1-0, FT 2-2
Scorers: Kirkwood 4, 47, Abercromby 54, McAvennie 62
United: McAlpine, Thomson, Malpas, Stark, Hegarty, Narey, Bannon, Holt, Coyne, Kirkwood, Dodds
St Mirren: Thomson, Hamilton, Clarke, Cooper, Fulton, McCormack, Fitzpatrick, Callachan, McCormack, Abercromby, McDougall
Subs: Scanlon; Reilly
A cracking contest produces four great goals. Sturrock nods down a McAlpine clearance and Kirkwood smashes in from twelve yards and surpasses that with a rising shot from 18 yards. Abercromby heads Saints back in contention. McAvennie sweeps in the leveller from close in.
Ref: A Waddell

**22 H CELTIC 3/3** — Att 15,326 — Pos 3, W, 2, Pts 31 — HT 1-0, FT 3-1
Scorers: Bannon 10, Kirkwood 51, Dodds 69, Aitken 87
United: McAlpine, Bonner, Malpas, Stark, Hegarty, Narey, Bannon^, Coyne, Sturrock, Kirkwood, Dodds
Celtic: Bonner, McGrain, Reid, Aitken, McAdam*, Sinclair, Colquhoun^, McStay P, McGarvey, MacLeod, McClair
Subs: Milne/Holt; Dobbin/McStay W
This is United's best display in ages. Bannon plays a one-two with Sturrock to fire in the first from 20 yards. Likewise, Kirkwood takes a Sturrock return pass to fire in off McAdam. Bonner kicks the ball against the post for Dodds to net. Aitken slots home from a McStay free-kick.
Ref: A Ferguson

**23 H HEARTS 11/3** — Att 10,058 — Pos 3, W, 5, Pts 33 — HT 2-1, FT 3-1
Scorers: Bannon 20, Coyne 24, 82, Kidd 6
United: McAlpine, Smith, Malpas, Stark, Hegarty, Narey, Bannon, Coyne, Sturrock^, Kirkwood, Dodds
Hearts: Smith, Kidd, Cowie, Jardine, MacDonald R Levein*, Bowman, Robertson, Bone, MacDonald A Mackay, Park
Subs: Holt/Milne
Kidd's one-two with Robertson sees him finish well. Bannon levels from a tight angle and crosses deftly for Coyne to head United in front. Milne's shot takes a deflection to deceive Smith and Coyne swoops. Despite some rough tackles by Hearts, Mackay is only one to be booked.
Ref: K Hope

# SCOTTISH PREMIER DIVISION    Manager: Jim McLean    SEASON 1983-84

## Match details

(United's league position is shown as "3" throughout; "Pos" = opponents' league position; "Pt" = United's cumulative points; "Res" = result.)

| No | Date | V | Opponent | Att | Pos | Pt | Utd | Res | F-A | H-T | Scorers, Times, and Referees |
|----|------|---|----------|-----|-----|----|-----|-----|-----|-----|------------------------------|
| 24 | 31/3 | A | HEARTS | 7,852 | 5 | 34 | 3 | D | 0-0 | 0-0 | Ref: H Alexander |
| 25 | 2/4 | A | DUNDEE | 12,732 | 8 | 36 | 3 | W | 5-2 | 3-2 | Malpas 24, Reilly 32, Dodds 36, Ferguson 23p, 45p [Bannon 56p, Milne 89]. Ref: A Ferguson |
| 26 | 7/4 | A | HIBERNIAN | 5,896 | 7 | 36 | 3 | L | 0-1 | 0-1 | Jamieson 11. Ref: L Thow |
| 27 | 14/4 | H | ST JOHNSTONE | 11,332 | 10 | 38 | 3 | W | 3-0 | 1-0 | Sturrock 27, Reilly 80, Coyne 86. Ref: D Downie |
| 28 | 18/4 | A | ABERDEEN | 19,562 | 1 | 38 | 3 | L | 1-5 | 1-3 | Reilly 34, Rougvie 10, 67, McGhee 27, 37, [Black 62]. Ref: H Young |
| 29 | 21/4 | H | DUNDEE | 13,244 | 8 | 39 | 3 | D | 1-1 | 1-0 | Clark 44, McCall 65. Ref: G Smith |
| 30 | 28/4 | A | MOTHERWELL | 1,870 | 10 | 41 | 3 | W | 3-1 | 2-0 | Dodds 8, Gough 28, Reilly 71, Gahagan 84. Ref: A Waddell |
| 31 | 30/4 | H | ST MIRREN | 5,347 | 6 | 43 | 3 | W | 2-0 | 0-0 | Holt 56, Reilly 84. Ref: K Hope |
| 32 | 2/5 | A | RANGERS | 5,000 | 4 | 44 | 3 | D | 2-2 | 1-1 | Sturrock 4, Dodds 86, Clark 24, Williamson 49. Ref: G Smith |
| 33 | 5/5 | H | ST MIRREN | 5,025 | 6 | 45 | 3 | D | 2-2 | 2-2 | Sturrock 19, Narey 41, McDougall 37, Jarvie 39. Ref: R Cuthill |
| 34 | 7/5 | H | ABERDEEN | 7,990 | 1 | 46 | 3 | D | 0-0 | 0-0 | Ref: D Syme |

## Line-ups

| No | Team | 1 | 2 | 3 | 4 | 5 | 6 | 7 | 8 | 9 | 10 | 11 | subs used |
|----|------|---|---|---|---|---|---|---|---|---|----|----|-----------|
| 24 | Dundee United | Gardiner | Stark | Malpas | Holt | Hegarty | Narey | Milne | Kirkwood | Clark | Munro * | Dodds | Reilly |
| 24 | Hearts | Smith | Kidd | Cowie | Jardine | MacDonald R / McLaren * | Bowman | Mackay | Bone | MacDonald A / Robertson | | | Levein |
| 25 | Dundee United | Gardiner | Stark | Malpas | Gough | Hegarty | Narey | Bannon | Kirkwood | Reilly | Sturrock * | Dodds | Milne |
| 25 | Dundee | Geddes | McGeachie | McInally | Fraser | Smith | MacDonald * / Ferguson | Richardson | McCall | McKinlay | Mackie ^ | | Glennie/Kidd |
| 26 | Dundee United | McAlpine | Stark | Malpas | Gough | Hegarty | Narey * | Bannon | Holt ^ | Reilly | Sturrock | Dodds | Kirkwood/Milne |
| 26 | Hibernian | Rough | Brazil | Schaedler | Sneddon! | Rae | Blackley | Callachan | Jamieson | Irvine | Rice ^ | Duncan ^ | Turnbull/McGachie |
| 27 | Dundee United | McAlpine | Stark | Malpas | Gough | Hegarty | Narey | Bannon | Milne * | Kirkwood | Sturrock ^ | Coyne | Taylor/Reilly |
| 27 | St Johnstone | Baines | Kilgour | Morton | Barron | Caldwell * | Rutherford | Gibson | Brogan | Reid ^ | Blair | Beedie | Lyons/Scott |
| 28 | Dundee United | McAlpine | Stark | Malpas | Gough * | Hegarty | Narey | Bannon | Kirkwood | Reilly | Coyne ^ | Dodds | Holt/Clark |
| 28 | Aberdeen | Leighton | Mitchell | Rougvie | Simpson | McLeish | Miller | Strachan | Black | McGhee ^ | Bell | Angus * | Weir/Stark |
| 29 | Dundee United | McAlpine | Stark | Munro | Holt | Hegarty | Narey | Bannon | Kirkwood | Reilly | Clark * | Dodds | Milne |
| 29 | Dundee | Geddes | McInally | McKinlay | Fraser! | Smith * | Glennie | Kidd | Richardson | McCall | Ferguson | Harris | Mackie |
| 30 | Dundee United | McAlpine | Malpas | Munro | Gough | Narey | Stark | Bannon | Holt | Reilly | Page * | Coyne | Dodds |
| 30 | Motherwell | Sproat | MacLeod | Black | McAllister | Kennedy | Boyd | Wishart | Rafferty | Harrow * | Lyall | Gahagan | Tracey |
| 31 | Dundee United | McAlpine | Malpas | Munro | Gough | Hegarty | Narey | Bannon | Holt | Reilly | Coyne * | Dodds | Sturrock |
| 31 | St Mirren | Money | Clarke | Winnie | McCormack / Fulton | Cooper | Alexander * | McAvennie | McDougall | Abercromby | Spiers | | Jarvie |
| 32 | Dundee United | McAlpine | Malpas | Munro | Gough | Hegarty | Narey | Bannon | Holt | Reilly | Sturrock * | Dodds | Taylor |
| 32 | Rangers | McCloy | Fraser | McClelland | McPherson | Paterson | Redford | Russell * | Williamson * | Clark | McCoist | Cooper | MacDonald/MacKinnon |
| 33 | Dundee United | McAlpine | Malpas | Munro | Gough | Hegarty | Narey | McGinnis | Holt | Reilly * | Sturrock | Dodds * | Bannon/Coyne |
| 33 | St Mirren | Money | Clarke | Winnie | Cooper | Fulton | McCormack / Jarvie * | | McAvennie | McDougall | Abercromby / Cameron ^ | | Spiers/Alexander |
| 34 | Dundee United | McAlpine | Malpas | Munro | Gough | Hegarty | Narey | Bannon | Holt | Coyne | Sturrock | Taylor | Stark/Falconer |
| 34 | Aberdeen | Leighton | McIntyre * | Rougvie * | Cooper | McLeish | Miller | Strachan | McKimmie | Cowan | Hewitt ^ | Weir | |

## Match reports

**24 — Hearts (A):** Nae goals, nae fitba, sums up this stalemate on a mudheap. Missing five players, Iain Munro debuts. Gardiner is rarely troubled, but conversely Clark skies United's only chance over. Bookings are level too – Robertson and R MacDonald of Hearts, Dodds and Kirkwood of United.

**25 — Dundee (A):** A mad minute for Malpas sees him handle and booked for Ferguson to net from the spot and then equalise with a low drive. Reilly taps United ahead. Dodds scores in like fashion before Ferguson hits a second penalty for Archie Knox's men. Bannon, from the spot, and Milne seal win.

**26 — Hibernian (A):** Hibs get stuck in as Jim McLean's side have Roma on their minds. Kirkwood hits the post, but Pat Stanton's side deservedly take the points thanks to Jamieson's head flick from Callachan's free-kick. Bookings galore – Bannon, Callachan, Dodds, McGachie and Blackley the culprits.

**27 — St Johnstone (H):** After the Italian job, it's back to bread and butter. Sturrock cracks a Hegarty free-kick into the roof of the net to subdue Saints. Late on Reilly scores from close range and then sets up Coyne to crash in a spectacular overhead kick. Saints' Blair, Beedie and Lyons sin and are booked.

**28 — Aberdeen (A):** Champions-elect Aberdeen crush United. Rougvie bizarrely scrambles in the first with his knees. McAlpine fists a McGhee 25-yarder into the net, but Reilly rallies United with a 25-yarder. McGhee heads home a third and Black scored similarly before setting up Rougvie's second.

**29 — Dundee (H):** Clark takes a return from Dodds to net via the woodwork which United hit twice more. McCall races on to a McKinlay pass and shoots past McAlpine. Fraser is sent off after a second booking near the end of a ding-dong derby. Dundee's Mackie and Glennie plus Reilly are booked.

**30 — Motherwell (A):** McLean, newly banished from the dug-out, misses a clinical win. Page breaks his leg a minute into his debut to mar the occasion. A Dodds header slips through Sproat's hands. Gough volleys a second and Reilly thumps home from close in. Gahagan goal is 'Wells's late consolation.

**31 — St Mirren (H):** As at Fir Park, McLean, searching for new faces, misses a comfortable victory. Hegarty hits the bar before Holt runs on to a crafty pass to score. Reilly gets a touch to a Hegarty flick for a second, but Bannon's spot-kick is saved to stop a third. Munro and Cooper are booked.

**32 — Rangers (A):** At ghost-like Ibrox, United fail to beat Gers for the fifth time. Sturrock rages a shot high into the net from a Dodds knock down. Clark's header trundles in and Williamson first times a McClelland cut-back home but Dodds, the only player booked, nets after McCloy saved from Sturrock.

**33 — St Mirren (H):** Three goals in four minutes set this game alight. Sturrock dribbles a superb solo first. McDougall levels with a header from Abercromby's cross and Jarvie's shot deflects over McAlpine. Narey's first goal of the season saves the day. Reilly plus Abercromby, Jarvie and Fulton are booked.

**34 — Aberdeen (H):** Having already deposed United as champions, the Dons equal United and Celtic's record Premier pointage. Leighton is at his international best to deny United, but Dons have best chances. Narey clears a Cowan effort off the line and Falconer hits the post. Rougvie is only booking.

| 35 | A | CELTIC | 3 | D | 1-1 | 10,281 | 2 | 47 |
|----|---|--------|---|---|-----|--------|---|----|

McAlpine / Malpas / Munro / Gough / Hegarty / Holt / Bannon / Narey / Coyne / Sturrock* / Taylor / Clark
Bonner / McGrain / Reid / Aitken / McStay W / MacLead / Colquoun* / McStay P / McClair / Burns / Melrose / Provan

Sturrock 78 / MacLead 75
Ref: D Syme

Celtic end the season undefeated at home. Runners-up spot is up for grabs, but for long periods, it was all so sedate with McLean again absent. MacLeod thunders in a free-kick to enliven it. Sturrock squares it getting on the end of a Coyne flick.

| 36 | H | RANGERS | 3 | L | 1-2 | 6,457 | 4 | 47 |
|----|---|---------|---|---|-----|-------|---|----|

McAlpine / Malpas / Munro / Gough / Hegarty / Holt / Bannon / Narey / Coyne / Sturrock* / Taylor* / Dodds
McCloy / MacKinnon / Dawson / McPherson / McClelland / Munro / Prytz^ / McCoist / Ferguson* / MacDonald / Cooper / Clark/Burns

Dodds 89 / Prytz 44p, McCoist 82
Ref: G Smith

Having quit his Scotland post, McLean sees Coyne hit the bar, but Prytz nets from the spot after Hegarty fouled McCoist, who later adds a second from Cooper's assist. Profligate United finally score through Dodds after a Malpas shot is blocked. MacDonald and Dawson are booked.

Home 10,421  Average  Away 10,705

## League Cup

| 2:1 | H | DUNFERMLINE | W | 6-1 | 5,324 | 3-0 |
|-----|---|-------------|---|-----|-------|-----|

McAlpine / Malpas / Kirkwood / Gough / Hegarty / Milne / Bannon / Narey / Taylor* / Holt / Dodds* / Clark/Stark
Whyte / Robertson / Lapsley / Smith / Dall / McCathie / Bowie / Rodier / Morrison / Perry / Stewart^ / Forrest/Donnelly

Gough 6, 12, Holt 32, Taylor 52, Morrison 63 [Dodds 60, Bannon 70]
Ref: M Delaney

Dunfermline are demolished. Gough's diving header and low drive from outside the box put United two up. Holt hits a cracking 30-yarder to make it three. Taylor's volley is deflected for number four. Dodds adds a fifth before Morrison pulls one back, but Bannon scores the sixth.

| 2:2 | A | DUNFERMLINE | W | 2-0 | 2,618 | 1-0 |
|-----|---|-------------|---|-----|-------|-----|

McAlpine / Malpas / Kirkwood / Gough / Hegarty / Milne / Bannon / Narey / Taylor* / Holt / Dodds / Clark
Whyte / McCathie / Lapsley / Hepburn / Dall / Donnelly / Bowie / Rodier / Morrison / Perry / Stewart

Gough 11, Dodds 69
Ref: A Waddell
(United win 8-1 on aggregate)

Five up, it took two McAlpine saves to shake United out of their lethargy against Tom Forsyth's troops. Left unmarked Gough heads in a Bannon cross and Dodds' glancing header from a Milne made it two as United stroll in. Pars Morrison and Kirkwood went into the ref's book.

## Section 1

| 1 | H | ALLOA | W | 5-0 | 4,483 | 2-0 |
|---|---|-------|---|-----|-------|-----|

McAlpine / Malpas / Kirkwood / Gough / Hegarty / Milne / Bannon / Narey / Taylor* / Holt / Dodds / Holt^/Britton
Hunter / Martin / Thomson / Munro / Houston / Lloyd* / Weir / Cole / McComb

Dodds 23, 73, 87, Reilly 36, 59
2
Ref: H Young

The Wasps resist until Dodds scores after they fail to clear their lines. Reilly whips in a second and latches onto a Narey lob to round Hunter for the third. Dodds completes his hat-trick, side-footing in a Bannon cross and tapping in when a Hegarty header slips through the keeper's arms.

| 2 | A | MORTON | D | 1-1 | 1,365 | 1-1 |
|---|---|--------|---|-----|-------|-----|

McAlpine / Malpas / Kirkwood / Gough / Hegarty / Milne / Bannon / Narey / Reilly* / Holt / Dodds / Stark
Kyle / Houston / Holmes / Miller / Welsh / Rooney / Robertson / Duffy / McNab / McNeil / Doak

Houston 3 (og), Robertson 12
3
Ref: T Muirhead

Despite a great start as Houston sends a Milne cross skidding into his own net, player/boss Alex Miller's gutsy Morton give as good as they get to end United's run of five wins. Robertson soon squeezes home a 25-yarder. McNab, who later forces Gough to clear off the line, is booked.

| 3 | H | MOTHERWELL | W | 4-2 | 5,731 | 4-1 |
|---|---|------------|---|-----|-------|-----|

McAlpine / Kirkwood / Stark / Gough / Hegarty / Milne / Bannon / Narey / Reilly* / Holt / Dodds* / Malpas/Taylor
Walker / Dornan / MacLeod / Carson / Edvaldsson / Rafferty* / Gahagan / Mauchlen / Gillespie / Ritchie^ / Harrow / McAllister/McFadden

Reilly 10, Gough 19, 24, Bannon 32p, Mauchlen 28, Gahagan 53
5
Ref: D Galloway

Four goals in a devastating 30 minutes leaves Well reeling. Reilly's composed finish from 12 yards and Gough fires home from 30 yards with Walker at fault as Gough hits another. Mauchlen reduces arrears from 35 yards. Reilly converts a penalty, but Gahagan grabs a late goal.

| 4 | H | MORTON | W | 3-0 | 6,645 | 2-0 |
|---|---|--------|---|-----|-------|-----|

McAlpine / Kirkwood / Malpas / Gough / Hegarty / Milne / Bannon^ / Narey / Johnstone* / Holt / Dodds / Reilly/Beaumont
McDermott / Houston / Holmes / Duffy / Welsh / McCallum* / McNab / Doak / Rooney / Clinging / McNeil / Hayes

Johnstone 25, 48, Milne 43
7
Ref: W Knowles

It's a memorable debut for ex-United fan Johnstone, scoring two spectacular goals. First is a thunderbolt off the underside of the bar from just inside the box. Milne hammers in a second before Johnstone takes a Dodds pass in his stride and flicks it over a defender before blasting home.

| 5 | A | ALLOA | W | 4-2 | 2,220 | 3-2 |
|---|---|-------|---|-----|-------|-----|

McAlpine / Kirkwood^ / Malpas / Gough / Hegarty / Milne / Bannon / Narey / Reilly / Holt* / Dodds / Johnstone/Phillip
Hunter / Thomson / Hagartt / Purdie / Martin / Houston / Paterson / Garner / Lloyd* / McComb* / Cole / Thompson/Jobson

Dodds 3, Reilly 17, Milne 22, Bannon 65p, Paterson 15, Garner 44p
9
Ref: M Delaney

Topping the section and a place in the last four are sealed with a less than classic display. Dodds header from Reilly's cross sees United in front but Paterson levels from close in. Reilly angles United back in front and Milne first times a great third. Garner nets from spot, as does Bannon.

| 6 | A | MOTHERWELL | W | 3-0 | 1,319 | 1-0 |
|---|---|------------|---|-----|-------|-----|

McAlpine / Malpas / Murray / Gough / Hegarty* / Milne^ / Bannon / McGinnis / Reilly / Holt / Dodds / Payne
Spraot / Dornan / MacLeod / Forbes / Carson / Mauchlen* / McAllister / Edvaldsson / Harrow / Alexander / Cole / Beaumont/Clark
Wark/Gillespie

Milne 20, McGinnis 47, Reilly 71
11
Ref: D Syme

All highly academic but an experimental United produce a display to please McLean. A fierce left-foot Milne drive from the edge of the box puts United in front. McGinnis scores his only goal for the club from a Gough pass and Reilly heads home a Bannon cross to round it all off.

| Qual | | P | W | D | L | F | A | Pts |
|------|---|---|---|---|---|---|---|-----|
| DUNDEE UNITED | | 6 | 5 | 1 | 0 | 20 | 5 | 11 |
| Motherwell | | 6 | 2 | 1 | 3 | 11 | 14 | 5 |
| Alloa | | 6 | 2 | 1 | 3 | 10 | 15 | 5 |
| Morton | | 6 | 1 | 1 | 4 | 7 | 14 | 3 |

# SCOTTISH PREMIER (CUP-TIES)

## Manager: Jim McLean — SEASON 1983-84

### League Cup (continued)

| | | | Date | Opponent | Att. | | F-A | H-T | Scorers, Times, and Referees |
|---|---|---|---|---|---|---|---|---|---|
| SF | H | 1 | 14/2 | RANGERS | 14,596 | D | 1-1 | 0-0 | Dodds 69, Mitchell 86. Ref: A Ferguson |
| SF | A | 2 | 22/2 | RANGERS | 35,950 | L | 0-2 | 0-1 | Clark 43, Redford 52. Ref: D Syme (United lose 1-3 on aggregate) |

**Line-ups**

| | 1 | 2 | 3 | 4 | 5 | 6 | 7 | 8 | 9 | 10 | 11 | subs used |
|---|---|---|---|---|---|---|---|---|---|---|---|---|
| SF1 United | McAlpine | Stark | Malpas | Gough | Hegarty | Narey | Holt | Milne | Kirkwood | Sturrock * | Dodds | Clark |
| SF1 Rangers | *McCloy* | *Nicholl* | *Dawson* | *McClelland* | *Paterson* | *Redford* | *Russell* | *Prytz ** | *Clark* | *McCoist* | *Cooper ** | *McPherson/Mitchell* |
| SF2 United | McAlpine | Stark | Malpas | Gough | Hegarty | Narey | Bannon * | Milne | Holt ^ | Sturrock | Dodds | Clark/Kirkwood |
| SF2 Rangers | *McCloy* | *Nicholl* | *Dawson* | *McClelland* | *McPherson* | *Redford* | *Russell* | *Prytz* | *Clark ^* | *McCoist* | *Cooper* | *Mitchell/Burns* |

SF1: Rangers' record of never losing a cup-tie to United continues. Gough's final touch after Dodds' header is parried in swirling mist. Fog lifts but gloom descends as Mitchell heads in Redford's cross. Holt, Stevens and Dodds of United plus Paterson are all booked in the non-stop action.

SF2: Hopes of a fourth final in five years evaporate in 11 minutes. Russell crosses to Clark, who chests the ball down and his shot on the turn found the far corner. Clark sends Redford to chip home and there is no way back although Sturrock hits the bar late on. Malpas is the only booking.

### Scottish Cup

| | | Date | Opponent | Att. | | F-A | H-T | Scorers, Times, and Referees |
|---|---|---|---|---|---|---|---|---|
| 3 | H | 6/2 | AYR UNITED | 4,441 7:9 | W | 1-0 | 0-0 | Sturrock 76. Ref: K Hope |
| 4 | H | 18/2 | HEARTS | 14,371 5 | W | 2-1 | 1-0 | Sturrock 28, Dodds 84, Robertson 70p. Ref: D Syme |
| QF | A | 17/3 | ABERDEEN | 22,000 1 | D | 0-0 | 0-0 | Ref: B McGinlay |
| QF R | H | 28/3 | ABERDEEN | 16,094 1 | L | 0-1 | 0-1 | McGhee 2. Ref: B McGinlay |

**Line-ups**

| | 1 | 2 | 3 | 4 | 5 | 6 | 7 | 8 | 9 | 10 | 11 | subs used |
|---|---|---|---|---|---|---|---|---|---|---|---|---|
| R3 United | McAlpine | Stark | Malpas | Gough | Hegarty | Narey | Bannon | Milne * | Holt | Sturrock | Dodds | Reilly |
| R3 Ayr | *Brown* | *Shanks* | *Hetherington* | *Morris ** | *McAllister* | *Collins* | *Christie* | *Connor* | *McNally* | *McN'ghton ** | *Murphy* | *Buchanan, Charnley* |
| R4 United | McAlpine | Stark | Malpas | Gough | Hegarty | Narey | Bannon | Milne | Kirkwood ^ | Sturrock | Dodds | Holt/Clark |
| R4 Hearts | *Smith* | *Kidd* | *Cowie* | *Jardine* | *Stevens* | *McLaren ** | *Mackay* | *Robertson* | *Bone !* | *Levein ^* | *Park* | *Bowman/Johnston* |
| QF United | McAlpine | Stark | Malpas | Gough | Holt | Narey | Bannon ^ | Kirkwood | Coyne | Milne * | Dodds | Clark/Page |
| QF Aberdeen | *Leighton* | *McKimmie* | *Rougvie* | *Cooper* | *McLeish* | *Miller* | *Strachan ^* | *Black* | *McGhee* | *Simpson !* | *Angus* | *Hewitt* |
| QF R United | McAlpine | Stark * | Malpas | McGinnis ^ | Holt | Narey | Holt | Kirkwood | Milne | Sturrock | Dodds | Clark/Taylor |
| QF R Aberdeen | *Leighton* | *McKimmie* | *Rougvie ** | *Cooper* | *McLeish* | *Miller* | *Strachan* | *Simpson* | *McGhee* | *Black* | *Angus* | *Mitchell* |

R3: Rustiness, not to mention a snow-covered surface, combine to make this a more difficult tie than anticipated. Sturrock's first goal of the season – from all of six inches – eventually ensures there is no slip up. The goal comes after Brown dropped a Reilly cross under pressure from Dodds.

R4: X-certificate stuff on and off the park with eight yellow cards, Bone sent off plus trouble on the terraces. Stevens blocks Hegarty's shot on the line, Sturrock forces the ball in. Narey handles, Robertson coolly converts the penalty. Hegarty heads on Narey's long ball for Dodds to strike.

QF: The woodwork twice foils the cup holders. Angus hit the top of the timbers from a free-kick and Clark strikes his own post from a corner. Best chance falls to Milne, who skies over from a Dodds flick. Gough is the only man booked in a game that only comes to life in the closing stages.

QF R: The Dons make it eight Scottish ties without defeat against United. Off to a bad start as McAlpine's poor clearance falls to Angus who plays McGhee in and he slams home from 18 yards. United sweat blood, but lack a cutting edge. Angus, Simpson and McGhee all receive cautions.

### European Cup

| | | Date | Opponent | Att. | | F-A | H-T | Scorers, Times, and Referees |
|---|---|---|---|---|---|---|---|---|
| 1:1 | A | 14/9 | HAMRUN SPART'S | 12,300 (Malta) | W | 3-0 | 2-0 | Reilly 2, Bannon 32, Stark 67. Ref: B Sinasi (Yugoslavia) |
| 1:2 | H | 28/9 | HAMRUN SPART'S | 8,213 | W | 3-0 | 2-0 | Milne 28, 47, Kirkwood 44. Ref: J Poucher (N Ireland) (United win 6-0 on aggregate) |
| 2:1 | A | 19/10 | STANDARD LIEGE | 26,000 (Belgium) | D | 0-0 | 0-0 | Ref: M Castillo (Spain) |
| 2:2 | H | 2/11 | STANDARD LIEGE | 16,674 | W | 4-0 | 2-0 | Milne 26, 43, Hegarty 52, Dodds 69. Ref: K Tritschler (West Germany) (United win 4-0 on aggregate) |

**Line-ups**

| | 1 | 2 | 3 | 4 | 5 | 6 | 7 | 8 | 9 | 10 | 11 | subs used |
|---|---|---|---|---|---|---|---|---|---|---|---|---|
| 1:1 United | McAlpine | Kirkwood | Stark | Gough | Hegarty | Narey | Bannon | Milne | Reilly * | Holt | Dodds ^ | Taylor/Clark |
| 1:1 Hamrun | *Brincat* | *Refalo G* | *Farrugia* | *Xuereb G* | *Zammit* | *Azzopardi* | *Refalo L* | *Salerno* | *Degiorgio* | *Xuereb R* | *Ciantar ** | *Grech* |
| 1:2 United | McAlpine | Kirkwood | Murray | Gough | Hegarty | Stark | Bannon | Milne | Holt | Sturrock * | Dodds | Payne |
| 1:2 Hamrun | *Brincat* | *Refalo G* | *Farrugia* | *Salerno* | *Zammit* | *Ivanov* | *Refalo L* | *Xuereb G* | *Gutman* | *Xuereb R* | *Degiorgio ** | *Azzopardi* |
| 2:1 United | McAlpine | Kirkwood | Stark | Gough | Hegarty | Narey | Bannon | Milne | Holt | Malpas | Dodds ^ | |
| 2:1 Standard | *Preud'homme* | *Jelikic ** | *Poel* | *Meeuws* | *Wintacq* | *Vandermis'n* | *Daerden* | *Plessers* | *Grundel* | *Hrubesch ^* | *Tahamata* | *Aussem/Delbrouck* |
| 2:2 United | McAlpine | Kirkwood | Stark * | Gough | Hegarty | Narey | Bannon | Milne | Holt | Sturrock * | Dodds | Reilly |
| 2:2 Standard | *Preud'homme* | *Jelikic* | *Wintacq* | *Poet* | *Meeuws* | *Vandermis'n* | *Tahamata* | *Plessers ** | *Aussems* | *Daerden* | *Grundel* | *Delengre* |

1:1: Opponents of modest ambition fail to make United sweat in the heat. Reilly's early opener from close range follows a melee. Bannon's header finishes off a fine move and Gough's header is blocked before Stark blasts in the rebound. G Refalo and G Xuereb are cautioned, as is Gough.

1:2: More damage limitation by the Maltese champions who have Brincat, Farrugia and G Refalo booked again. Milne chips a clearance at the near post from 15 yards. The visitors' barrier is breached again when Kirkwood's shot takes a deflection. Milne squeezes in the third from a tight angle.

2:1: Jim McLean's deep defensive tactic work to perfection as Standard lose their bearings. A Milne cross rocks the top of the bar. Holt, one of the heroes in tangerine, is the name noted by the ref.

2:2: United celebrate their 50th European tie in style, destroying Standard. Milne runs amok. His flying header from Bannon's cross has United in front and his delightful chip makes it two. Milne sets up Hegarty, who nods in his corner and is involved before Dodds prods in Gough's cross.

## European Cup

| | | | Date | Att | Res | HT | United scorers / *Opponents* |
|---|---|---|---|---|---|---|---|
| QF 1 | A | RAPID VIENNA | 7/3 | 15,000 | L | 1-2 | 0-1 | Stark 25 — *Hagmayr 77, Kranjckar 86* |
| QF 2 | H | RAPID VIENNA | 21/3 | 17,442 | W | 1-0 | 1-0 | Dodds 21 |
| SF 1 | H | AS ROMA | 11/4 | 20,543 | W | 2-0 | 0-0 | Dodds 48, Stark 60 |
| SF 2 | A | AS ROMA | 25/4 | 68,060 | L | 0-3 | 0-2 | *Pruzo 23, 40, Di Bartolemi 58p* |

(Austria) Ref: B Dotchev (Bulgaria)
Ref: R Wurtz (France) (United win on away goals)
(Italy) Ref: S Kirschen (East Germany)
Ref: M Vautrot (France) (United lose 2-3 on aggregate)

**Line-ups (United / Opponent):**
McAlpine/Feurer, Stark/Lainer, Gough/Pregesbauer, Malpas/Garger *, Bannon/Kranjcar, Narey/Kienest, Hegarty/Weber, Gough/Pregesbauer, Sturrock/Krankl, Dodds/Keglevits ^, Milne/Holt, Wilfurth/Hagmayr

McAlpine/Feurer, Stark/Lainer, Gough/Pregesbauer, Malpas/Garger *, Bannon/Kranjcar, Narey/Kienest, Hegarty/Weber, Gough/Pregesbauer, Sturrock/Krankl, Dodds/Keglevits ^, Milne/Holt, Wilfurth/Hagmayr

McAlpine/Tancredi, Stark/Oddi, Gough/Nela, Malpas/Righetti, Bannon/Conti, Narey/Di Bartolemi Maldera, Hegarty/Di Bartolemi Maldera, Gough/Nela, Sturrock */Cherica, Dodds/Pruzzo, Milne/Cerezo, Dodds/Graziani, Sturrock */Cherica, Coyne

McAlpine/Tancredi, Stark */Nappi, Gough/Nela, Malpas/Righetti, Bannon/Conti, Narey/Maldera, Hegarty/Falceo, Gough/Nela, Sturrock */Pruzzo ^, Milne/Cerezo *, Conti, Kirkwood/Cerezo *, Sturrock ^/Di Bartolemi Graziani, Holt/Clark, Cherico/Oddi

Even losing a late goal fails to dampen tangerine optimism for a semi spot. Stark flashes a low 25-yard drive into the bottom corner for the all-important away goal. Home pressure tells as Hagmayr heads home and Kranjcar nets after McAlpine denies Krankl. Hegarty is only booking.

More perspiration than inspiration, as Stark's away goal is the order of the day. Dodds does the donkey-work by scoring the all-important winner. Accepting Stark's crisp pass, he wheels to net his eighth Euro counter. Despite high stakes, Bannon and Wilfurth are the only cautions.

A night to remember as the Italian aristocrats are humbled. Sturrock touches the ball back to Dodds who shoots low into goal from eight yards. From a second Sturrock lay-off, Stark unleashes a swerving 30-yarder which totally deceives Tancredi to set up European final dreams.

After Milne's early miss from a Bannon cross, it is downhill thereafter. Pruzzo rises to head in Conti's corner. Pruzzo chests down and wheels to prod in and square the tie. The inevitable winner comes when skipper Di Bartolemi nets from the spot after McAlpine brought down Pruzzo.

## League Table

| | | P | W | D | L | F | A | W | D | L | F | A | Pts |
|---|---|---|---|---|---|---|---|---|---|---|---|---|---|
| 1 | Aberdeen | 36 | 14 | 3 | 1 | 46 | 12 | 11 | 4 | 3 | 32 | 9 | 57 |
| 2 | Celtic | 36 | 13 | 5 | 0 | 46 | 15 | 8 | 3 | 7 | 34 | 26 | 50 |
| 3 | DUNDEE UTD | 36 | 11 | 3 | 4 | 38 | 14 | 7 | 8 | 3 | 29 | 25 | 47 |
| 4 | Rangers | 36 | 11 | 7 | 0 | 26 | 18 | 8 | 4 | 6 | 27 | 23 | 42 |
| 5 | Hearts | 36 | 5 | 9 | 4 | 23 | 23 | 8 | 1 | 9 | 15 | 24 | 36 |
| 6 | St Mirren | 36 | 8 | 6 | 4 | 34 | 23 | 6 | 3 | 9 | 21 | 36 | 32 |
| 7 | Hibernian | 36 | 7 | 4 | 7 | 21 | 21 | 5 | 3 | 10 | 24 | 34 | 31 |
| 8 | Dundee | 36 | 6 | 1 | 11 | 28 | 42 | 5 | 4 | 9 | 22 | 32 | 27 |
| 9 | St Johnstone | 36 | 6 | 1 | 11 | 19 | 33 | 4 | 2 | 12 | 17 | 48 | 23 |
| 10 | Motherwell | 36 | 2 | 5 | 11 | 15 | 36 | 2 | 2 | 14 | 16 | 39 | 15 |
| | | 360 | 79 | 45 | 56 | 296 | 237 | 56 | 45 | 79 | 237 | 296 | 360 |

## Head-to-head

| | P | W | D | L | F | A | Pts | Cup W | D | L |
|---|---|---|---|---|---|---|---|---|---|---|
| v St Johnstone | 4 | 4 | 0 | 0 | 14 | 2 | 8 | 0 | 0 | 0 |
| v Motherwell | 4 | 4 | 0 | 0 | 11 | 4 | 7 | 2 | 0 | 0 |
| v Celtic | 4 | 2 | 2 | 0 | 7 | 4 | 6 | 2 | 0 | 0 |
| v Hearts | 4 | 2 | 2 | 0 | 4 | 1 | 6 | 0 | 0 | 0 |
| v Hibernian | 4 | 3 | 0 | 1 | 9 | 1 | 6 | 1 | 0 | 0 |
| v Dundee | 4 | 3 | 0 | 1 | 10 | 5 | 6 | 0 | 0 | 0 |
| v St Mirren | 4 | 2 | 1 | 1 | 6 | 8 | 5 | 0 | 0 | 0 |
| v Aberdeen | 4 | 1 | 1 | 2 | 3 | 8 | 3 | 2 | 0 | 1 |
| v Rangers | 4 | 0 | 2 | 2 | 3 | 6 | 2 | 2 | 0 | 1 |

## Odds and Ends

Quadruple wins: (1) St Johnstone.
Quadruple losses: (0).

Win from behind: (3) Dundee (a), Hearts (h), Dundee (a).
Lost from in front: (1) Rapid Vienna (EC).

High spots: Coming within a goal of emulating Celtic and reaching the European Champions Cup final.

Beating Motherwell on the opening day as the League Flag was raised. Winning 2-1 at Pittodrie to make it five straight wins at the start of the season. This was Dons' only home league loss on their way to the title. Not conceding a goal in any of the four European Cup home ties. Winning the opening five league games of the campaign which, combined with six wins at the end of the previous season, constitutes the best sequence in league games in the club's history.

Low spots: Not performing against AS Roma in the intimidating atmosphere of the Olympic Stadium in Rome.
The poor record against Rangers. Apart from losing to them in the semi-final of the League Cup, they were the only side United failed to beat in the league, despite finishing above the Ibrox giants.
Going down 0-4 to St Mirren at Love Street, the heaviest ever defeat suffered at Saints' hands in any Premier contest.

Hat-tricks: (0).
Ever Presents: (1) Hegarty.
Leading scorer: Dodds (15).

## Appearances and Goals

| | Appearances | | | | | | | | Goals | | | | |
|---|---|---|---|---|---|---|---|---|---|---|---|---|---|
| | Lge | Sub | LC | Sub | SC | Sub | Eur | Sub | Lge | LC | SC | Eur | Tot |
| Bannon, Eamonn | 32 | 1 | 9 | | 3 | | 8 | | 7 | 3 | | 1 | 11 |
| Beaumont, David | 1 | | 2 | | | | | | | | | | |
| Britton, Ian | | 1 | | | | | | | | | | | |
| Clark, John | 4 | 5 | | | | 3 | | 3 | 1 | | | | 1 |
| Coyne, Tommy | 13 | 5 | | | | | 1 | 1 | 3 | | | | 3 |
| Dodds, Davie | 31 | | 9 | | 4 | | 8 | | 15 | 7 | 1 | 3 | 26 |
| Flavell, Bobby | | 1 | | | | | | | | | | | |
| Gardiner, John | 2 | | | | | | | | | | | | |
| Gough, Richard | 33 | | 10 | | 3 | | 8 | | 3 | 5 | | | 8 |
| Hegarty, Paul | 36 | | 10 | | 3 | | 8 | | 4 | | | 1 | 5 |
| Holt, John | 26 | 6 | 9 | 1 | 3 | 1 | 4 | 3 | 2 | 1 | | | 3 |
| Johnstone, Derek | 2 | 2 | 1 | 1 | | | | | 2 | | | | 2 |
| Kirkwood, Billy | 24 | 2 | 8 | 1 | 3 | | 8 | | 9 | | | 1 | 10 |
| McAlpine, Hamish | 34 | | 10 | | 4 | | 8 | | | | | | |
| McGinnis, Gary | 2 | 2 | 1 | | | | 1 | | | | | | |
| Malpas, Maurice | 33 | 1 | 9 | 1 | 4 | | 6 | | 1 | | | 1 | 2 |
| Milne, Ralph | 19 | 6 | 10 | | 4 | | 7 | 1 | 5 | 3 | | 4 | 12 |
| Munro, Iain | 9 | | 1 | | 1 | | | | | | | | |
| Murray, Derek | 2 | | 1 | | | | 1 | | | | | | |
| Narey, David | 34 | | 9 | | 4 | | 7 | | 1 | | | | 1 |
| Page, Jimmy | 1 | | | | | | | | | | | | |
| Payne, Graeme | | 1 | | 1 | | 1 | | | | | | | |
| Phillip, Iain | | 1 | | 1 | | | | | | | | | |
| Reilly, John | 15 | 4 | 5 | 1 | 1 | 1 | 1 | 1 | 7 | 5 | | 1 | 13 |
| Stark, Derek | 23 | 2 | 3 | 2 | 4 | | 8 | | 3 | | 3 | 3 | 6 |
| Sturrock, Paul | 15 | 2 | 2 | 3 | | 5 | | 4 | | 2 | | | 6 |
| Taylor, Alex | 5 | 4 | 3 | 1 | 1 | | 1 | 1 | 1 | 1 | | | 2 |
| (own-goals) | | | | | | | 1 | | | 1 | | | 1 |
| 27 players used | 396 | 47 | 110 | 18 | 44 | 7 | 88 | 11 | 67 | 29 | 3 | 14 | 113 |

A ticket to hell, Rome, 25 April 1984

LIST OF SUBSCRIBERS AND VOTES FOR THE MOST IMPORTANT UNITED PLAYER 1982-83

| | | | |
|---|---|---|---|
| Steve Barclay | David Narey | Eamonn Malone | Derek Stark |
| Brian Boardman | Eamonn Bannon | William Marren | Ralph Milne |
| Tom Cairns | Billy Kirkwood | John Mill | Ralph Milne |
| Dr Colin M Campbell | Paul Sturrock | David Mitchell | Jim McLean |
| Stuart Chalmers | Eamonn Bannon | Martin Mooney | Eamonn Bannon |
| Iain Craig | Ralph Milne | Gavin Muir | David Narey |
| John Cruickshank | Paul Sturrock | Niall J Mulligan | David Narey |
| Gordon Cuthbert | Paul Hegarty | Stewart Page | David Narey |
| Paul Doherty | David Narey | George & Helen Paton | Paul Hegarty |
| Mark Dorward | David Narey | Islay Reid | David Narey |
| Alasdair Easson | Ralph Milne | James Reid | Eamonn Bannon |
| Ross Forbes | Paul Hegarty | Bruce Robertson | David Narey |
| William Gibb | | Paul Scrimger | Ralph Milne |
| Kenny Grant | Eamonn Bannon | Kevin Sheehan | Ralph Milne |
| Kevin Green | Paul Sturrock | Jon Steadman | David Narey |
| Stuart Herd | Paul Hegarty | Derek Thoms | Ralph Milne |
| Hugh Jenkins | Hamish McAlpine | Michael Toner | Hamish McAlpine |
| Mr E Johnston | Jim McLean | Kevin White | David Narey |
| Johnny Kirkland | Ralph Milne | Gary White | Paul Hegarty |
| Graeme Liveston | Paul Sturrock | Keith S Wilson | Eamonn Bannon |
| Blair Louden | David Narey | Andrew Winton | Paul Sturrock |
| Ian Napier MacLeod | Paul Sturrock | Paul Zarembski | Ralph Milne |
| Scott McCarthy | Paul Hegarty | | |
| Pauline McDonald | | 1st | DAVID NAREY |
| James McGeary | David Narey | 2nd | RALPH MILNE |
| Peter D McIntyre | Paul Sturrock | 3rd | PAUL STURROCK |